Introduction

You can read about the world in a book or watch programmes on the television, but until you get out there and grasp it with both hands, the Earth might as well be flat.

There are endless places to explore, people to meet and experiences to be had, and setting off on a gap year will open up a world of opportunity and adventure.

How do you decide what to do?

Not long ago you could pretty much guarantee that a gap year would include a round-the-world flight and a stint working in Australia, but modern gap years are much more varied. There is now more emphasis on getting to know a country, taking part in volunteer work or pushing your boundaries through adventure travel. With so many options available, it can be difficult to decide which one is right for you.

Rather than bombarding you with every possible option, itinerary and detail, this book keeps it simple. Planning a gap year can be confusing enough without having things overcomplicated!

So, where do you start?

You may only have a few months to spare, or are planning on taking a whole year out, but either way you will want to make the most of your time away. From booking flights and planning an itinerary, to choosing what to do and how to pay for it, this book will help you put the basics in place.

It will give you the inspiration you need to make all those essential decisions. with helpful continent guides and chapters on volunteering and working abroad. As well the fun stuff, this book offers important advice on health and safety and a comprehensive help list to get your travel planning underway.

Whether you are leaving behind school, university or your career, jetting off to explore the world is an exciting and life-changing prospect. However excited you are though, it can feel a bit scary to leave behind the safety and comfort of home. While a gap year is tinged with uncertainty, that is part of the fun. If you are in doubt, listen to these wise words from Mark Twain, one of America's most famous literary icons:

'Twenty years from now you will be more disappointed by the things you didn't do than by the ones you did do. So throw off the bowlines. Sail away from the safe harbor. Catch the trade winds in your sails. Explore. Dream. Discover'.

The things you discover about yourself and the world around you on your gap year will last a lifetime and it is an adventure that you will never forget.

So start reading and making some exciting decisions and get ready to have the time of your life. Happy planning!

Disclaimer

When planning a gap year, you should always consult your GP regarding the vaccinations and booster injections you will need. This guide gives a brief overview of the vaccinations you can receive, but professional medical advice is recommended.

GAP YEARS

The Essential Guide

Emma Jones

Gap Years – The Essential Guide is also available in accessible formats for people with any degree of visual impairment. The large print edition and eBook (with accessibility features enabled) are available from Need2Know. Please let us know if there are any special features you require and we will do our best to accommodate your needs.

First published in Great Britain in 2012 by
Need2Know
Remus House
Coltsfoot Drive
Peterborough
PE2 9BF
Telephone 01733 898103
Fax 01733 313524
www.need2knowbooks.co.uk

Contents

Chapter One

Practicalities

Are you ready for a gap year?

There are plenty of reasons for taking a gap year but the main one should be because you want to. Don't decide that you 'should' take one or let your mum or best friend persuade you that it's the best thing to do. Young people are under a lot of pressure with student fee hikes and high youth unemployment, so it is more important than ever that you make the best use of your time and money. A gap year can build your confidence, change your outlook on the world and add skills and experience to your CV, but only embark on the adventure if you are sure it is right for you.

You should also consider what level of support and structure you need. If you are an experienced traveller you may be happy to plan it all yourself, but if you haven't left home alone before, it may be a good idea to think about an organised programme or tour.

Choosing what to do

If you are set on taking a gap year then you need to have a clear idea of what you are going to do with it. Whether you are delaying university or your career, you need to make the most of it. The best way to make this decision is to take a thorough look at all the options. Gather brochures and books, scour websites and talk to other people who have taken a gap year to ensure that you are able to make an informed decision. Your gap year is as individual as you are but here are some elements you might consider including:

'When I decided to take a gap year I had no idea where to start. Having some guidance would have been a huge help.'
Tracey, 32.

Travel

The main reason why most people take a gap year is to get out and see the world. You know that once you get settled into a career, or have other commitments, it will be more difficult to take time out to travel, so this is your time to explore. You need to think carefully about where you want to go, how much you can realistically fit in and plan an itinerary.

Working abroad

Working abroad is a great way to see the world and get paid for it. It can help you get to know a country, learn a language or gain international experience for your CV. There are many options ranging from seasonal work to cruise ships, working visas or internships. These all take planning and commitment but can help combine two key aspects of a gap year – money and travel.

Working in the UK

You may have to work for a few months and save some money before you set off. Or perhaps you would rather dedicate your entire gap year to earning money or working on your career before university. Deciding to work for the year is admirable, but you should ask yourself how you will feel when your friends leave for university or travelling and you are left at home.

Volunteering

Volunteering abroad has soared in popularity over recent years. Volunteering allows you to give something back while getting to know the locals and immersing yourself in the culture. These programmes can be expensive, so it is worth shopping around and finding out exactly where your contribution is going.

Need2Know

How do you plan an itinerary?

With so much to do and see, you could spend decades travelling the world but never see it all – so how do you decide where to go? Your itinerary is going to be guided by two main considerations: what you want to do and how much money you have to do it. Start by asking yourself a few questions:

- Is there anywhere you've always wanted to go?
- What major sights would you like to see?
- What do you enjoy doing?
- How much time can you spare?
- How much time would you like to spend in each place?
- How much money do you have?

Although traditionally referred to as a 'gap year', the length of your trip may vary considerably. A few months can be just as rewarding if planned carefully, while, if you have the time and funds, an extended trip can allow you to really explore the world. Be sure to give yourself enough time in each place and always add a few more days on than you think you actually need.

'You need to think carefully about where you want to go, how much you can realistically fit in and plan an itinerary.'

You may decide that you want to concentrate on one region of the world or try to fit in as many countries as possible. Whatever your philosophy, you need to try and balance your trip. Decide on the major sights or cities that you want to visit and then give yourself plenty of time around these to travel, relax or take in your surroundings.

How do you get around the world?

Round-the-world flights

The most popular way to get across the world is by buying a round-the-world flight. These work out much cheaper than buying individual flights and are usually fairly flexible. There are various restrictions but the basic rules are similar to the following:

- You must start and end your journey in one place.

- You must keep travelling in the same direction around the world.

- Your ticket is valid for one year.

- You have to choose your destinations before you travel.

The best thing to do is talk to a travel agent as there are many different options and prices depending on how many stops you make, or which 'zones' you travel in. Your ticket is going to be cheaper if you stick to the major hubs and most popular destinations, for example:

- London – Bangkok – Sydney – LA – London.

Many passes also allow you to insert an overland segment so you can fly into one city and out of another within the same region. For example:

- London – Bangkok – overland to Singapore – Sydney – LA – overland to New York – London.

If you are going to do it this way you need to leave yourself plenty of time to travel between the two locations, or make sure that your ticket is flexible enough to allow date changes.

By sea

While a round-the-world flight is the cheapest and easiest option, circumnavigating the world by sea can be an awesome experience. Your choices are to travel by cruise ship (expensive), freighter ship (not very glamorous) or crewing a yacht (hard work). If you are serious about this idea then research your options and remember that it is only a good idea for those of you who have time on your hands and don't get seasick!

Overland

The most adventurous option is to travel overland. While this is easy in some parts of the world, others will prove more difficult and you either need to be a seasoned traveller or go with an organised tour. The best option is to throw in a few flights and combine them with some overland travel along the way.

Who will you travel with?

Travelling alone

Travelling alone can be a liberating experience and allow you to make all your own choices without having to compromise. There is a huge network of backpackers around the world who meet through hostels and continue their journeys together, so you won't be alone for long. Seeing you go off to travel the world alone is a parent's worst nightmare, but try to calm their nerves by reminding them that thousands of people go off travelling alone every year and that you are prepared and sensible,

Boy/girlfriends

Many people choose to take a gap year with their boyfriend or girlfriend. On one hand it is good to have the support of someone you are close to, but it is a very intense environment for a relationship to withstand. Nothing is going to ruin a gap year quicker than breaking up. If you have been together for a while then it may be a good way to test your staying power, while fledging couples are ill advised to set off together.

Friends

Travelling with a friend is quite similar to travelling with a boyfriend or girlfriend. You may get on really well when you see each other at school or hanging out at the weekends, but all day every day is a different matter. Think about it carefully and try to pick a trustworthy friend who you have known for a good amount of time. If you are planning to go with two or more friends then consider the group dynamics and the practicalities of making joint decisions.

'The most rewarding part of my gap year was living with my host family and being accepted into another culture.'

Craig, 20.

Organised trips

The safest and most secure way to travel is to go on an organised tour. These will always cost more and allow less freedom, but will give you more support and guidance. Do your research to find out people's past experiences of the company and pick one that suits your age, interest and budget. Organised trips give you a ready made set of travel companions, so they can be a great idea if you are travelling alone.

What should you pack?

'It's bad enough trying to decide what to pack for a week's holiday, let alone a year travelling the world. When you are going backpacking it is a whole new set of rules. You need items that multitask and take up minimal space.

Backpack

Investing in good basic items will pay off. Choose a backpack that isn't too big for your frame and has good support and ventilation. Think about access to pockets and whether you can reach items without having to take the whole thing apart. Backpacks with detachable bags and straps are best. Karrimor and Eastpak are both trusted brands to consider but the most useful thing you can do is visit an outdoor supplies store such as Blacks (see the help list) for some personal advice.

Clothing

Anyone trying to choose a year's worth of outfits is going to struggle, especially when you have to fit it all in one bag. Clothing needs to be multi-functional, take up minimal space and to not need ironing. Make sure you consider the climates and customs of the places you are visiting. Long-sleeved cotton tops and trousers will always come in handy, as will any clothing that you can layer.

'It's bad enough trying to decide what to pack for a week's holiday, let alone a year travelling the world. When you are going backpacking it is a whole new set of rules.'

Other essentials

- Sleeping bag – choose a lightweight, compact one that is still warm and waterproof.

- Waterproof – it may not be the trendiest item but you will be thankful when you are waiting for your next bus in a downpour!

- Walking shoes – when you have been on your feet all day, having a good pair of walking shoes will seem like the best investment. These don't need to be expensive but should be supportive and waterproof.

- Torch – the dark can make anywhere seem scary, so make sure you have a good quality, compact torch to hand.

- Money belt – the safest place for your money is close to your body, so buy a belt that can fit snugly underneath your clothing.

- Water bottle and purifying tablets – investing in a sturdy water bottle will save you money and purifying tablets mean you will always have a supply of safe water to drink.

- A lock – as you will often be staying in shared accommodation and travelling by bus, a sturdy lock is an essential.

Use the packing checklist at the end of this chapter to make sure you have got everything you need. (For health and safety essentials, see chapter 4.)

Flights, visas and passports

You need to make sure that you have the basics in place so that you don't get caught out at the first hurdle.

Flights

Look for the best deals on flight comparison websites (see the help list) and keep an eye on prices so you can book them when they drop. If you are making a number of different stops, it is usually much cheaper to buy a specialist round-the-world ticket. Check the restrictions, as a lot of the round-the-world deals are quite flexible and allow you to change the dates and times along the way, while regular flights will not do this. Get into the habit of reconfirming your flight 48 hours beforehand.

Visas

Some countries require you to have a visa giving you permission to enter and stay there for a certain amount of time, especially if you are planning to work or study. Making sure that you have the right visa for each country that you will visit and for what you intend to do there is vital. Many countries, such as the United States, are very strict about these rules and if you are caught with the wrong visa you can be instantly sent home and banned from returning. Contact the embassy of the country you are planning to visit to find out what visa you may need, the process for getting one and how much it will cost. Costs will vary but they are generally a few hundred pounds. The best thing to do is apply for all your visas well in advance so you don't get caught out or have to think about it on the road. If your plans change while you are travelling then check that your visas are still valid. See www.projectvisa.com to get started.

Passports

Make sure that you have a valid passport that lasts for at least six months after the date you are going to return home. A new 10-year passport costs £77.50 and you can apply at your local post office or online at www.passport.gov.uk/passport. If it is your first passport, you will need to attend an interview. The whole process takes about six weeks. If you have had your passport for a while and the photo no longer resembles you closely, you should get it changed. To do this, you will have to renew your passport which costs the same as getting a new one but is worth the expense to save any confusion with immigration officials! It is essential to have two photocopies of your passport so you can leave one with your parents and take the other one away with you. You should always keep this copy in a separate place to the original.

Action points

- Do your research: find out what is on offer.
- Invest in good basic equipment.
- Visit www.roundtheworldflights.com to start planning your trip.
- Check that your passport is valid.
- Find out what visas you will need at www.projectvisa.com.

Packing checklist

Essential

- [ ] Walking shoes
- [ ] Waterproof
- [ ] Sleeping bag
- [ ] Torch
- [ ] Water bottle
- [ ] Towel
- [ ] Long-sleeved top
- [ ] Lightweight trousers
- [ ] Short-sleeved top
- [ ] Warm, thin jumper
- [ ] Swimwear
- [ ] Socks
- [ ] Underwear
- [ ] Sandals/flip-flops
- [ ] Shorts
- [ ] Lock
- [ ] Photocopy of passport
- [ ] Toiletries
- [ ] Money belt

Recommended

- [ ] Lighter/matches
- [ ] Washing line
- [ ] Lightweight scarf
- [ ] Hat
- [ ] Sunglasses
- [ ] Ear plugs
- [ ] Sewing kit
- [ ] Power adaptors
- [ ] Pocket knife
- [ ] Phrasebooks and guidebooks
- [ ] Mosquito net
- [ ] Pillow
- [ ] Alarm clock
- [ ] Water purification tablets

Optional

- [ ] Camping mat
- [ ] Digital camera
- [ ] Plastic cutlery
- [ ] Photos from home
- [ ] Journal
- [ ] Address book
- [ ] Tent
- [ ] Mobile phone
- [ ] Mp3 player

Need2Know

Summing Up

- To plan the best gap year, you need to get the basics right. Do your research to find out what is on offer and consider your options carefully, including who you will travel with, where you will go and how you will fund it.

- Invest in good basic equipment such as a backpack and sleeping bag and be realistic about what you can pack.

- Make sure that your passport is valid, that you have the right visas and that you have some idea of an itinerary.

- Once you have the practical issues in place, you can concentrate on planning a life-changing gap year and enjoying what the world has to offer.

'Once you have the practical issues in place, you can concentrate on planning a life-changing gap year and enjoying what the world has to offer.'

Chapter Two

Volunteering and Studying

A gap year is a great way to see the world and earn some money, but more and more people are adding an element of volunteering or studying to their adventures. This allows you to get to know a country and its people, give back and add/build some skills or languages on your travels. Employers like to see that you have done more than just sunbathe on your year out, and this is one way to broaden your CV and create interesting talking points.

There are many different types of volunteer work, so it is worth considering which is right for you. This may be something that you are interested in, have experience of or just suits your skills or personality the best.

Working with children

Working with children is a popular choice for volunteer work and can be very rewarding. Whether it is teaching English, helping out in an orphanage or working with street children, the bonds you make will stay with you forever. However, try to remember that it can also be very heart-wrenching to see the condition that some children live in – you need to learn not to get too attached.

Conservation

If you love animals or are keen on environmental issues then a conservation placement might be right for you. These usually take place in some of the world's most stunning places and give you access to areas you would never normally visit.

Specialist

Whether you are studying medicine, journalism or marine biology, there are opportunities to put your specialist skills to good use. Taking part in a specialist placement will be a boost to your CV and help you get a new perspective on your career choices.

Practical

'Whether it is digging wells or building houses, doing physical work leaves you with a tangible result to show for your efforts. It will be hard work and tiring, but is a great way to feel like you have achieved something worthwhile.'

Some people prefer to get their hands dirty and do some practical work. Whether it is digging wells or building houses, doing physical work leaves you with a tangible result to show for your efforts. It will be hard work and tiring, but is a great way to feel like you have achieved something worthwhile.

How do you choose a volunteer programme?

Search the Internet for volunteer placements and you will be bombarded with thousands of different options. So how do you know which one to go for? There are a number of things that you need to consider when deciding which programme to opt for.

Do your research so that you know what is available. Decide what is important to you and then ask questions so you can be clear about what you are signing up to. A good place to check for legitimate companies is www.theyearoutgroup.org where all the members have signed up to a code of practice. See the help list for some more reputable volunteer organisations.

Cost

Volunteer programmes can vary wildly in price. If you are booking one through a specialist company then you will be paying thousands of pounds, whereas if you arrange it locally it may only be a few hundred. The important thing is to know what you can afford, what your priorities are and what you are getting for your money.

Location

Due to the nature of volunteer work it is likely that you will be based in the poorest or most remote areas of the world, however location can still vary greatly. Think about whether you want to be in a city or rural location. This will affect the type of volunteer work that you are able to do. Do you have a particular country or area of the world that you are interested in? That is a good place to start.

Length of placement

Some people don't have the time or inclination to do a long-term volunteer placement but would still like to have a go. There is a whole industry of volunteering for one or two weeks. Although many of these placements can work out to be expensive, they are convenient and allow you to get a taster without any commitment. However, to get the most out of any volunteer placement, you really need to do it for at least a month so that you can settle into your surroundings and get to know people. How long you commit to will depend on your own circumstances. You may decide to devote a whole year to volunteer work or choose a couple of different shorter placements.

Values and vision

If you have strong feelings or beliefs in certain areas then you ought to choose a volunteer placement that matches them. For example, if you are strongly religious you may want to choose a company that shares your values. Or perhaps you believe poverty should be dealt with in a certain way and want to work with an organisation that upholds your beliefs.

The best thing to do is talk to other people who have volunteered with the same organisation. There are many Internet forums where you can find people who are willing to share their experiences with you.

Values of volunteering

Volunteering is a very different kind of experience than just visiting a country. It is a great way to immerse yourself in the culture that you are visiting by getting to know local people and seeing the reality of life at ground level. You will get a true understanding of the places you visit rather than just skimming the surface or seeing them from a tourist's perspective.

Donating money to charity is great but helping out personally is a much more rewarding experience. It can give you a whole new perspective on life and make you question your own values and ideals. Putting yourself in an unfamiliar situation and presenting yourself with new challenges can teach you a lot about your strengths and capabilities. Volunteering is a great way to test your limits, develop your confidence and figure out who you are as a person. Your experiences will stay with you when you return home and help to shape your opinions on the world.

As well as being a great personal experience, volunteering can also boost your career. It gives you international experience in working with people of different cultures which is important in today's global workforce. You may also use your time volunteering to develop new skills such as teamwork and project management.

'As well as being a great personal experience, volunteering can also boost your career. It gives you international experience in working with people of different cultures which is important in today's global workforce.'

What should you expect?

It may sound obvious, but the places you will volunteer in will not be the same as home. It is easy to think that you will be fine but you need to be realistic about what you are signing up for and what you are able to handle. You may be in a remote area, very close to extreme poverty and living without running water – could you cope?

Accommodation

Because the nature of volunteer work often takes you to remote and poor locations, the accommodation you stay in is likely to be less modern than you are used to. It can vary greatly but you need to ask where you will be staying and decide what you are willing to experience. Would you be happy living with strangers who don't speak English? Can you cope without running water?

Work

While you have signed up to volunteer, you don't want to be taken advantage of. Find out what you will be expected to do and how many hours a day you will be committing to. Part of your trip is about seeing the country and experiencing the local culture, so you need to make sure you will have time to do this. Also, be sure that you are offered enough training to prepare you for the work you will be doing, whether this is on the job or before you start.

Poverty

A lot of the places you will volunteer in are going to be very poor. If you have not experienced extreme poverty before it can be a big shock to the system. Seeing it close up in person is very different to seeing it on the television and it is something you need to prepare yourself for. Remember that, although your volunteering will make a useful contribution, you are not going to be able to solve these people's problems.

Where is your money going?

A lot of volunteer programmes can be expensive, so it is important that you know where your money is going. If you organise it locally then your money should be going directly to the project. If you organise it through a big company then don't be afraid to ask questions:

- What percentage of your fee goes directly to the project?
- Where does the rest of it go?

- How is the money managed?
- What do you get for your fee?

Organising independently

Organising your volunteer work independently is not for the faint-hearted but can be one of the best ways of doing it. It can save you a lot of money and ensure that what you are paying is going directly to those who need it.

This option is not a good idea if you are an inexperienced traveller or have worried parents at home. Even if you have travelled a lot, you need to have your wits about you, trust your instinct and make sure you do a lot of research before you commit to anything.

While many big companies will make donations from your fee to the project, you may find that spending the same amount locally will do a lot more good.

Remember though, by organising volunteer work independently you don't have the back up or in-country support of a big organisation – you have to be comfortable looking after yourself and making your own decisions if things go wrong.

Studying

Another common thing to choose to do is study abroad. This may be to get stuck into the culture, pick up a new skill or learn a language and is a great way to meet other people and spend some quality time in one place. Embrace your chosen subject and make the most of any social events or extra activities that are run in conjunction with it. A popular way to study abroad is through a university programme, but there are also many private organisations that offer a great variety of courses abroad. For a comprehensive directory to start looking for ideas, try www.studyabroadlinks.com.

Language courses

Language courses are especially popular, as being surrounded by a language is the best way to pick it up. It's also great to be able to communicate with the locals. These courses vary from a few days to months, and can often be combined with a stint of volunteering. Try and give yourself a head start by learning a bit before you go, but be realistic about your level, as being stuck in 'advanced Spanish' when you only know how to order a beer is not going to help you!

Cultural courses

Cultural courses can be a brilliant way to find out more about the country that you are visiting. Whether it is a cooking course, dance or a local tradition, it can give you a great insight into the area. These courses will usually be a bit shorter but, again, are often offered in conjunction with language courses or volunteering.

Skills

You may want to top up your skills to earn money while you are travelling or pursue or expand a hobby. Perhaps lifeguarding or outside survival is your kind of thing. Be sure you know exactly what the course will cover, check out their safety record and make sure that their certification is valid in other parts of the world.

While studying abroad is a learning venture in itself, think carefully about the subject you choose. There is nothing wrong in picking something just for fun, but it is also worth thinking about how it will benefit you when you return home and embark on your career.

'Cultural courses can be a brilliant way to find out more about the country that you are visiting. Whether it is a cooking course, dance or a local tradition, it can give you a great insight into the area.'

Action points

- Think about what type of volunteer work would suit you.
- Ask key questions about the volunteer programme.
- Talk to other volunteers and check out recommendations.
- Find courses in the countries you want to visit.
- Check the safety record and accreditation of practical courses.

Questions to ask volunteer programmes

Experience

- [ ] What will I gain from it?
- [ ] What skills will I learn?
- [ ] What is the aim of the project?
- [ ] Who will I be helping?
- [ ] Can I talk to some past volunteers?

Money

- [ ] How much will it cost?
- [ ] What does that include?
- [ ] How much more will I need?
- [ ] How much goes to the project?
- [ ] Where does the rest go?

Conditions

- [ ] Where will I be staying?
- [ ] How easy is it to get around?
- [ ] Will I be sharing with others?
- [ ] What is the standard of accommodation?
- [ ] Are there any safety concerns?

Work

- [ ] What exactly will I be doing?
- [ ] How many hours will I work?
- [ ] What training will I receive?
- [ ] Who will I be working with?
- [ ] Is there in-country support?

Summing Up

▦ Volunteering has become a very popular way to see the world and give something back. It allows you to immerse yourself in a culture, get to know the locals and see the reality of a country.

▦ Think about what kind of volunteer work would suit you and research suitable placements.

▦ Make sure that you are realistic about what to expect, the work involved and the commitment that you are making.

▦ If you are considering organising a placement independently, be sure you check the organisation out thoroughly and if going with a large company, find out where your money is going.

Chapter Three

Working

Unless you have another source of income, the chances are that you will have to work at some point during your gap year. You may choose to do this before you go away or combine it with your travels. Either way, there are a number of different options to consider and some exciting opportunities to gain more than just pocket money from your gap year job.

Seasonal work

Seasonal work is a popular way to earn some money and have some fun for a few months. Some people even make it a way of life; working a summer season somewhere sunny and then a winter season. Seasonal work doesn't usually pay very well but it is a great experience and your earnings will cover your expenses so you will not end up out of pocket. Across the world there are plenty of opportunities to take on seasonal agricultural work following the harvests. This kind of work, usually spending hours picking fruit or vegetables in the fields, is hard and not well paid. However, it is usually easy to pick up, very flexible and doesn't involve much thought or experience.

Summer season and holiday reps

Once the school holidays get started, thousands of families rush to holiday camps and resorts around the world. Summer camps in America are big business and you will be looking after a group of children while they enjoy an activity-filled break. It is a good way to live and work in the country for a short amount of time and your visa will usually allow you an extra couple of weeks to travel around before flying home.

'Opportunity is missed by most people because it is dressed in overalls and looks like work.'
Thomas A. Edison.

Similar to camp supervisors, there are plenty of jobs as holiday reps. Not all are 18-30's style, but can still be hard work and stressful. You will have to work all hours, dealing with guests' problems and complaints. However, you will get the chance to relax and have a bit of fun at the same time.

There are also many entertainment jobs available on holiday parks across the world. Whether you can sing, dance or juggle, it can be a fun way to spend your summer and a good learning ground if you want to develop your skills.

Winter season

'A popular way to earn some money is to teach English abroad. There are a lot of programmes that you can sign up to which take you to some amazing places.'

Winter season work is usually based in and around ski resorts which are plentiful across Europe in countries including France, Switzerland and Austria. Further afield, Canada and the USA have some very big and well-known resorts in places like Colorado and Banff (see the help list for web resources). These resorts come alive as people flock to them over the winter months and they need a lot of staff to run them. Whether you have a specialist skill such as ski instruction or want to work in the bar or chalets, the bonus is that you are likely to be given a free ski pass so you can spend your free time on the slopes.

Teaching English

A popular way to earn some money is to teach English abroad. There are a lot of programmes that you can sign up to which take you to some amazing places. Usually you will have to be willing to commit to at least a few months, but a year or more is more common.

Learning English is very popular across the world, so there are a lot of opportunities to work with both adults and children. Consider which age group you feel happiest teaching and also whether you want to be based in a school, community group or giving private lessons.

To teach English abroad you will usually need to have a TEFL qualification (see ESL Café in the help list). You can pay to do this on your own or it will be included in the more prestigious programmes. During this training you will learn some techniques for teaching but you will also develop your own methods on the job. Before accepting a teaching position, check what you will be required to do, what class sizes and support you will have and how many hours you will have to work. Teaching English can be a very well paid occupation but remember that you will have to commit to it and it may limit the travelling that you are able to do.

Finding temporary work abroad

Many people decide to spend a period of time in one country and find some work while they are there to fund the rest of their travels. First, you need to check what restrictions there are on your visa as some will limit the amount of time you can work for one employer or the type of work you can do. Hospitality, administration and the travel industry are the most common areas to find work in, but you don't need to limit yourself to these. Start looking around for opportunities – ask other travellers, look for adverts in your hostel, scour the Internet and approach some employment agencies.

Working visas

Unfortunately, in most cases, working abroad is not as easy as just showing up and getting a job. With the EU regulation, working in Europe is fairly simple, but if you want to go further afield, you will need to apply for a work visa and requirements vary greatly.

Europe

Thanks to the European Union, it is easy to gain work across Europe without a visa. Anyone from a member of an EU country can go to another one and work without restrictions. If you are looking for temporary work as you travel, it is very useful to speak the language, although you can organise work through many UK companies without needing to know the language.

'Travelling the world and getting paid for it – what could be better than that?'

Melanie, talking about her time working on cruise ships.

Australia

Australia has long been the most popular destination for people on their gap years. As well as the sea and sunshine, its appeal has a lot to do with the ease of getting a working visa. If you are a British national under 30 you can apply for a working holiday visa. This means you can stay in Australia for up to 12 months and work for up to six months with each employer. You can apply online and have to enter Australia within 12 months of the visa being issued.

North America

America has notoriously strict immigration laws. If you are found working without an appropriate visa, you will be shipped back to England and banned from returning. Usually, both in America and Canada, the only way to do it is to apply through a recognised programme that will allow you to do seasonal work or organise work with a specific employer. There is not the option, as with Australia, of going over and picking up work while you are there.

Working in the UK

Internships

You may decide that instead of spending your gap year travelling, you would prefer to get a head start on your career. This will put you a step ahead of your peers and can be a great way to build invaluable contacts.

Firstly, you need to decide if you want to do an internship here or abroad. Internships are very popular in America and there are lots of opportunities over there.

Do your research and find out what programmes are available. If there is a particular company that you want to work for then find out how they recruit interns and put together a strong application.

Finding vacancies

Where do you start? If you are looking for a local job to save some money, look in the newspaper, visit the job centre or ask friends. You may want to consider joining some employment agencies as well who will look for suitable work for you.

If you want to work as an intern or trainee in a bigger firm then you will need to find out about schemes. Contact companies in the industry you are interested in and ask about vacancies. Most information will usually be on their websites, so that is a good place to start.

Writing a CV

Your CV is probably the first contact you will have with future employers, so it is important that it makes a great first impression. A CV needs to include details on your education and qualifications, work experience and any relevant pastimes. Don't panic if you have never had a job before, it is all about presenting your transferable skills.

Were you on the school council? That shows you can take on responsibility, make a commitment and work as part of a team. Are you a keen runner? That shows motivation and determination. Look at what you've done while you were at school and how those skills could help you in the world of work.

See the page overleaf for help on putting your own CV together.

How to write a CV

The basics

- Keep it short – ideally one page, no more than two.
- Use a simple layout and font.
- Use a sensible email address.
- Include entries with most recent first.
- Never lie.

Personal profile

Talk about your main attributes and skills, what work you are looking for and why you would be good at it.

Employment history

- Include company name, location, job title and date period you worked.
- Concentrate on what you learnt/were responsible for/added to the company – rather than the ins and outs of what you did daily.

Education

- Keep it concise – employers don't need to know about every module.
- Leave out the negative but never lie.

Achievements and skills

- Don't go too far back – a book prize you won in Year 5 doesn't count!
- Stick to three or four points and don't exaggerate.
- Only include foreign languages if you can hold a basic conversation.

Hobbies

- Choose things that say something about your personality and capabilities – avoid hobbies like 'hanging out with friends'. Also, only include things you still do.

Working to save

In an ideal world, money would be no object. However, in reality you will need to think about how you are going to pay for your gap year. A popular route is to spend some of your year working at home to save up the money for travelling.

Getting into the habit of saving is the hardest part. You need to be strict with yourself and make a regular contribution to your savings account. Work out how much money you need to live on and then transfer the rest to a savings account as soon as you get paid. This will stop you having the temptation to spend it.

Your bank will be able to advise you on the best options and help you set up a savings account. Another good source of information and practical tips on saving money is www.moneysavingexpert.com.

Living at home

If you have just finished school and are planning your gap year, you are probably itching to get away from home. If you have been living away from home at university, then living with your parents again may not seem very appealing. However, when you are trying to save hard for your gap year, it is the best option.

Sit down with your parents and agree a set of rules that you are both happy with. They may want you to contribute towards the household costs, but it will still be a lot less than if you were living elsewhere. Try and be tolerant with each other and remember that it is only for a set amount of time.

Work and travel

Another option for working and travelling is to do both at the same time and choose a job that allows you to see the world. This is a bigger commitment than applying for a summer job or taking on some temporary work, but it also comes with some great opportunities.

'In an ideal world, money would be no object. However, in reality you will need to think about how you are going to pay for your gap year.'

Nanny

If you have a childcare qualification, it could be a great idea for you to become a nanny. Lots of families employ nannies to look after their children in the UK, abroad and while they travel. There are agencies that can help you find vacancies and organise visas and legalities for you such as Childcare International (see the help list for details).

Cruise ships

Cruise ships offer a superb way of combining work and travel. There are all sorts of jobs – from waiters and bar staff to beauty therapists, photographers and sports coaches. Your food and accommodation will be taken care of so you don't have any expenses and can spend your money enjoying the amazing places you sail into.

You can apply for cruise ship jobs directly with the cruise line or through a hiring agent, as they are always looking for new staff as the industry expands. Crown Recruitment is a good agency who hire for Royal Caribbean, Carnival and Azamara (see the help list for details).

Crewing yachts

Having sailing experience is a bonus but yachts also need other staff such as chefs and cleaners. Crewing a yacht is hard work but can allow you to get a taste of the high life by visiting some of the world's wealthiest ports.

Most people find jobs in this line of work by turning up at ports and asking around but you can also look at www.crewseekers.net where many vacancies are advertised.

Action points

- Decide if you want to work at home or abroad.
- Work out what your skills and attributes are and spend time creating a CV.
- Do your research to find out what jobs are available.
- Make sure you have the appropriate working visa.

Summing Up

- Most people will work at some point in their gap year to help them fund their time away. Whether you choose to work before you leave or take a job that allows you to travel or work abroad, you need to think carefully about your choice.

- You may decide to spend the whole time concentrating on working, in which case you need to do even more research to make sure you find a suitable job.

- There are some amazing opportunities to earn money while seeing the world and furthering your career, and a job doesn't just need to be a means to an end.

Chapter Four

Health and Safety

You want to remember your gap year for the rest of your life – but for all the right reasons. Catching a nasty disease, being mugged or left stranded abroad are probably not the type of memories you are planning to make. It may be the boring side of planning your trip, but making sure you are safe and healthy is essential if you want to enjoy all the fun parts. Check out what vaccinations you need for the areas of the world you are visiting and be aware of common scams and mishaps so that you can do your best to prevent them from happening to you.

Disease prevention

It is important that you take the correct precautions against disease and get the right vaccinations for wherever in the world you are travelling. Sometimes you can get these for free from your GP, otherwise you may have to pay.

For some areas of the world, certain precautions are essential while others may only be advised, especially if you are just visiting certain parts of a country. Make sure you visit your GP at least eight weeks before you are due to travel so you have time to get everything you need.

'It is important that you take the correct precautions against disease and get the right vaccinations for wherever in the world you are travelling.'

Malaria

Malaria is a serious disease that you catch from mosquito bites in many tropical areas. Wearing long clothing, using a strong mosquito spray and a mosquito net can all help prevent you catching it, but you should also take a course of malaria tablets. You will need to start these before you go to the affected area and continue taking them once you leave.

Yellow fever

Yellow fever is a viral infection transmitted by mosquitoes and is most common in Sub-Saharan Africa and tropical areas of South America. The vaccine is one simple injection that lasts around 10 years and some countries require proof that you have been vaccinated before they will let you in.

Hepatitis A

Hepatitis A is caught from contaminated food and water or from person to person through poor hygiene. Make sure that the water you drink is safe and avoid anything that may have been washed in contaminated water such as salad or fruit. A vaccination will protect you for up to a year and then a booster shot will make sure you are covered for the next 20 years.

Typhoid

Typhoid is caused by salmonella bacteria through food that has been contaminated with faeces or urine. A single vaccine will protect you for up to three years.

Meningococcal meningitis

Meningococcal meningitis is passed on through respiratory excretion such as coughing or sneezing. It is difficult to prevent but you can get a vaccine against it which is advised if you are visiting areas where there have been outbreaks e.g. Saudi Arabia, India, Nepal and some parts of Sub-Saharan Africa.

Tetanus and polio

Both of these diseases are vaccinated against under the child immunisation programme, so most people should already be protected. If you have not had these vaccinations or are at particular risk, talk to your GP.

Jetlag

When you are travelling around the world you are going to enter lots of time zones and gain and lose hours as you go. All these time changes can take their toll on your body. There are various schools of thought about how to deal with jetlag but having a sleep on the plane, avoiding alcohol and drinking lots of water will all help. Trying to regulate your body clock by staying up until night-time in your new location will also help you get over it a bit quicker.

Altitude sickness

Some popular tourist destinations – e.g. Cusco and Machu Picchu in Peru – are at a much higher altitude than you are probably used to. While some people won't notice any difference, others can be affected quite severely by altitude sickness which can leave you feeling dizzy, sick and disorientated. The best way to combat it is to acclimatise slowly at intermediate altitudes and go back down if you are feeling unwell. There are altitude sickness tablets you can take – Acetazolamide being a common one – or in South America, chewing coca leaves is the accepted remedy.

Safe sex

Safe sex is essential wherever you are in the world and the best way to stay safe is to plan ahead.

- Condoms – the best thing to do is to take a supply of condoms with you from the UK. If you are going to buy them abroad, make sure that they have the CE symbol that means they meet European standards, or choose well-known, respected brands if further afield. If you decide to sleep with someone then make sure that a condom is used.

- The pill – if you are on the pill, visit your GP and get a supply for your whole trip. When you are travelling with a lot of time changes, knowing when to take your pill can be confusing. Try to do the maths and take your pill within 12 hours of the normal time. Remember that the pill does not protect you against sexually transmitted infections (STIs).

'There are various schools of thought about how to deal with jetlag but having a sleep on the plane, avoiding alcohol and drinking lots of water will all help.'

- STIs and AIDS – nobody can be counted as 'safe' because of what they look like or where they come from, so you always need to protect yourself. If you think that you may have contracted an STI, you need to find a local clinic and get checked out as it may get worse if you leave it until you return home.

What precautions should you take?

Trying to fit all your clothes in your backpack may seem hard enough, but you need to make sure that you leave room for a few safety essentials. Having the basics to hand can make a big difference when you are in a tricky situation and prevention is always better than cure.

Mosquito spray

If you are visiting humid countries, the jungle or anywhere known for mosquitoes, you need to buy some good repellent. Not only will bites leave you in a lot of discomfort, you also run the risk of catching malaria – not a fun prospect. Be sure to spend the extra pounds on a strong spray that contains a high percentage of DEET (the most common active ingredient found in insect repellent) as many others have little effect.

Safety alarm

Although no substitute for staying safe, a safety alarm can be a good back up and help you gain attention if you find that your safety is threatened. There are many options but a pocket-sized alarm with a strap to attach to your bag can be the most practical choice. Some police stations or student unions give these out for free, so it is worth checking before you buy one.

Emergency numbers

Do you know how to phone for an ambulance in Thailand? It is a good idea to check what the local emergency numbers are in the countries that you are visiting. Also, make sure you know how to contact your local embassy and have the number of your travel insurance company handy.

First aid pack

Having some basics with you will be helpful when you get a blister, cut or graze and don't have access to any medical supplies. A basic first aid pack should include:

- Plasters.
- Bandages.
- Antiseptic cream.
- Cotton wool.
- Sterile dressings.
- Adhesive tape.
- Disposable gloves.
- Scissors.
- Tweezers.
- Safety pins.

It is also a good idea to go on a first aid course so that you know how to deal with emergency situations and carry out basic procedures.

See the end of the chapter for a complete health and safety checklist which will ensure that you are fully prepared.

Diarrhoea and rehydration tablets

You may have heard of 'Delhi belly' and it sounds quite funny until you actually experience it! Because the quality of the water is not as good in some countries and you will be eating different foods, you can be prone to getting diarrhoea. As well as being very uncomfortable, it can quickly lead to dehydration, so it is good to have the ability to minimise its effect.

Painkillers and allergy pills

Yes, you will be able to buy painkillers abroad but it is much easier to deal with brands and doses that you are familiar with. It is also a good idea to take some allergy pills as you never know what you may have an adverse reaction to.

Safe travel

Across the world there is a lot of political instability and you should always check with the foreign office for advice on which countries are safe to travel to. While some are quite obvious, there can be unrest in regions that you are unaware of and certain areas of countries should be best avoided, even if the rest are safe to travel to.

Terrorism

Unfortunately, terrorism is a realistic concern in today's world. Part of the terror is that you cannot predict the attacks and there really is nowhere that you can consider 'safe'. This is not meant to scare you but to point out that you should not let your fears stop you from travelling, as an attack could just as well happen in your home town. Security has increased in airports and major tourist destinations, but it is still worth being vigilant and reporting any suspicious activity.

Natural disasters

There have been some major natural disasters in recent years and nobody could have failed to be shocked by the tsunami that devastated areas of Asia. Like terrorism, natural disasters can be difficult to predict but it is worth checking for any details on recent activity in places you are planning to visit. Take note of any serious weather warnings, make sure you are adequately prepared and do not take unnecessary risks by thinking it won't happen to you.

Drug smuggling

You have no doubt seen the stories on the news of young people being sentenced to life in jail for drug smuggling abroad. Some people choose to take that risk while others are coerced into it – but the authorities often do not care about your reasons. Many foreign jails have terrible conditions and it is not somewhere you want to end up. Even a recreational amount of cannabis can land you in serious trouble, so be very careful about using drugs abroad – the best way to stay safe is by not being involved with drugs at all!

Scams

It would be nice to think that everybody is friendly and helpful, and most are, but unfortunately there is still a small percentage who are out to rip you off. It is good to meet new people and socialise with the locals, but you also need to be aware of some common scams.

- Fraud – whether it is your passport or your bank card, you need to be extra careful when you are abroad. A common scam is for a shopkeeper to take your card into the back in order to scan it and then get you to sign the receipt. While they are back there though, they make an extra copy for a further amount and then forge your signature. Always ask them to bring the machine out to where you can see it.

- Keep your luggage with you – when you are travelling around the world your luggage is the home of all your worldly possessions and the last thing you

'Natural disasters can be difficult to predict but it is worth checking for any details on recent activity in places you are planning to visit.'

want to do is lose them. Some dodgy taxi drivers will wait for you to get out and then drive off with your luggage in their boot. Instead, keep it with you on the seat of the car.

- Check your change – when you are dealing with a foreign currency it is easy to get confused and not be exactly sure how much things cost or how much change you are due. Some retailers will take advantage of this by short-changing you, so try to be aware of what you are owed and count it before you leave.

- Stick with your hotel – a lot of travellers have found that when they give the address of their hotel or hostel to a taxi driver, they claim that it no longer exists. They may seem helpful, offering to take you to a different one, but this is a scam and they will be on commission to take tourists to it. Check in advance that the place exists by calling them or looking on the Internet, then be firm with your taxi driver that you want to be taken to it.

'When I had my bag stolen in South America I was so happy that my mum had badgered me into getting travel insurance.'

Ele, 18.

Travelling alone

Travelling alone can be a scary prospect – often more for your parents than for you! Plenty of people do it every year but you need to make sure that you stay safe and don't put yourself in any unnecessary danger. Tell someone where you are going to be and inform your hostel or another traveller if you are going anywhere remote.

It is a good idea to make sure that you always have a charged mobile phone with you and stay in regular touch with friends and family at home so they know where you are. Also, be sure you have enough cash to make a call or catch a taxi in an emergency.

Be careful not to give too much personal information away to strangers and be wary about telling taxi drivers that you are travelling alone. Stay in reputable hostels and make sensible travel choices so you don't end up in any sticky situations.

Women travellers

In certain areas of the world, women may need to adapt their behaviour and dress appropriately in order to respect local customs. In more conservative countries, women are expected to cover up completely. It is advisable to act in a moderate way to avoid any unwanted attention.

Wherever you are travelling, it is important as a female traveller to be sensible – don't walk alone at night, only use reputable travel firms and be careful about who you befriend. If you make responsible choices there is no reason why you cannot have a safe, fun experience travelling alone.

Trusting your instinct

If something doesn't feel right then it probably isn't. Trusting your instinct is one of the best things that you can do to stay safe. Our 'sixth sense' acts as an early warning system as our unconscious mind registers danger before our conscious mind has a chance to notice. Don't feel stupid or scared for trusting your instinct. You want your gap year to be a fun and memorable experience for all the right reasons and erring on the side of caution will help keep it that way.

Action points

- Check the foreign office website for up-to-date travel advisories.
- Visit your GP at least eight weeks before you set off to get all the relevant vaccinations.
- Make a simple health and safety kit.
- Never put yourself in an unnecessarily dangerous situation.
- Trust your instinct.

Health and safety checklist

Essential

☐ Vaccinations

☐ Vaccination certificates

☐ Mosquito repellent

☐ Antiseptic wipes

☐ Plasters

☐ Painkillers

☐ Allergy pills

☐ Diarrhoea tablets

☐ Sunscreen

☐ Travel insurance policy

☐ Emergency contact numbers

☐ Prescription medication

Recommended

☐ Condoms

☐ Safety alarm

☐ Malaria tablets

☐ Cold medicine

☐ Indigestion remedies

☐ Rehydration sachets

☐ Insect bite cream

☐ Tweezers

☐ Blister plasters

Optional

☐ Contraceptive pill

☐ Sanitary products

☐ Toilet paper

☐ Bandages

☐ Cystitis relief

☐ Altitude sickness medicine

Summing Up

- Health and safety may be the boring bit, but it is also the most important in making sure your trip runs smoothly. The last thing you want to do is abandon your gap year because of something that you could have prevented.

- Make sure that you find out about the places you want to visit, how safe they are and what vaccinations you will need.

- As well as carrying essential health and safety items with you, trust your instinct and don't put yourself in any situations that may be unsafe.

'Health and safety may be the boring bit, but it is also the most important in making sure your trip runs smoothly. The last thing you want to do is abandon your gap year because of something that you could have prevented.'

Chapter Five

Money

Planning for a gap year is an exciting time but paying for it can be a little less enjoyable! Whatever you decide to do with your year, you need to think about how you are going to pay for it.

How much money will you need?

How much you spend can vary wildly depending on the level of luxury that you are looking for and whereabouts in the world you are going. Costs for different areas of the world are covered in their relevant chapters further along in the book, but an average daily budget, staying in hostels, eating reasonably and having a few trips and activities would be around £15-20 for developing countries and £35-40 for developed countries.

To work out how much money you are going to need for your trip you need to do your research. Find out average prices for flights, accommodation, volunteer programmes and any other major costs in the areas of the world you want to visit. Then look at the cost of living for each place and how much you will need for everyday expenses while you are there. On top of that you need to add some money for activities, socialising, treats and emergency funds.

Flights

Flights are going to be your biggest single cost, so it is important that you get the best deal. Some round-the-world flights offer great savings and can be found for as little as £900. Check out www.roundtheworldflights.com to find the best value flight for your trip or talk to a travel specialist such as Trailfinders (see the help list for details). If you go on the most common routes, e.g. Asia – Australia – America, then it can be quite cheap, but once you start adding less popular places, it can soon add up. As you will book your major flights before you leave, you will already have paid this expense. However, you still need to leave some money for any flights you may want to take locally.

Other travel

Once you have arrived in a country, you are still going to need to travel around it. Travelling by bus is usually the cheapest option but if you are going to travel long distances in Australia or America, it can be worth buying a car or camper van and selling it when you are done.

'Travelling by bus is usually the cheapest option but if you are going to travel long distances in Australia or America, it can be worth buying a car or camper van and selling it when you are done.'

Equipment

It is worth investing in a good backpack as it can make a big difference to your comfort. The same goes for a sleeping bag and a good pair of walking shoes. These costs will need to be paid out before you leave but will definitely give you your money's worth (see chapter 1 for information on buying equipment).

Accommodation

The cost of your accommodation can vary wildly. Camping is the cheapest but in some areas it is not safe to do so. There are hostels available in all backpacker destinations but the quality can be very different, so it is good to find recommendations. If you would like to treat yourself to some better accommodation along the way, make sure you have budgeted it in.

- Camping – as the cheapest way to bed down for the night you may choose to stay on a campsite, or set up in an unofficial location. The downside of camping is that you will have to carry your equipment with you and this can add a lot of extra bulk and weight to your backpack.

- Home stays – home stays are popular if you are volunteering or learning a language and can be a cost-effective way to stay and get to know the locals. Families will usually be assigned by the organisation you book with.

- Couch surfing – there has been a growth in 'couch surfer' websites, where other travellers agree to let you stay in their homes. Many of the popular sites such as www.couchsurfing.org have review sections where you can see what other people have said about the hosts. This is by no means a guarantee of safety but can help you vet people.

- Hostels – hostels are the most popular kind of accommodation for travellers. They are plentiful and can be found in every city or tourist trail in the world. The cost and standard can vary wildly, so it is good to get recommendations or stick to listings in trusted guide books. You will usually be sleeping in a same-sex dorm but in some hostels it is possible to book a private room at an extra cost, which can work out well if you are travelling with a partner or friends.

- Guesthouses – guesthouses are often small, family-run places that have been set up in a home. They usually offer good value for money and include breakfast. If you are travelling alone this can work out expensive but with friends or a partner, it can be a reasonable option.

- Hotels – although you may associate hotels with expense, you can get a lot more for your money in some areas of the world. You may also find that after months in shared hostels, you might be willing to splash out a little bit more for a night of comfort.

Programmes and visas

If you are going on an organised volunteering or work programme, this is going to be a big expense which you will have to pay for in advance. Make sure that you do your research and know what is included in the cost as the extra expenses can all add up. Consider the cost of living for the region you will be staying in so you can work out how much more money you may need.

If you need to get a visa to work in or visit a country, you need to consider that expense too. Find out how much these will cost in advance so you are fully prepared and can factor it into your budget.

Trips

While travelling, you may decide to take a trip because you don't have much time, are travelling alone or want to go somewhere difficult to reach. The price of trips will depend on where you are in the world and whether you book it locally. Look into costs in advance and make sure you know what you are getting for your money and if you will have to pay out anything extra for food or activities. While you can always find someone who will do it for less, remember that the cheapest isn't always the best value.

Food

'A few basic meals and some lacklustre hostels meant I could afford the really memorable moments.'

Sarah, 22

You have to eat, so this area of budgeting is essential! If you are happy to make your own meals and buy food from markets, you can get by on quite a small budget. However, if you would like the occasional meal out, or are travelling in more expensive countries such as America or Europe, then it can become a major expense.

Activities

Travelling around the world gives you the opportunity to experience some amazing activities. Decide on the things that you really want to do and make sure that you have enough money to do them so that you are not left disappointed. Be careful about going for the cheapest providers as you want to make sure they are safe and reliable. The best thing to do is to ask other travellers or enquire at your hostel.

Part of the fun of travelling is meeting new people and you are going to want to socialise. A few drinks in a local bar is not going to break your budget, but you need to make sure that you don't build your budget too tightly to have a bit of fun. Hostels often have reasonably priced drinks and will arrange social events. In tourist areas, prices will shoot up, so you may only want to hang out there for one slowly sipped drink!

Travel insurance

Travel insurance is not an area to scrimp on. Of course you hope that nothing bad will happen but if it does, you want to make sure you can access the best help available. Your bank or home insurer may be able to offer you travel insurance but some companies will only insure travellers for shorter trips. Shop around for the best deals on a comparison site such as Insure My Trip (see the help list for details).

Insurance will cost more if you are travelling outside Europe and many companies have a further premium for travelling in North America. By agreeing to pay a higher amount yourself before the company pays out, you will be able to lower the cost of your insurance. Never lie about any details on your application as this can invalidate your claim.

* Sports cover – remember that most policies will not cover any kind of sports or high-risk activity unless you pay extra. This means that all the bungee jumping, skydiving and white water rafting that you want to do won't be covered unless you specifically buy insurance for it.

* Repatriation and medical bills – in some countries, such as the United States, medical bills can be astonishingly high, so you don't want to run the risk of having to pay them. Take a look at how much the insurance covers and if anything – such as pre-existing conditions – is excluded. Also, find out whether it only covers in-country treatment or if it will pay for repatriation back to the UK.

* Personal items – cheaper travel insurance policies will not give any cover for the loss of personal items and those that do will have set limits and often group items together under one claim. Read the fine details of these and if you are travelling with an expensive camera or other equipment, make sure it is named separately.

Managing your money

Once you have worked out how much money you are going to need for your gap year, you can start figuring out how you are going to save it. Perhaps you have savings, your parents are willing to contribute to your trip or you are planning to work while you are away to contribute to your fund. If you still need to save money before you leave then you must work out how much you can afford to put aside and regularly transfer this to a savings account.

How do you budget?

While you are away you need to keep an eye on what you are spending. If you only have limited funds, the last thing you want to do is run out of money halfway round the world! By working out a weekly budget and sticking to it, you will make sure that you have enough spare cash to spend on the exciting stuff. Use the budgeting form at the end of this chapter to work out how much money you will have to work with, then keep a log of what you spend so you can see where your money is going. It is easy to get carried away when you are travelling – remember to concentrate on your priorities and make sure you have money for the things you really want to do.

Keeping money safe

Whether you are at home or thousands of miles away, you should always be keeping your money safe. However, when you have been away for a while it can be easy to get a bit blasé about where you stash your cash. The best thing you can do is buy a money belt which will sit flat under your clothes so your money is always close by. If you are staying in communal accommodation, make sure you have a locked compartment to keep it in.

Access to money

When you are travelling you want to make sure that you always have enough money. You also need to be careful about how much money you have on you at once. The best way to handle it is to have a combination of different methods. You should always make sure that you have a reasonable amount of cash on you so that you are not caught out. In most areas of the world though, you will be able to access your money at a cashpoint and this often gives you the best exchange rate. However, it is good to have a back up in case you lose your card or it does not work. Take a few travellers cheques with you in sterling or US dollars so you can cash them anywhere.

Changing currency

As you travel around the world, you are probably going to need a number of different currencies. It is not worthwhile leaving home with all of these – instead pick them up along the way. One of the easiest ways to get money in different countries is to use your cash card. Travelling with some US dollars is also a good idea as many people often prefer to receive these than their local currency.

When you do need to change money you can visit a bank or travel exchange, or many hotels or hostels will also run this service. Before changing any money, have an idea of what the current exchange rate is so that you do not get a bad deal. You will always have to pay some sort of charge, so plan how much you will need as you go along to avoid making too many small transactions and losing out.

Money-saving tips

- Flights – keep checking sites as prices can change a lot. Have a look just after midnight when tickets are released and mid-week when prices are often lower.

- Accommodation – staying out of the centre is always cheaper. Keep your eyes open for special offers and consider taking up those offers of a sofa to sleep on from friends you have made along the way.

- Food – go where the locals go, avoid the tourist areas and look for 'meal of the day' offers. Buy food from the street vendors and local markets and make use of cooking facilities in hostels.

- Activities and attractions – look out for discount cards, student discounts and money off vouchers. Take advantage of any free museums and galleries or specific days or evenings when they offer discounted entry.

- Shopping – bargaining is common in many countries and is to be expected. Make sure you are not showing a lot of wealth through your dress or jewellery, then decide what you want to pay and start significantly lower to give haggling room.

'One of the easiest ways to get money in different countries is to use your cash card. Travelling with some US dollars is also a good idea as many people often prefer to receive these than their local currency.'

Action points

- Open a savings account and set up a monthly direct debit.
- Use the form opposite to work out how much money you will have.
- Buy a money belt and keep your money safe and secure at all times.
- Find out the cost of living for each destination (see the continent guides).
- Create a weekly budget.

Budgeting

Overall budget

Money from savings

Money from parents

Amount you expect to earn before you go

Amount you expect to earn while travelling

Total

Expenses

Flights

Other travel

Equipment

Accommodation

Programmes and visas

Trips

Food

Socialising

Activities

Travel insurance

Emergency funds

Total

Travelling budget

Daily cost of living

Number of days

Total

Summing Up

■ Money makes the world go round and helps you go around the world. It would be great if you had an endless supply, but the chances are you will need to budget and prioritise.

■ Do your research so you know how much the cost of living will be in the areas of the world you are visiting.

■ Then try and work out how much money you will need – leaving some room for activities, socialising and emergencies.

■ Make sure that you keep your money safe and always have access to some back-up funds.

Chapter Six

Asia

Popular with gap year travellers for its cheap hostels and backpacking trail, Asia is a continent that offers culture, relaxation and value for money. Step away from the tourist trail and you will find genuine, welcoming people who make this continent what it is. Fabulous food, ancient sites and beautiful beaches have marked Asia as a firm favourite.

Where to go

When you think of travelling in Asia you are probably automatically drawn to Thailand or India, but the continent stretches all the way over to Saudi Arabia and Yemen. The most popular area is still Southeast Asia where you can fly into the hub of Bangkok and spend your time on the beaches or in the eclectic cities. Circle north to take in the culture of Vietnam and Cambodia or pick the clean class of Singapore and head south to enjoy the beauty of Indonesia. If the language and traditions of the east intrigue you, fly into high-rise Hong Kong before stepping out into the sprawl of China and up to Beijing to walk on the Great Wall. Fly over to Japan to get a taste of its intriguing past and the high-tech future before flying out of Tokyo. It is possible to spend your whole trip just in India which can prove to be addictive with its mix of people, food, landscapes and culture. If you are feeling more ambitious, head over to the Middle East but make sure you have done your research to navigate this less travelled region.

'Fabulous food, ancient sites and beautiful beaches have marked Asia as a firm favourite.'

What to see

Taj Mahal, India

This iconic mausoleum in Agra is just as impressive close up – if you can see it clearly through the hazy smog caused by pollution in the city.

Hong Kong at night

The lights on the high-rise buildings reflect in the river and present an image in sharp contrast with the small boats and homes that float on it.

Reclining Buddha, Thailand

There is more to Bangkok than cheap bars and hostels and this striking Buddha, the largest in Thailand, sits in Bangkok's oldest Buddhist temple.

Washing in the Ganges, India

The mass of Hindus making the pilgrimage to perform the traditional washing away of their sins in this sacred river is a dazzling sight to see.

Angkor Wat Temple, Cambodia

This collection of over one hundred temples dating from the 12th century is overrun by the jungle and looks like something out of an Indiana Jones movie.

Things to do

Have a curry on the beach

Curry may be the UK's national dish but what better place to eat it than where it originated, combined with the other love of the Brits – sun, sea and sand.

Get a suit tailor-made in Hong Kong

Look like you can afford a trip to Saville Row by investing in the super talented but cut-price services of a tailor in Hong Kong or Thailand.

Ride on an elephant

It may not be the most comfortable of rides but riding on an elephant has to be the ultimate in exotic travel!

Walk along the Great Wall of China

Stretching around 4,000 miles, it's the only manmade structure that can be seen from space – that should be reason enough to take a bit of a stroll.

Buy some silks

Whether you want to use them as a scarf, for curtains or as a present for your mum, the silks in Asia are stunning.

'India is the cradle of the human race, the birthplace of human speech, the mother of history, the grandmother of legend, and the great grandmother of tradition.'

Mark Twain.

Customs, laws and language

Asia is the largest and most populated continent (it is home to 60% of the world's population) and with this comes a diverse mix of countries and cultures. From the conservative societies of the Middle East to cosmopolitan hubs like Hong Kong and Singapore and the world powerhouse of China, there is no one set of rules that will cover you for them all.

Southeast Asia is very popular with backpackers for its spiritual, laid-back approach to life and the friendly welcoming nature of its people. Initially, India can be a bit overwhelming but if you strip away the outer images, you will find an enchanting set of people. In China and Japan you will find that people are much more proud and private and it may take you a little longer to get to know them.

'The main hubs of Asia are usually included on a round-the-world ticket, so it pays to stop off at places such as Bangkok, Hong Kong or Singapore.'

In Japan and Hong Kong and the major cosmopolitan cities, you can get away with speaking English but if you are travelling into mainland China or countries such as Cambodia, you will struggle without a few simple phrases. Obviously, Japanese and Chinese are not the easiest languages to learn but you should be able to pick up a few phrases even if you can't read it.

Areas further west and in the Middle East are much more conservative and strictly religious. A lot of countries in this area are Muslim and have conservative views about dress and behaviour. Make sure you have long, loose fitting clothes and women should have something to cover their head. If you are going to visit these areas, be careful not to behave by Western standards. Alcohol is often forbidden and you can be locked up for being too intimate in public. The main language is Arabic but English is widely spoken.

Getting there and getting around

The main hubs of Asia are usually included on a round-the-world ticket, so it pays to stop off at places such as Bangkok, Hong Kong or Singapore. The area has also been receiving more low cost airlines, so even if you are travelling directly or within the region, you can find some good deals. Try www.airasia.com or www.jetstarasia.com.

Japan and China have extensive rail networks but outside of these countries you will probably be relying on the bus system, taking a few internal flights or choosing an organised tour. There are many companies that serve this region of the world but they vary in price considerably depending on whether they are run locally or by a foreign company.

Health and safety

There has been a lot of unrest in this region recently, so it's important to check for foreign office travel advisories before visiting any of the more unstable countries such as Sri Lanka or Tibet. However, Southeast Asia is generally a fairly safe destination for travellers.

In China there has been a lot of tension about human rights issues and although it is safe to travel around, you may be wise to bite your tongue sometimes so you don't cause offence or get in trouble with the authorities.

There are a number of vaccinations recommended for this area of the world, so check in with your GP who will be able to advise you on what you need. The basic recommendations are hepatitis A, hepatitis B, tetanus, measles and typhoid vaccinations. You also need to be careful about what you eat and drink in the region as no one wants to suffer the infamous Delhi belly! Try to stick to bottled water and avoid any food that may have been washed in water or seems poorly cooked.

Costs

Although it can cost quite a lot to get there, once you are in Asia, living is quite cheap (depending greatly on which country you are visiting). While your money will go a long way in Thailand and India, you won't get much for it in the likes of Dubai or the bigger cities in the region. You can live for as little as £5 a day in India, Nepal and Indonesia, but this can easily jump to over £30 if you are staying somewhere more cosmopolitan.

Accommodation and food costs vary wildly depending on what level of luxury you are looking for. This area of the world has some of the most expensive hotels in the world – in Dubai for example – and also some of the cheapest backpacking hostels. You can pick up some amazing street food or enjoy a curry on the beach in Goa for next to nothing, while some people will be splashing out hundreds of pounds for a meal in a top restaurant.

Asia is a great place for picking up silks and clothing. In Thailand and Hong Kong you can get a suit made for a fraction of the price you would pay for the service in the UK. It is a good idea to carry some US dollars with you as these are often popular, especially if you are buying produce at the markets.

Living and working

Asia is a common destination for people wanting to teach English and there are a number of relatively well-paid programmes in Japan, www.jetprogramme.org being a popular one. You will also find a lot of volunteer programmes in the region, many working with children or animals. You should do your research before signing up to any of these but they are a great way to really get to see the local culture.

In recent years, Dubai and the Middle East have been attracting a lot of work, and people are drawn out there because of the tax-free living. They are not the best places to pick up casual work but if you are planning to spend a solid portion of your time in one place, they can be a great place to work and save.

Action points

- Budget more for visits to the cosmopolitan cities in the region.
- Pack layers and long clothes for conservative countries.
- Check with the foreign office for any civil unrest.
- Learn a few key phrases for countries where you can't guess at the language.
- Pick areas that suit your personality.

Summing Up

- There are some well-worn backpacker roads in Asia and it is a laid-back and spiritual place to travel.

- Don't find yourself limited to the south east though, as there is plenty to see further afield.

- Start your trip from one of the cosmopolitan hubs such as Bangkok and Hong Kong, but make sure you experience the countryside and culture away from the big cities.

- Head in the direction that suits your interests and personality – whether it is partying, culture or relaxation.

- Watch: *The Beach* directed by Danny Boyle.

- Read: *Wild Swans: Three Daughters of China* by Jung Chang.

- Surf: www.thingsasian.com.

Chapter Seven

Africa

Africa may only be a small step from Europe but it is a whole different world that will assault your senses and give you a new reality check. From the sights and souks in North Africa down to the vast stretches of desert and vibrant city of Cape Town, Africa will enchant you.

Where to go

A popular and relatively safe place to start is Cape Town which has a great laid-back trendy appeal. Move east along the famous garden route or north to Kruger National Park for some animal spotting. From here you can continue up to see the stunning Victoria Falls in Zambia, the dunes of Namibia or the 'warm heart of Africa' by heading up to Malawi. Most people go to Africa for safari where Kenya and Tanzania are the best bet. This area is also good for a quick beach break by popping over to the Kenyan resorts or on to Zanzibar. North Africa also offers some great sights – from the pyramids in Egypt, over to the souks of Marrakech in Morocco. If you're feeling adventurous, head south from here and take in the whole of the continent which is much more about the people and the experience than ticking things off along the way.

What to see

Masai Mara, Kenya

This immense national reserve is especially famous for its views of the formidable wildebeest migration.

'The person who has not travelled widely thinks his or her mother is the only cook.'
African proverb.

Table Mountain, South Africa

Looming over Cape Town, the hanging mist makes this imposing mountain look all the more impressive.

The Pyramids, Egypt

A wonder of the ancient world, the pyramids are a truly unique sight and cannot be seen anywhere else in the world.

Mount Kilimanjaro, Tanzania

Even if you don't have the time, inclination or money to climb it, a trip to Mount Kilimanjaro is still mesmerising.

Victoria Falls, Zambia

Straddling the border of Zambia and Zimbabwe, the immense amount of water tumbling over these Falls is immense.

Things to do

Feel lost in the Namibian desert

With the largest sand dunes in the world, it is difficult to know which way is out! It is an awesome feeling to be just a dot in the desert.

Buy some local crafts

Some of the local indigenous crafts are so intricate and based on generations of experience that you will always have a unique souvenir.

Go on safari

There's nothing quite as amazing as watching a lion or giraffe in their natural habitat. It may be a bit pricey but it's worth every penny.

Ride a camel

It's not particularly comfortable but it is a unique experience that you won't get on the beach at Blackpool.

Start haggling in the souks

Unlike in your local supermarket, haggling is an expected part of the culture and can bag you a great bargain!

Customs, laws and language

Africa is often portrayed as a scary continent and although there has been a lot of war and corruption over the years, it is still a great place to visit.

The majority of people are humble and hard-working and are also very hospitable, despite often being very poor themselves. Generally, wherever you go, you will be made to feel welcome by the infectious charm of the locals. Many countries are still very conservative, especially in the Muslim areas of the north, so it is important to respect their cultures and cover up.

There are a wide range of languages and dialects spoken across Africa but French is prevalent in the west. In the majority of places, even in small remote villages, you will be able to get by with English and a few signs and actions!

'Out of all the places I visited, Africa was the one that got under my skin and I can't stop thinking about.'
James, 27.

Getting there and getting around

Flights to Africa can be expensive and although they can be included on round-the-world tickets, they are not the most common and therefore push the price up. It can be worth travelling to France and flying from there with www.airfrance.com because with various former French colonies on the continent, travelling there is more common.

Although flights to Africa can be long, as you are going down instead of across the world, the time change is only a few hours so you will not suffer from much jet lag.

The best way to travel depends on your whereabouts and how far you want to go. Away from the main tourist areas and large cities, a lot of the roads are very poor so if you want to drive independently, you need to plan your route carefully. There are buses available but the rides can be a bit rocky and often overcrowded so aren't advised, although South Africa does have a good bus network. See www.bazbus.com.

If you are going any distance then you should consider getting a flight or joining an organised tour. Both can be pricey and tours can feel limiting, but they are sometimes the best way to visit more remote areas.

'Although flights to Africa can be long, as you are going down instead of across the world, the time change is only a few hours so you will not suffer from much jet lag.'

Health and safety

Unfortunately, Africa is one of the worst continents for both disease and political unrest. This should not put you off visiting but you must make sure that you get all the correct vaccinations and check with the foreign office before travelling. Hepatitis A and B, boosters of tetanus, measles and polio, meningococcal meningitis, typhoid and yellow fever vaccinations are all recommended. As well as vaccinations, you will need to take malaria tablets for most countries on the continent. Sub-Saharan Africa has the highest HIV rate in the world, so you also need to be particularly vigilant about practising safe sex.

Africa can still be a dangerous and unwelcoming place if you end up in the wrong place, so always be sensible about where you travel to. It is important to remain vigilant and, unless you are sticking to the main tourist centres, it is not the best place to travel alone, especially if you are a woman.

Costs

Although flights to Africa can be quite expensive, once you get there costs are generally cheap. Basic living costs would be around £5-15 per day unless you are visiting places such as Cape Town, Botswana and Namibia where this can rise drastically. Obviously though, it depends on what you want to do. There are some amazing locations to stay in and one of the most popular things to do in Africa is to go on safari. You can do variations of this on a budget but it is still going to be quite expensive and something that you should budget for in advance.

Haggling is the done thing in Africa and you will be expected to barter for your goods. Always start at a price much lower than you are willing to pay. This can feel a bit overwhelming at first, especially if the stall owners are being particularly pushy. Only do what you are comfortable with and if the situation feels aggressive then walk away.

Africa isn't as well set up for the backpacker as more popular destinations such as Asia, so outside the main hubs, hostels and low cost accommodation can be of a varying standard. You can get some really cheap, tasty food across the continent, and even in big cities like Cape Town the restaurants are still great value.

Living and working

Unless you have organised a specific job in advance, Africa is not an easy place to live and work. It is a popular destination for volunteer work but make sure you know what the living conditions are like and be prepared to face up to scenes of poverty.

Africa is also popular for tour guide work as there is so much call for safaris and organised trips. Companies have different requirements but will usually need you to have travelled extensively in the area and been on their tours. There are some specific training schemes available but make sure you sign up with a reputable company and are given the support and training that you need.

Action points

- Be sure you have the correct vaccinations and malaria tablets.

- Check with the foreign office for areas of unrest.

- If you want to go on safari, make sure you have budgeted for it in advance.

- If you are volunteering, be clear about what you are signing up for.

- Plan your travel in advance.

Summing Up

- Africa is an infectious place that will get under your skin.
- Don't be put off by its image but do be sensible about where you travel and how you get there.
- It is also important that you have the correct vaccinations to stay healthy.
- Whether you want to play it safe and enjoy the great city of Cape Town or are ready to explore further into the continent, be ready for some culture shocks.
- Watch: *Long Way Down* with Ewan McGregor and Charley Boorman.
- Read: *Out of Africa* by Karen Blixen.
- Surf: www.africaguide.com.

Chapter Eight

North America

They are our allies and the provider of many of our TV shows, but there is still something oddly alluring about North America. With its big ideals, big roads and even bigger meals, everything is turned up a notch or two in the 'land of plenty'.

Where to go

If you are looking for the high life then fly into LA, hire a car and drive up the coast to San Francisco and over to Las Vegas, taking in the Grand Canyon on your way. Or for east coast cool, start off in New York, pop to Washington for some political culture and fly down to Miami to party. To see more of the 'real' America, jump on a bus and cruise down the iconic Route 66 or head south and experience the charms of New Orleans and Louisiana. Don't forget Canada though! A trip coast to coast by plane, train or automobile takes you through some stunning scenery. Get a taste for the outdoors by taking a trip out into the vast wilderness, have a European moment in Quebec and end up in Vancouver for the perfect mix of the city and outdoors lifestyle.

'With its big ideals, big roads and even bigger meals everything is turned up a notch or two in the "land of plenty".'

What to see

New York City, New York

It's the city that never sleeps because there's so much to see and do – climb the Empire State Building, explore Central Park or take a trip across the Hudson River.

LA Walk of Fame, California

Yes, it's tacky, but while you are in LA, try to find the handprints of your favourite star – or you may even spot the real thing!

Grand Canyon, Arizona

This vast expanse is breathtaking and if you can afford a helicopter ride over the top, it will blow you away.

Las Vegas, Nevada

Whether you enjoy gambling or not, you can't help but be amazed by the attitude of this city and the size of everything it has on offer.

Niagara Falls, Ontario, Canada

It may be surrounded by tacky, flashy attractions but donning the plastic poncho and taking to the water is still worth the trip.

What to do

Take a road trip

North America is vast and the best way to see it is to get out on the open road and stop off at all the random places along the way.

Shop on Fifth Avenue

OK, so it may just be window shopping but wandering down Fifth Avenue is a classic New York experience.

Gamble in Las Vegas

You don't have to be a high roller to enjoy a few free drinks and soak up the atmosphere of the most famous casinos in the world.

Go to a rodeo

Could you get anything much more American? Yeeeehaaah! Ride 'em cowboy!

Have pancakes

If the Americans know how to do one thing, it's make a good meal. Find some space to indulge in a sumptuous breakfast.

Customs, laws and language

Although it may seem that England is just an extension of America, you will be surprised to see how different their attitudes and customs can be. At least you have a leg up on the language – well, once you master your elevators, eggplants, sidewalks, zucchinis and SUVs. North America is so vast, with the state of Texas alone being larger than the UK, that there is great diversity. The people that you meet in New York are a world away from those in Kansas and it is this mix that makes it such an interesting country.

Remember that you cannot drink until you are 21 in America, which can be a bit of a shock to the system. They are very strict about asking for ID, so you should always carry some with you. If you don't have it on you, it is unlikely that you will get served anywhere.

Canada, which is often forgotten next to its loud, brash neighbour, has more English influence and is more reserved. Quebec is French speaking and has a very European vibe about it, although in most areas, especially the main cities, you will be able to get by speaking English.

'The most riveting thing about New York is that anything can happen there.'

Bill Bryson.

Getting there and getting around

Flights to North America are relatively cheap and can usually be bought as part of a round-the-world ticket. They don't have the same cheap flight culture that we do, so flights within the country can work out a bit pricey. There are many bus networks such as www.greyhound.com which are the cheapest way to travel, but remember it is a long way between major cities. Their trains are expensive and not that extensive, unless you are on the east coast.

Another option, and the best way to see the country, is to hire a car, but you will need to be over 25. One way to do it is to use a company that transports people's personal cars for them if they need them moved across the country but don't want to do the drive. The company will assign you a specific car and destination and although you will have to cover the petrol costs and be expected to arrive in a certain amount of time, the car use is free. Visit www.autodriveaway.com.

Health and safety

Generally, North America is a safe place to travel around, although you need to be careful in the major cities, just like anywhere in the world. Beware of pickpockets, keep your wits about you and make sure you don't end up in a cheaper area of the city just to save a few pounds.

If you are going to travel to more remote areas to hike and climb, especially in sparsely populated regions of Canada, then you need to make sure you are prepared. Have the correct equipment and make sure that you tell someone where you are planning to go. For more extreme expeditions, it is best to go on an organised trip.

Costs

The cost of living is generally cheaper in North America than the UK, but it really depends on the fluctuating exchange rate just how much of a bargain you get. Clothes and eating out are particularly good value, although travel tends to work out a bit more. You can get by on around £25 per day, but it will vary greatly depending on whether you are in a big city or a rural outpost. If you want to take up some activities or travel remotely in Canada, you will need to boost your budget.

Even in the big cities across North America you can still find some budget backpacker accommodation and motels en route can be a bargain. Even though fast food, which the continent is famous for, often doesn't work out as the cheapest option, eating out is still much cheaper than in the UK.

Tipping is big in America and you will be expected to add on 15-20% in a restaurant, although sometimes this is done automatically. You will also be expected to tip taxi drivers and leave an extra dollar or two when you buy a round of drinks, which can soon add up.

Working and living

The USA is quite strict about handing out working visas but if you are a student or are being sponsored by a company or work programme, then there are lots of opportunities. It is a great place to live and work because language is not a problem. There are vast differences in different areas of the country and the attitude to working life in New York is poles apart from Kansas.

There is some interesting seasonal work available in North America and a popular option is working at a summer camp such as www.campamerica. co.uk. These can be quite claustrophobic as you are looking after children for up to 12 weeks but they are also a lot of fun and allow time for travel. Another big draw are the internships which are huge in the US and also in Canada. Getting a placement at a large respected company will give you invaluable international experience and look great on your CV. Visit www.bunac.org.

'Even though fast food, which the continent is famous for, often doesn't work out as the cheapest option, eating out is still much cheaper than in the UK.'

Action points

- Expect to spend more than you would in poorer areas of the world.
- Make sure that you have the correct visa for visiting or working.
- Remember to tip staff in restaurants and bars.
- Consider combining your trip with some seasonal work or an internship.
- Don't forget Canada!

Summing Up

- It may not be the most exotic of gap year destinations but there is still plenty to see and learn in North America.

- The cities are bigger and brasher than ours and the small towns more remote and conservative.

- Road-tripping is the best way to see the USA although the east coast is fairly compact for rail or bus travel.

- Don't strike Canada off the list as it has some great cities (Vancouver and Quebec) and some outstanding scenery, especially if you love to be outdoors.

- Watch: *Stephen Fry: In America.*

- Read: *On The Road* by Jack Kerouac.

- Surf: www.roadtripusa.com.

Bolivian salt flats

It takes a while to really believe that this massive landscape of salt from dried up lakes is not ice and then a while longer to take in this crazy feat of nature.

Amazon rainforest

Home to some of the most isolated tribes in the world, South America isn't complete without a journey into the jungle.

Galapagos Islands, Ecuador

If you are a wildlife lover then a trip to these islands is a must, especially for the turtles.

Rio de Janeiro, Brazil

One of the most flamboyant cities in the world, Rio does everything to the extreme.

Things to do

Learn Spanish

With so many countries to choose from, you will soon be able to say more than just 'beer please'.

Take a tango lesson

Even if you can't speak like a South American, you can move like one by perfecting your dance moves.

Walk the Inca Trail

It is a challenging and tiring trip but the pain will all be worthwhile when you see the sunrise over Machu Picchu.

Go to Rio carnival

It's the ultimate place to let loose, so drink, dance and be merry at this party of all parties.

Enjoy a margarita

Sitting by the pool sipping a margarita is the epitome of a luxury beach break, but in Mexico it doesn't need to break the bank.

Customs, laws and language

The majority of central and Southern America speak Spanish, while the odd ones out are the Brazilians who speak Portuguese instead. In the main tourist traps you will find that you can get by with English but if you are going off the beaten track, it is a good idea to brush up on your Spanish skills you learnt at school!

The South Americans are often known for their friendly and welcoming demeanour and this is generally true, although female travellers should be cautious and take extra care, especially if travelling alone.

While the whole of the continent is friendly, there is quite a difference between the more traditional communities where family and customs are important and the eclectic mix of the big cities like Rio. Be prepared to adjust your behaviour accordingly depending on the areas that you are heading for.

'Try and embrace the local culture by visiting markets, going salsa dancing and trying out your Spanish – however limited!'

Getting there and getting around

Flights to South America can often be included on a round-the-world ticket, but flying directly there can be quite pricey. Within the continent, flights are still quite expensive, so overland travel, especially by bus, is very popular. Although the journeys can be very long, the network is well set up, with many companies serving meals and even playing bingo en route. In some cases, because of the terrain or sheer distance, it may be worth splashing out on an internal flight.

South America does not have a vast rail network, apart from a few limited routes and tourist services. It is possible to hire a car but the distances are vast. There are many organised tours across South America which are a good idea if you don't have much time, would like the expertise of a guide or are visiting places you can't go without one, such as the Inca Trail. Visit www.incatrailperu.com for more information.

'There are many organised tours across South America which are a good idea if you don't have much time, would like the expertise of a guide or are visiting places you can't go without one.'

Health and safety

It is a good idea to check the political situation before travelling to some countries in South America – Colombia is especially unstable. The Darien Gap, which connects Central and South America, is the scene of numerous robberies and kidnappings and is definitely worth paying the airfare to avoid.

Health wise, you need to be careful about drinking the water in many countries and if you are visiting tropical areas be sure you have all the necessary vaccinations. Recommended ones are hepatitis A and B, rabies, typhoid, yellow fever and boosters for tetanus and measles. If you are visiting Machu Picchu or other mountainous areas, you are likely to suffer from some altitude sickness.

South America is generally not a dangerous place but some people will try their luck and attempt to scam you. Be careful not to mark yourself out as a tourist and leave valuables well hidden.

Costs

South America is generally fairly-budget friendly but it all depends on where you are visiting. Peru, Bolivia and Ecuador are particularly cheap and you can live comfortably on £10 per day. Argentina, Brazil and Chile are a bit pricier but you should still be fine on £15-20 per day. If you would like to do any big trips such as visiting the jungle, going to the Galapagos Islands or hiking the Inca Trail then budget for this in advance and shop around for the best deals – which can often be found locally.

There is a huge network of hostels across the continent and it is good to gather recommendations as you go. Home stays are also popular and can be a great way to save money and get to know the locals. You can buy some great food from the local markets but basic fare in local restaurants is also a cheap option. Haggling is normal in this area of the world but is not as aggressive as in Africa and they will stop when they reach a price they are not happy with. Travelling around South America is generally quite cheap but activities and accommodation on the 'gringo trail' can be overpriced so it is worth shopping around.

Living and working

South America is a popular destination for language courses such as www.linguaschools.com which are often combined with a stint of volunteering. The South Americans are very friendly and family-orientated and lots of these courses will be combined with a home stay. Don't expect the same standards of décor and luxury that you are used to at home, but you will always be well looked after, treated as part of the family and fed regularly. Try to embrace the local culture by visiting markets, going salsa dancing and trying out your Spanish – however limited!

Action points

- Learn some Spanish before you go.
- Be prepared for some long bus rides.
- Devote enough time to really see this exuberant continent.
- Make sure you have the correct vaccines – especially for tropical areas.
- Avoid more dangerous areas such as the Darien Gap.

Summing Up

- South America is a continent packed with fun. There are some amazing things to see and do, but also some great people to meet.

- The 'gringo trail' has developed for a reason as it takes you through some of the top places, but to get a real sense of places try and divert at least a little bit.

- It is easy to get around by bus and you can live on quite a small budget unless you want to party in the big cities or enjoy the resorts on the beaches of Mexico.

- Watch: *The Motorcycle Diaries* directed by Walter Salles.

- Read: *In Patagonia* by Bruce Chatwun.

- Surf: www.saexplorers.org.

'South America is a continent packed with fun. There are some amazing things to see and do but also some great people to meet.

Chapter Ten

Australia, New Zealand and the Pacific

Australia is traditionally the most popular gap year destination as it has always been easy to get a working visa. It offers a chance to enjoy the sun, sea and sand while earning some money along the way. Hang out in the backpacking haunts of Sydney, get down with nature at the Great Barrier Reef or experience the vast nothingness of the outback – Australia is so much more than beer and barbecues!

However, you must not forget about New Zealand and the Pacific Islands as both offer some truly stunning destinations. The idyllic islands of Fiji and Tahiti and the wide landscapes of New Zealand lure visitors into never wanting to leave.

'God bless America. God Save the Queen. God defend New Zealand and thank Christ for Australia.'

Russel Crowe.

Where to go

The east coast of Australia is the most popular destination and takes in Sydney, where you will probably fly into, Melbourne and the Great Barrier Reef. It's a shame to miss out on the middle though, so circle up past Ayres Rock and Alice Springs if you have the time. Western Australia is very remote which is good if you like that sort of thing, but can take a lot out of your journey, so think about whether it is worth it. New Zealand is split into the North Island, where Auckland is, and the South Island, home to Milford Sound. Both are worth a visit and are home to some amazing scenery and a whole host of outdoor activities. It would be a mistake to travel this far round the world without taking in one of the Pacific Islands. Take your pick and remember that some of the less well known ones can give a cheaper and more authentic experience.

What to see

Sydney Opera House

This performing arts centre is one of the 20th century's most distinctive buildings and is at the heart of the city with great views of the harbour and bridge.

Great Barrier Reef

If you think that little dots of sand with a palm tree in the middle are only real on postcards, then you need to come here to see the real thing.

Ayres Rock

You have to travel a long way to see it but this feat of nature is a symbol of the size and scale of Australia.

Bondi Beach

Famous for its surfing, this is one of the most popular destinations for young backpackers – many would say this is what Australia is all about.

Milford Sound, New Zealand

This amazing fjord, set in a national park, is New Zealand's most popular destination, great for adrenalin junkies and nature lovers alike.

Things to do

Go diving

If you love to dive then there is nowhere better than the Great Barrier Reef. If you can't dive, here is a great place to learn!

Have a barbecue on the beach

Join in the Aussie culture and get down to the beach for a beer and some al fresco dining.

Climb Sydney Harbour Bridge

There is no better place to view Sydney than from on top of the famous Harbour Bridge.

'There is no better place to view Sydney than from on top of the famous Harbour Bridge.'

Cuddle a koala

Make sure you do this in a zoo or animal park as koalas in the wild can be quite vicious, but captive, they are awfully cute!!

Start surfing

You can't go to Australia and not go surfing, so sign up for a lesson and learn how to catch those waves without making a fool of yourself!

Customs, laws and language

Australians are famed for their laid-back attitude and will soon be inviting you to a barbecue on the beach. Although they technically speak English, there are a lot of variations, but you will soon pick up on the local slang.

New Zealand has a great mix of cultures originating from many European countries and they all share a great love for the outdoors.

People of the South Pacific Islands are very friendly and welcoming. These remote destinations have their own language and ingrained culture where family and tradition are important. French is widely spoken but you should be able to get by speaking English most of the time.

Getting there and getting around

Australia and the South Pacific is a long way away from England! You haven't got much choice but to fly there unless you fancy a very long boat trip. The best way to visit is by buying a round-the-world flight. These usually don't work out much more than buying a standard return but allow you to stop off in a number of places on the way.

Australia is vast and it takes a long time to travel from one place to the next, especially if you want to visit central or western Australia. Travelling up and down the east coast can be done by hiring a car. Another popular choice is to buy a camper van. Alternatively, there are lots of bus companies that you can join to take you around such as www.ozexperience.com, and the same applies in New Zealand. If you have limited time then you should consider investing in a few internal flights.

The islands of the South Pacific are always an option on round-the-world flights and it is well worth adding one on as getting there independently can be very expensive.

Health and safety

Another reason why Australia and New Zealand are popular gap year destinations is because they are relatively safe and with few health risks. Sharks and poisonous spiders are dangerous but the biggest risk is the scorching sun, so make sure you cover up and use a high factor sun cream while you are out and about.

If you are going further afield than mainland Australia and New Zealand, it is worth getting vaccinated against tetanus, hepatitis A and B, typhoid and measles.

Tahiti has one of the lowest crime rates in the world, so you can generally expect to be safe when you travel around this region of the world. However, make sure you tell someone if you are planning to go off into the more remote areas and ensure that you have plenty of water and supplies.

Costs

Australia used to be very budget-friendly, but prices have risen as the dollar has got stronger. The good news is that it is well set up for backpackers, with a lot of hostels, cheap bus travel and student discounts. You can expect to get by on around £20 a day but, as you will probably stop off and work somewhere along the way, your costs will vary and you will have a chance to save up.

There are many hostels in Australia and the climate is good for camping, although the popular option of buying a camper van can be a budget friendly way to travel and sleep.

If you want to visit Tahiti, expect to pay out a lot more. Although other islands such as The Cook Islands can be a good cheaper alternative, you still need to expect to push your budget.

Living and working

Australia is a very popular place for Brits to go and work because it is easy to get a working holiday visa (see www.immi.gov.au/visitors/working-holiday). There is a lot of work available but there are restrictions on the type of work that you can do and for how long.

You will generally find it easy to find somewhere to live as there is a huge British expat community and many temporary visitors. You will never feel too far from home but it can be a good idea to try not to rely on this – make friends with the locals instead.

The Pacific Islands are popular for environmental volunteering and you can be working in some idyllic locations, although these types of trips can be a bit pricey.

Action points

- Include the Pacific Islands on a round-the-world flight.
- Factor in enough time to earn some money.
- Don't get caught up in the expat community – meet the locals.
- Get active in New Zealand.
- Wear high factor sun cream.

Summing Up

- Australia is the eternal backpacker haven and has earned its reputation for its easy working visas, safe environment, stunning scenery and outgoing people.

- While you are in this corner of the world, try to fit in a visit to New Zealand which is a great destination for adrenalin junkies and nature enthusiasts.

- The islands of the South Pacific are also definitely worth a stop as they are paradise on Earth!

- Watch: *Australia* directed by Baz Luhrmann.

- Read: *Down Under* by Bill Bryson.

- Surf: www.bugpacific.com.

'Australia is the eternal backpacker haven and has earned its reputation for its easy working visas, safe environment, stunning scenery and outgoing people.'

Chapter Eleven

Europe

Most people will have visited Europe when they were growing up, so it doesn't seem as exotic as far-flung destinations. However, by stepping from one country to the next, it is easy to experience a huge variety of culture, language and scenery without ever changing currency or showing your passport. History, food and architecture are on show around every corner, and east and west offer very different experiences.

Where to go

Western Europe may not seem very exotic but it has a lot to offer and is easy to navigate by train, car or cheap flight networks. Start in the romantic heart of Paris before heading south to Spain and indulging in the variety that this vast country has to offer. Make like a movie star and cross through the south of France before heading down to Italy and ferry-hopping over to the Greek islands. If that's all old hat to you then explore Eastern Europe. Croatia with its stunning coastline is a good place to start and then take a look at Bosnia, Serbia and Romania which are much more than ex-war torn countries. Bulgaria is also a great budget choice. If you are not drawn by the sun and sea then the Baltic countries are something a bit different. Fly into Tallinn, take the ferry over to Finland (or start in the hedonistic Amsterdam) and head up through Copenhagen and on to Sweden for some clean living. Further afield, Russia is an interesting trip. Fly to Moscow or St Petersburg to whet your appetite or consider an organised trip if you want to go further afield.

'The Europe I saw on my gap year was not the same English-centric place I remember as a kid. It's a shame so many people overlook it for far-flung destinations.'
Amy, 23.

What to see

Eiffel Tower, France

It's a classic and always will be. Whether you are with a lover or on your own, there is still a sense of romance about this famous attraction.

Colosseum, Italy

It is amazing to think how long this Roman amphitheatre has been standing for – imagine the gladiatorial games that it was once home to.

Northern Lights

There's nothing else like this natural phenomenon, so head to northern Scandinavia between September and April for the chance to marvel at it.

Sistine Chapel, Italy

Classy and classic, you'll be blown away that Michaelangelo painted this ceiling upside down.

The Kremlin, Russia

A fascinating insight into Russia, this fortified governmental building sits at the heart of Moscow.

Things to do

Take a gondola ride in Venice

Join the other tourists and jump on a gondola. It is a great way to see another view of the city and you might even get sung to!

Go skiing

Whether you are a beginner or a pro, it's always an adrenalin kick and a chance to see some amazing scenery.

Have a sauna in the snow

Such a Scandinavian thing to do, this experience is fun, exhilarating and great for the skin!

Greek island hopping

The stunning beaches and picture perfect villages are all just a short ferry trip away.

Soak up the culture

Art, music, fashion and food – Europe has it all on offer round every corner, so seek it out and soak it up.

'The great thing about Europe is that you can experience so many different languages and cultures in a short space of time.'

Customs, laws and language

The great thing about Europe is that you can experience so many different languages and cultures in a short space of time. Most people have studied French or Spanish at school, so you should be able to get by with the basic phrases in Western Europe, although Eastern Europe and Scandinavia are a different matter.

The English have got a bit of a reputation in Europe for being 'Brits abroad' and you may find in some places they try to take advantage of this. However, as long as you are friendly and respectful then you can expect a warm welcome in most places as the Europeans are very family-orientated.

In Germany and some Eastern European countries, people can come across as a bit rude and abrupt. Don't be put off by this as they are perfectly friendly and it is just a cultural difference. Scandinavians are often very outgoing and welcoming and love to have a good time.

'Over the last few years, the cheap flight market has exploded, meaning that it has never cost less to fly to Europe.'

Getting there and getting around

Over the last decade, the cheap flight market has exploded, meaning that you can often fly to Europe for less than a train fare to Newcastle. A great bonus of this is that you can buy single flights instead of returns as you are unlikely to want to fly home from the same airport. Just check which airports they fly into as often they can be so far away from your intended destination that you pay just as much again on taxis into the city.

For the eco-conscious, travelling by train is a great way to see Europe. Rail passes can be the most economical choice as they give you unlimited travel within your chosen countries. You can buy them online at www.raileurope.com or in person at stations across Europe. The train system on the continent is extensive, reliable and a relatively cheap way of getting around. Another option is to drive which gives you flexibility but, with the price of petrol, may not be the cheapest way to do it.

Health and safety

Generally, Europe is quite a safe place to travel in and is free from lots of the worst diseases and political problems. However, it is recommended that you have an up-to-date tetanus shot and, if you are travelling to many Eastern European countries, it is suggested that you have the hepatitis A vaccination too.

In the major cities, you can be vulnerable to pickpockets and muggings. Like any city, stay away from the less desirable areas and don't have your valuables on display. The metros can be the worst places for pickpockets so never leave things in easy-to-reach pockets and turn your bags around so they can't get into them without you noticing.

Costs

Since the majority of Europe has now signed up to the Euro, it has become more expensive to visit many countries. Eastern Europe is still great value but if you want to stay in Italy or France, it can cost you as much as in the UK. Expect to budget about £25 a day in Western Europe if you stay in hostels and eat cheaply. In some areas of Eastern Europe, you can still get by on as little as £10-15 a day.

Europe's markets are a great place to pick up fresh fruit and vegetables at bargain prices and if you pick the restaurants that the locals visit, you can still get some very reasonably priced meals – often with a glass of wine thrown in! Accommodation in the main cities isn't all that cheap, but if you travel over to Eastern Europe you can stay in some good hotels for less.

Living and working

Because of the EU, it is easy to go and work in many European countries. There is a lot of seasonal work to pick up either in the holiday industry or in agriculture and it is easy to go over there for a few months. If your language skills are good, you may decide to stay for longer and settle into a more permanent job. Check out www.eurojobs.com.

Europe is a popular place to study or take language classes and it is a great way to soak up the culture. Studying at university for a year is often possible as part of a university course and this can be an ideal way to integrate into the country. There are often a lot of expat communities, especially in the major cities, but you will pick up the lingo a lot quicker if you force yourself to speak it every day and mix with the locals.

Although it used to be quite cheap to live in Europe, the Euro exchange rate means that you will find many places are not much cheaper than living in the UK.

Action points

▪ Protect your valuables from pickpockets on the metro.

▪ Check which airport your cheap flight arrives at.

▪ Brush up on your language skills.

▪ Go to Eastern Europe with no preconceptions.

▪ Budget more while the Euro rate is poor.

Summing Up

- People from across the world flock to Europe every year and just because it is on your doorstep you shouldn't rule it out as a worthy gap year destination.

- Western Europe has a lot to offer in terms of culture and scenery. However, if you want something a bit different, Eastern Europe and Russia are the places to visit.

- Also, don't forget about Scandinavia which can give you a new perspective on the best way to live and a fresh attitude to life.

- Watch: *Before Sunrise* directed by Richard Linklater.

- Read: *A Year in Provence* by Peter Mayle.

- Surf: www.guideforeurope.com.

Chapter Twelve

Readjustment

When you are on your gap year, every day is filled with new, exciting experiences that are a world away from your old life at home. At some point though, you are going to have to return to reality and leave your travels behind. Although you may have missed your friends and family, getting back home always ends up being an anticlimax. Life has stayed the same, there is nothing exciting to do and nobody seems interested enough in all your adventures. It can take time to settle back down again but knowing you will have these feelings, and taking constructive steps to deal with them, can make the transition a little bit easier.

Staying in touch

Staying in touch on your travels not only lets your friends and family know that you are safe, it also allows you to share your adventures and maintain a relationship with them while you are away.

It can be difficult to keep regular contact with everyone but the wonders of modern technology make it a lot easier. Even the remotest outposts now have Internet connection, although a quick phone call will always be welcomed by your nearest and dearest.

Skype

Skype is a great invention that means you can make phone calls through the Internet. All you need to do is sign up at www.skype.com, then it is free to make and receive calls. You will both have to be online in order for it to work, so you will need to arrange a day and time in advance.

'I never travel without my diary. One should always have something sensational to read in the train.'
Oscar Wilde.

Phones

Making calls from a UK mobile can be very costly, so find out about the charges beforehand. If you are staying in a country for any length of time, it can be worth buying a cheap local mobile. Don't forget about phone cards though. These are usually much cheaper, can be picked up easily and used on any payphone.

Email and social networking

If your parents are not very technically savvy, give them a crash course in email or Facebook before you leave. It is the cheapest and easiest way to stay in touch. While group emails and status updates are a good way to keep friends and family up to date, taking the extra time to reply individually will always be appreciated.

Blogs

Setting up a blog or online diary can be a great way to let your friends and family follow your adventures and be a dedicated place to share photos and videos. There are some sites, like www.travelpod.com that are designed for this, or you can set up a simple blog through www.wordpress.com This can also be a great way to record your travels to look back on when you return.

Although it is tempting to take your laptop and mobile phone away with you, in reality you don't want to be burdened with them. They take up space, are at risk of being stolen and will be expensive to use abroad. Nowadays it is easy to access the Internet or phone from almost anywhere in the world so you can always stay in touch.

Down in the dumps

It is only natural that when you get home from your gap year you will feel down. You have just had an amazing time and coming back to the boredom of everyday life is going to be a let down. Your perspective on life is likely to have changed and your old town, friends and life may seem uninspiring.

Remember that just because you are home, it doesn't mean the fun has ended. Now is the time to start looking towards the future and planning your next adventure. Instead of seeing your friends and family as boring, spend time with them, fill them in on your adventure and catch up on what they have been doing.

If you are feeling low, go for a walk, look at your photos or start researching your next step. The best thing you can do is focus on all the great things that are to come instead of what you have left behind.

How can you preserve your memories?

Your year has no doubt been packed with lifelong memories that you will still be talking about to your grandchildren. It is natural that you will want to preserve these as much as possible. Photos are a great way to keep memories alive but so often they just languish on the computer. Make the effort to buy some photo albums and print off your favourites. This will be a great way of reliving your experiences and sharing them with others.

While you were away you may have kept a diary or journal. This is a lovely thing to look back on when you are older, so take good care of it. Perhaps you could make it into a scrapbook or add to your thoughts now you are back. If you kept an electronic diary or blog, consider printing it out so that you have a tangible piece of writing that you can store away for the future.

Also, along the way, you are bound to have made many friends from across the world. With technology, it is so easy to keep in touch with people that you must make sure you do so. Then, the next time that you get itchy feet you will have someone to stay with!

'When you arrive home from your gap year you will probably be planning your next adventure, spurred on by other travellers you have met along the way.'

Itchy feet

However many amazing places you see, there will always be more that you want to visit. When you arrive home from your gap year you will probably be planning your next adventure, spurred on by other travellers you have met along the way.

Having this feeling means that it can be difficult to settle down, so you need to plan some trips to keep you satisfied. Even if it is just within the UK to visit friends or to go to a new city, it will give you something to focus on.

Get a globe, buy some guide books or go to the library and start thinking about your next adventure. Even if you don't have the time or funds to do it any time soon, it gives you something to fill that void.

Dealing with a change of perspective

'When you travel you will see and experience so many new things and meet people from all different cultures and backgrounds. It can really open your eyes to the world and leave you with a fresh perspective and a new set of opinions.'

When you travel you will see and experience so many new things and meet people from all different cultures and backgrounds. It can really open your eyes to the world and leave you with a fresh perspective and a new set of opinions.

This new perspective can make it difficult to fit back in with your old set of friends and can lead you to question the beliefs of your family. It is good that you have discovered more about the world, but don't judge everyone by your new view. Inflicting your views on your friends and family will only alienate you. Instead, think about how you can use them constructively.

Consider reading up on the things you have learnt or taking a course that suits your new outlook on life. Start planning another trip so that you can go back to the place that inspired you, or put your experience to good use in a volunteer project. Another important thing to think about is choosing a career path that fits in with your new view of the world. However, remember while you feel strongly about these things now, your commitment may fade over time, so don't blow off your current plans until you are sure.

How do you settle into university?

If you have taken your gap year before you go to university, it can be tricky settling back down to study.

If you look back at the person you were before you went on your gap year, you probably feel very different now. Travelling and spending time away from home helps you grow up and gives you a new perspective on the world.

One thing you may find is that your peers seem a lot younger than you. Although it will only be by one year, having come straight from home, they will not be as worldly wise.

The thing to remember is that there are so many people to meet at university that you are guaranteed to find someone who has the same outlook as you. Try not to look down upon other students who have not taken time out – look for common ground that you can enjoy together.

Instead of constantly looking back at your gap year and being unable to settle, focus your energies on making the most of this new experience and embracing university life.

Finding a job

When you return from your gap year, the reality of everyday life can hit you hard. Whether you have left education and need to get started on your career, or just need some part-time work to pay off debts or see you through college, it can be a daunting prospect. Okay, working is not going to be as exciting as travelling the world, but there is a lot to look forward to. You can use your new experiences, outlook on the world and time away to help you find the job you want.

Modern employers, far from looking down on gap years, now realise that they produce more well-rounded and confident employees. What you need to do is emphasise what you have learnt from your experiences and how these translate into skills you can use for employment. Ask yourself:

- What do I enjoy doing?
- What am I good at?
- What am I interested in?
- How can I adapt my skills to the workplace?
- How can I illustrate my experience with examples?

Once you have thought up the answers to these questions, compose a CV that shows what you have learnt and the skills that you have gained. Try to use solid examples in interviews of times that have been challenging or where you have been forced to think up a new solution or work well with others.

Fitting back into your career

If you are a bit older and took a career break, the thought of going back to the everyday grind can make you want to run for the hills.

You may find that your gap year has given you new focus and drive and reaffirmed how you feel about your career. However, you may find that you have been left questioning a lot of the things that you took for granted before your trip.

Don't make any rash decisions, return to your job and take time to process all your feelings before you act on them. See if there is any way of adapting your current job or grasping opportunities within the company.

If not, do your research to find out what else is out there and what you would need to do to make the transition. It is great that you are inspired but think carefully about how you will feel in a year's time when you come down off your gap year high, and whether you are willing to commit to long-term changes.

Looking to the future

When you have taken a gap year and had a life-changing trip, it can be easy to keep looking back and reminiscing about all the experiences you had. There is nothing wrong with this, of course you want to remember the fun times, but you also need to focus on the future.

You may already have something that you are coming back to, such as an old job or a place at university and, if so, you need to make the most of it. Share your travels with your friends but make sure you work hard at fitting into your new reality.

If you have no firm plans then now is the time to make some. Think about what you would like to be doing this time next year and start figuring out how to make that happen. Yes, you have had an amazing year but there are many more to come and you don't want to be that person that spends their whole life talking about one year. Instead, fill your life with lots of amazing years.

Action points

- Stay in touch with family and friends, and make an effort to catch up with them when you get back.

- Be prepared to feel low and frustrated when you get back.

- Make a scrap book, print off your photos and preserve your journal.

- Take time to think about what you want to do next and take practical steps to make the changes.

How has it changed your perspective on the world?

Reflection form

What was your favourite country and why?

Where did you feel most inspired?

Describe the most interesting person you met on your trip.

What were your top three sights?

1.

2.

3.

Describe your favourite day of the trip.

What has your gap year taught you about yourself?

How has it changed you?

Give an example of when you:

. . . had to think on your feet.

. . . faced a new situation.

. . . worked with people from other cultures.

. . . were put outside your comfort zone.

What practical skills have you learnt?

How has it changed your perspective on the world?

Summing Up

- Arriving back home to your old life can make you feel like the walls are closing in around you. However, far from being the end of your adventures, it is only the beginning.

- Now you know what you are capable of and what the world has to offer, you can start looking towards an exciting future. Whether it is embracing university, changing career or planning your next travels, start taking practical steps towards achieving it.

- Try not to dwell on what you have left behind but preserve your memories so you can always look back and remember the great times you had.

Help List

When you've got the whole world to research, it can be difficult to know where to start. Here is a list of useful websites and organisations that can help you on your way.

Flights

Airtreks

www.airtreks.com
This site is a good place for round-the-world flights and also has a useful 'planning your trip' tool.

Expedia

www.expedia.com
Expedia is an extensive travel portal which is useful for booking flights, hotels or car hire and comparing what's on offer.

Round The World Flights

www.roundtheworldflights.com
Tel: 0207 704 5700
An easy-to-use website that allows you to design your own round-the world-flight. Great for getting ideas and comparing different routes and prices, but if you need some help you can always give them a call.

Skyscanner

www.skyscanner.net
This travel portal concentrates on budget airlines, so it is a really good tool for finding cheap flights across Europe.

STA Travel

www.statravel.co.uk
Tel: 0871 230 0040
STA are specialists in student and gap year travel. They can offer some good discounts and worldwide advice.

Trailfinders

www.trailfinders.com
Trailfinders are well known for their tailor-made travel packages and, with their extensive knowledge and enthusiasm, can help you organise the trip that you are looking for.

Other travel

CrewSeekers International

www.crewseekers.net
Find out all you need to know about working on a yacht and search out yacht owners who are currently seeking staff.

Freighter World Cruises, Inc

www.freighterworld.com
info@freighterworld.com
Find out about the different routes available on freighter ships, what to expect and how to book your journey.

Rail-Europe

www.raileurope.co.uk
The one-stop shop for finding out everything about rail travel across Europe, from timetables to tickets and routes.

Money

International Student Travel Confederation

www.aboutistc.org
This is the place to get yourself an international student card which can give you access to a host of discounts across the world.

Moneygram

www.moneygram.com
Moneygram allows you to transfer money across 190 countries, so it's the perfect back up if you find yourself stranded.

XE

www.xe.com
This website has a simple tool that allows you to find out the exchange rate for any two currencies.

Working abroad

Any Work Anywhere

www.anyworkanywhere.com
An easy-to-use site that allows you to search by location and job type to find a number of different programmes and recruiters worldwide.

Childcare International

www.childint.co.uk
Tel: 0800 652 0020
An international agency that finds work for qualified childcare professionals. It offers a list of vacancies and details of what is required from you.

Crown Recruitment

www.workonship.co.uk

shipjob@aol.com

This recruitment agency supplies a wide variety of staff for Royal Caribbean and Carnival, two of the world's largest cruise lines.

Jobs Abroad

www.jobsabroad.com

A comprehensive search engine providing hundreds of links to jobs and recruitment companies around the world.

Monster

www.monster.com

A good place to look for more permanent jobs and career opportunities in Europe and America.

Seasonal work

Camp America

www.campamerica.co.uk

A detailed and straightforward website that lays out what to expect from signing up to work on American summer camps.

Ski Staff

www.skistaff.co.uk

jobs@skistaff.co.uk

If you are looking for a winter season job then this is the website to visit. It has details on job vacancies and links to specialist companies.

Teaching English

British Council

www.britishcouncil.org/teacherrecruitment.htm
The British council offers opportunities for teaching English abroad and also gives advice on how to gain a TEFL qualification.

Dave's ESL cafe

www.eslcafe.com
This website is a great hub of information for all things related to teaching abroad and has a jobs board and interactive forum.

Internships

Bunac

www.bunac.org
Tel: 0207 251 0662
A popular and long-running gap year company that arranges a variety of jobs, work placements and volunteer programmes around the world.

Mountbatten Institute

www.mountbatten.org
Tel: 0845 370 3535
The Mountbatten Institute offers a renowned internship programme in New York, allowing students to spend a year working at top US companies.

Volunteering

Madventurer

www.madventurer.com

Tel: 0191 232 0625

Madventurer offer a mix of volunteer work and adventure travel, all taking place in small groups with good in-country support.

Raleigh

www.raleighinternational.org

info@raleighinternational.org

Tel: 0207 183 1270

Raleigh has been running challenging expeditions for 25 years, combining volunteer work, adventure travel and physical activity.

Travellers worldwide

www.travellersworldwide.com

Tel: 01903 502595

As well as an extensive list of volunteer opportunities, this site has contact details for language and cultural courses.

Communication

Facebook

www.facebook.com

This social networking site allows you to create a personal profile, upload pictures and keep in touch with your friends.

Skype

www.skype.com

Visit this site to download the Skype software for free or to sign into an existing account and start making calls.

Book List

A Year in Provence
By Peter Mayle, Penguin, London, 2000.

Down Under
By Bill Bryson, Black Swan, London, 2001.

In Patagonia
By Bruce Chatwin, Summit Books, London, 1977.

On the Road
By Jack Kerouac, Viking Press, New York, 1957.

Out of Africa
By Karen Blixen, Penguin, London, 1999.

Wild Swans: Three Daughters of China
By Jung Chang, HarperPerennial, London, 2004.

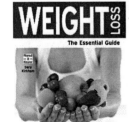

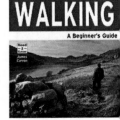

Contents

The Scientific Process

'How Science Works' is all about the scientific process — how we develop and test scientific ideas.
It's what scientists do all day, every day (well except at coffee time — never come between scientists and their coffee).

Scientists Come Up with **Theories** — Then **Test Them**...

Science tries to explain **how** and **why** things happen. It's all about seeking and gaining **knowledge** about the world around us. Scientists do this by **asking** questions and **suggesting** answers and then **testing** them, to see if they're correct — this is the **scientific process**.

1) **Ask** a question — make an **observation** and ask **why or how** whatever you've observed happens.
   E.g. Why does sodium chloride dissolve in water?

2) **Suggest** an answer, or part of an answer, by forming a **theory** or a **model** (a possible **explanation** of the observations or a description of what you think is actually happening).
   E.g. Sodium chloride is made up of charged particles, which are pulled apart by the polar water molecules.

3) Make a **prediction** or hypothesis — a **specific testable statement**, based on the theory, about what will happen in a test situation.
   E.g. A solution of sodium chloride will conduct electricity much better than water does.

4) Carry out **tests** — to provide **evidence** that will support the prediction or refute it.
   E.g. Measure the conductivity of water and of sodium chloride solution.

The evidence supported Quentin's Theory of Flammable Burps.

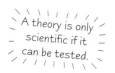

A theory is only scientific if it can be tested.

...Then They **Tell** Everyone About Their **Results**...

The results are **published** — scientists need to let others know about their work. Scientists publish their results in **scientific journals**. These are just like normal magazines, only they contain **scientific reports** (called papers) instead of the latest celebrity gossip.

1) Scientific reports are similar to the **lab write-ups** you do in school. And just as a lab write-up is **reviewed** (marked) by your teacher, reports in scientific journals undergo **peer review** before they're published.

   Scientists use standard terminology when writing their reports. This way they know that other scientists will understand them. For instance, there are internationally agreed rules for naming organic compounds, so that scientists across the world will know exactly what substance is being referred to.

2) The report is sent out to **peers** — other scientists who are experts in the **same area**. They go through it bit by bit, examining the methods and data, and checking it's all clear and logical. When the report is approved, it's **published**. This makes sure that work published in scientific journals is of a **good standard**.

3) But peer review **can't guarantee** the science is **correct** — other scientists still need to **reproduce** it.

4) Sometimes **mistakes** are made and bad work is published. Peer review **isn't perfect** but it's probably the best way for scientists to self-regulate their work and to publish **quality reports**.

...Then **Other Scientists** Will **Test** the Theory Too

1) Other scientists read the published theories and results, and try to **test the theory** themselves. This involves:
   - Repeating the **exact same experiments**.
   - Using the theory to make **new predictions** and then testing them with **new experiments**.

2) If all the experiments in the world provide evidence to back it up, the theory is thought of as **scientific 'fact'** (for now).

3) If **new evidence** comes to light that **conflicts** with the current evidence the theory is questioned all over again. More rounds of **testing** will be carried out to try to find out where the theory **falls down**.

> This is how the **scientific process works** — **evidence** supports a theory, loads of other scientists read it and test it for themselves, eventually all the scientists in the world **agree** with it and then bingo, you get to **learn** it.

This is exactly how scientists arrived at the structure of the atom — and how they came to the conclusion that electrons are arranged in shells and orbitals. It took years and years for these models to be developed and accepted — this is often the case with the scientific process.

A2-Level
Chemistry

The Revision Guide
Exam Board: OCR A

Editors:
Amy Boutal, Mary Falkner, David Hickinson, Paul Jordin, Sharon Keeley, Simon Little,
Michael Southorn, Hayley Thompson.

Contributors:
Mike Bossart, Robert Clarke, Ian H. Davis, John Duffy, Lucy Muncaster, Jane Simoni, Paul Warren.

Proofreaders:
Barrie Crowther, Julie Wakeling.

Published by Coordination Group Publications Ltd.

ISBN: 978 1 84762 267 9

With thanks to Laura Stoney for the copyright research.

Groovy website: www.cgpbooks.co.uk
Jolly bits of clipart from CorelDRAW®
Printed by Elanders Hindson Ltd, Newcastle upon Tyne.

Based on the classic CGP style created by Richard Parsons.

The Scientific Process

If the **Evidence** Supports a Theory, It's **Accepted** — for Now

Our currently accepted theories have survived this '**trial by evidence**'. They've been tested **over and over again** and each time the results have backed them up. **BUT**, and this is a big but (teehee), they never become totally indisputable fact. Scientific **breakthroughs or advances** could provide new ways to question and test the theory, which could lead to **changes and challenges** to it. Then the testing starts all over again...

And this, my friend, is the **tentative nature of scientific knowledge** — it's always **changing** and **evolving**.

In 1865, when Kekulé suggested the structure of benzene was a ring of carbon atoms, joined by alternating single and double bonds, it was widely accepted — it was the best fit for the evidence at the time. It was only once electrons had been discovered and orbital theory was developed that scientists came up with the modern 'delocalised model', which explains the behaviour of benzene better than Kekulé's model. See page 4.

Evidence Comes From **Lab Experiments**...

1) Results from **controlled experiments** in **laboratories** are **great**.
2) A lab is the easiest place to **control variables** so that they're all **kept constant** (except for the one you're investigating).
3) This means you can draw meaningful **conclusions**.

For example, if you're investigating how temperature affects the rate of a reaction you need to keep everything but the temperature constant, e.g. the pH of the solution, the concentration of the solution, etc.

...But You **Can't** Always do a Lab Experiment

There are things you **can't** study in a lab. And outside the lab controlling the variables is tricky, if not impossible.

- *Are increasing CO_2 emissions causing climate change?*
  There are other variables which may have an effect, such as changes in solar activity. You can't easily rule out every possibility. Also, climate change is a very **gradual process**. Scientists won't be able to tell if their predictions are correct for donkey's years.

- *Does eating food containing trans fatty acids increase the risk of heart disease and strokes?*
  There are always differences between groups of people. The best you can do is to have a **well-designed study** using **matched groups** — **choose two groups** of people (those who eat a lot of trans fats and those who don't) which are **as similar as possible** (same mix of ages, same mix of diets etc.). But you still can't rule out every possibility. Taking newborn identical twins and treating them identically, except for making one consume a lot of trans fats and the other none at all, might be a fairer test, but it would present huge **ethical problems**.

Samantha thought her study was very well designed — especially the fitted bookshelf.

See pages 16-18 for more about fats and fatty acids.

Science Helps to Inform **Decision-Making**

Lots of scientific work eventually leads to **important discoveries** that **could** benefit humankind — but there are often **risks** attached (and almost always **financial costs**).

Society (that's you, me and everyone else) must weigh up the information in order to **make decisions** — about the way we live, what we eat, what we drive, and so on. Information is also used by **politicians** to devise policies and laws.

- Scientific advances mean **hydrogen fuel cells** can now be used to power cars (see page 85). They sound better for the **environment** than conventional engines because their only waste product is **water**. But you need lots of **energy** to produce the **hydrogen** and **oxygen** in the first place, so maybe they're not so good after all.
- Pharmaceutical drugs are really expensive to develop, and drug companies want to make money. So they put most of their efforts into developing drugs that they can sell for a good price. Society has to consider the **cost** of buying new drugs — the **NHS** can't afford the most expensive drugs without **sacrificing** something else.
- **Synthetic polymers** are very useful — they're **cheap** to produce and very **durable**. But they're **hard to dispose of** (they don't break down easily). So we need to make choices about how we can best dispose of plastics and whether we should try to **reduce** the amount that we use, or work to develop more **biodegradable plastics** (see page 23).

So there you have it — how science works...

Hopefully these pages have given you a nice intro to how science works, e.g. what scientists do to provide you with 'facts'. You need to understand this, as you're expected to know how science works yourselves — for the exam and for life.

Benzene

We begin A2 chemistry with a fantastical tale of the discovery of the magical rings of Benzene.
Our story opens in a shire where four hobbits are getting up to mischief... Actually no, that's something else.

Benzene has a **Ring Of Carbon Atoms**

Benzene has the formula **C_6H_6**. It has a cyclic structure, with its six carbon atoms joined together in a ring.
There are two ways of representing it — the **Kekulé model** and the **delocalised model**.

The **Kekulé Model** Came First

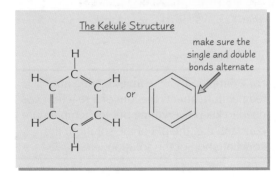

The Kekulé Structure

make sure the single and double bonds alternate

or

1) This was proposed by German chemist Friedrich August Kekulé in 1865. He came up with the idea of a **ring** of C atoms with **alternating single** and **double** bonds between them.

2) He later adapted the model to say that the benzene molecule was constantly **flipping** between two forms (**isomers**) by switching over the double and single bonds.

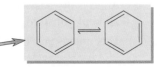

3) If the Kekulé model was correct, you'd expect there to always be three bonds with the length of a **C–C bond** (147 pm) and three bonds with the length of a **C=C bond** (135 pm).

4) However **X-ray diffraction studies** have shown that all the carbon-carbon bonds in benzene have the **same length** of 140 pm — i.e. they are **between** the length of a single bond and a double bond.

5) So the Kekulé structure **can't** be completely right, but it's still used today as it's useful for drawing reaction mechanisms.

Apparently Kekulé imagined benzene as a snake catching its own tail. So here's a picture of a man charming some snakes.

The **Delocalised Model** Replaced Kekulé's Model

The bond-length observations are explained with the delocalised model.

1) The delocalised model says that the **p-orbitals** of all six carbon atoms **overlap** to create **π-bonds**.

2) This creates two **ring-shaped** clouds of electrons — one above and one below the plane of the six carbon atoms.

3) All the bonds in the ring are the **same length** because all the bonds are the same.

4) The electrons in the rings are said to be **delocalised** because they don't belong to a specific carbon atom. They are represented as a circle inside the ring of carbons rather than as double or single bonds

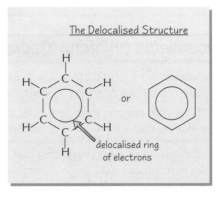

The Delocalised Structure

or

delocalised ring of electrons

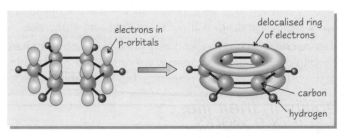

electrons in p-orbitals

delocalised ring of electrons

carbon

hydrogen

Benzene is a planar (flat) molecule — it's got a ring of carbon atoms with their hydrogens sticking out all on a flat plane.

Benzene

Enthalpy Changes Give More Evidence for Delocalisation

1) Cyclohexene has **one** double bond. When it's hydrogenated, the enthalpy change is **–120 kJmol⁻¹**. If benzene had three double bonds (as in the Kekulé structure), you'd expect it to have an enthalpy of hydrogenation of –360 kJmol⁻¹.

2) But the **experimental** enthalpy of hydrogenation of benzene is **–208 kJmol⁻¹** — far **less exothermic** than expected.

3) Energy is put in to break bonds and released when bonds are made. So **more energy** must have been put in to break the bonds in benzene than would be needed to break the bonds in the Kekulé structure.

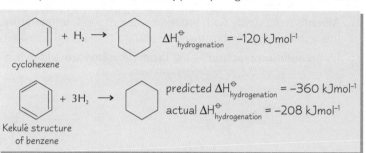

4) This difference indicates that benzene is **more stable** than the Kekulé structure would be. This is thought to be due to the **delocalised ring of electrons**.

See page 70 for more about enthalpy changes.

Aromatic Compounds are Derived from Benzene

Compounds containing a **benzene ring** are called **arenes** or **'aromatic compounds'**. Don't be confused by the term 'aromatic' — although some of them are smelly, it's really just a term for compounds that have this structure. Arenes are **named** in two ways. There's no easy rule — you just have to learn these examples:

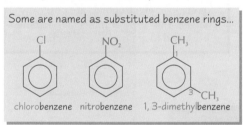

Practice Questions

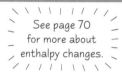

Q1 Draw the Kekulé and delocalised models of benzene.
Q2 Give two pieces of evidence for the delocalised electron ring in benzene.
Q3 What type of bonds exist between C atoms in the delocalised model?

• bonds same length
• enthalpy shows more energy put in
π bonds

Exam Questions

1 a) The diagram represents the compound methylbenzene.
What is its chemical formula? [1 mark]

b) What name is given to compounds that contain a ring like this? [1 mark]

c) Name compounds A, B and C, shown on the right. [3 marks]

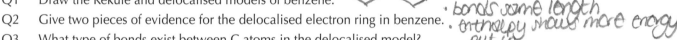

2 a) In 1865, Friedrich Kekulé proposed the structure shown for a benzene molecule.
What does this model imply about the C-C bond lengths in the molecule? [1 mark]

b) What technique has been used to show that the bond lengths suggested by the Kekulé structure are incorrect? [1 mark]

c) How does this technique show that Kekulé's structure is incorrect? [1 mark]

Everyone needs a bit of stability in their life...

The structure of benzene is bizarre — even top scientists struggled to find out what its molecular structure looked like. Make sure you can draw all the different representations of benzene given on this page, including the ones showing the Cs and Hs. Yes, and don't forget that there's a hydrogen at every point on the ring — it's easy to forget they're there.

Reactions of Benzene

Benzene is an alkene but it often doesn't behave like one — whenever this is the case, you can pretty much guarantee that our kooky friend Mr Delocalised Electron Ring is up to his old tricks again...

Alkenes usually like Addition Reactions, but Not Benzene

1) **Alkenes** react easily with **bromine** water at room temperature. The reaction is the basis of the test for a double bond, as the orange colour of the bromine water is lost.

2) It's an **addition reaction** — the bromine atoms are added to the alkene.

For example:

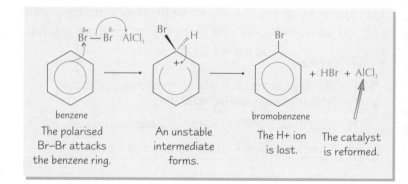

3) If the Kekulé structure (see page 4) were correct, you'd expect a **similar reaction** between benzene and bromine. In fact, to make it happen you need **hot benzene** and **ultraviolet light** — and it's still a real **struggle**.

4) This difference between benzene and other alkenes is explained by the **delocalised electron rings** above and below the plane of carbon atoms. They make the benzene ring very **stable**, and **spread out** the negative charge. So benzene is very **unwilling** to undergo **addition reactions** which would destroy the stable ring.

5) In alkenes, the C=C bond is an area of **high electron density** which strongly attracts **electrophiles**. In benzene, this attraction is reduced due to the negative charge being spread out.

> Remember, **electrophiles** are positively charged ions or polar molecules that are **attracted** to areas of negative charge.

6) So benzene prefers to react by **electrophilic substitution**.

Arenes Undergo Electrophilic Substitution Reactions...

1) With Halogens using a Halogen Carrier

1) Benzene will react with bromine, Br–Br, in the presence of aluminium chloride, $AlCl_3$.

2) Br–Br is the **electrophile**.

3) $AlCl_3$ acts as a **halogen carrier** (see below) which makes the **electrophile stronger**.

Without the halogen carrier, the electrophile doesn't have a strong enough positive charge to attack the stable benzene ring.

4) A Br atom is **substituted** in place of a H atom.

5) Chlorine Cl–Cl will react in just the same way.

benzene — The polarised Br–Br attacks the benzene ring. / An unstable intermediate forms. / bromobenzene — The H+ ion is lost. / The catalyst is reformed.

> **Halogen carriers make the Electrophile Stronger**
> 1) Halogen carriers accept a **lone pair of electrons** from the electrophile.
> 2) Halogen carriers include **aluminium halides**, **iron halides** and **iron**.
> 3) **E.g.** Aluminium chloride combines with the bromine molecule like this in the example above: $AlCl_3 + Br-Br \rightarrow AlCl_3Br^{\delta-}-Br^{\delta+}$

Reactions of Benzene

2) With Nitric Acid and a Catalyst

When you warm **benzene** with **concentrated nitric** and **sulfuric acid**, you get **nitrobenzene**.

Sulfuric acid works as a **catalyst** — it helps make the nitronium ion, **NO$_2^+$**, which is the **electrophile**, but is regenerated at the end of the reaction mechanism.

$$HNO_3 + H_2SO_4 \rightarrow H_2NO_3^+ + HSO_4^-$$
$$H_2NO_3^+ \rightarrow NO_2^+ + H_2O$$

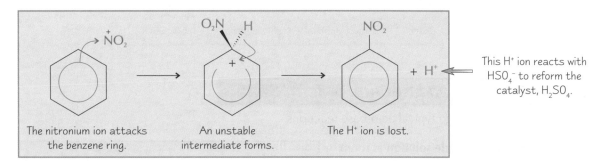

The nitronium ion attacks the benzene ring.

An unstable intermediate forms.

The H$^+$ ion is lost.

+ H$^+$

This H$^+$ ion reacts with HSO$_4^-$ to reform the catalyst, H$_2$SO$_4$.

If you only want one NO$_2$ group added (**mononitration**), you need to keep the temperature **below 55 °C**. Above this temperature you'll get lots of substitutions.

Practice Questions

Q1 What type of reaction does benzene tend to undergo?

Q2 What makes benzene resistant to reaction with bromine?

Q3 Which substances are used as halogen carriers in substitution reactions of benzene?

Q4 Which two acids are used in the production of nitrobenzene?

Exam Questions

1 Nitrobenzene is a yellow oily substance used in the first step of the production of polyurethane. It is made from benzene by reaction with concentrated nitric and sulfuric acids.

a) Draw the structure of nitrobenzene. [1 mark]

b) 1,3-dinitrobenzene is made by the same process if the temperature is higher. Draw its structure. [1 mark]

c) What kind of reaction is this? [1 mark]

d) Outline a mechanism for this reaction. [3 marks]

2 In the Kekulé model of benzene, there are 3 double bonds. Cyclohexene has 1 double bond.

a) Describe what you would see if benzene and cyclohexene were each mixed with bromine water. [1 mark]

b) Explain the difference that you would observe. [2 marks]

c) To make bromine and benzene react, they are heated together with iron(III) chloride.

i) What is the function of the iron(III) chloride? [1 mark]

ii) Outline a mechanism for this reaction. [3 marks]

What are you looking at, punk?

Arenes really like Mr Delocalised Electron Ring and they won't give him up for nobody, at least not without a fight. They'd much rather get tangled up in an electrophilic substitution — anything not to bother The Ring. Being associated with The Ring provides Arenes with stability but also serious respect on the mean streets of... err... Organic Chemistryville.

8

Phenols

A phenol is the aromatic version of an alcohol. Don't drink them though — they'd get your insides a bit too clean.

Phenols Have Benzene Rings with –OH Groups Attached

Phenol has the formula C_6H_5OH.
Other phenols have various groups attached to the benzene ring:

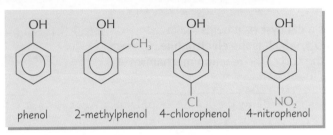

phenol   2-methylphenol   4-chlorophenol   4-nitrophenol

Number the carbons starting from the one with the –OH group.

Phenol reacts with Bases and Sodium to form Salts

Phenol is weakly acidic, so will undergo typical acid-base reactions.

1) Phenol reacts with **sodium hydroxide solution** at room temperature to form **sodium phenoxide** and **water**.

2) Phenol **doesn't react** with **sodium carbonate** solution though — sodium carbonate is not a strong enough base.

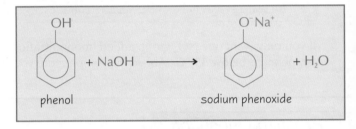

phenol   sodium phenoxide

3) **Sodium phenoxide** is also formed when **sodium** metal is added to liquid phenol. **Hydrogen gas** fizzes off this time.

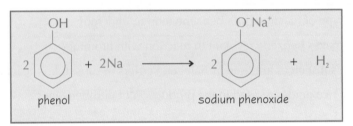

phenol   sodium phenoxide

Phenol Reacts with Bromine Water

1) If you shake phenol with orange bromine water, it will **react**, **decolorising** it.

2) Benzene **doesn't** react with bromine water (see page 6), so phenol's reaction must be to do with the **OH group**.

3) One of the pairs of electrons in a **p-orbital** of the oxygen atom **overlaps** with the delocalised ring of electrons in the benzene ring.

4) This increases the **electron density** of the ring, especially at positions 2, 4 and 6 (for reasons you don't need to know), making it more likely to be attacked by the bromine molecule in these positions.

5) The hydrogen atoms at 2, 4 and 6 are **substituted** by bromine atoms. The product is called 2,4,6-tribromophenol — it's insoluble in water and **precipitates** out of the mixture. It smells of antiseptic.

This is an electrophilic substitution reaction.

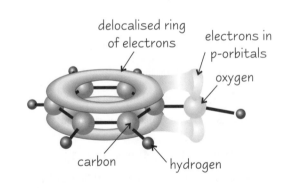

delocalised ring of electrons

electrons in p-orbitals

oxygen

carbon   hydrogen

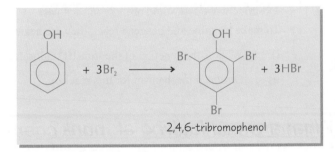

2,4,6-tribromophenol

Phenols

Phenol has many Important Uses

Phenol is a major chemical product, with more than 8 million tonnes being produced each year.

1) The first major use was as an **antiseptic** during surgery. Joseph Lister was the first to use it to clean wounds. It wasn't used like this for long though as it was too damaging to tissue. It's still used today in the production of **antiseptics** and **disinfectants** such as TCP™.

2) Another important use is in the production of **polymers**. Kevlar® (see page 24) and polycarbonate are both produced from substances made from phenol. Bisphenol A is used to make polycarbonates, which are used in things like bottles, spectacle lenses and CDs.

3) One of the earliest "plastics" was **Bakelite**™, a polymer of phenol and formaldehyde. It is a resin with good insulating properties and was used to make things like telephones and radio casings. Today, similar compounds are used to make all sorts of objects including saucepan handles, electrical plugs, dominos, billiard balls and chess pieces.

4) Bisphenol A is used in the manufacture of resins called **epoxies**. These have a variety of important uses including **adhesives** and **paints**. They're also really important in electronic circuits where they're used as electrical insulators.

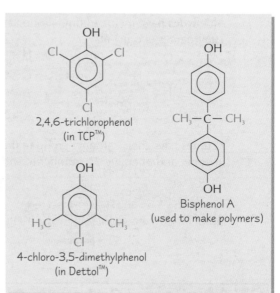
2,4,6-trichlorophenol (in TCP™)

4-chloro-3,5-dimethylphenol (in Dettol™)

Bisphenol A (used to make polymers)

Practice Questions

Q1 Draw the structures of phenol, 4-chlorophenol and 4-nitrophenol.

Q2 Write a balanced equation for the reaction between phenol and sodium hydroxide solution.

Q3 Write a balanced equation for the reaction between phenol and bromine (Br_2).

Q4 Give three uses of phenol.

Exam Questions

1 a) Draw the structure of 2-methylphenol. [1 mark]

b) Write an equation for the reaction of 2-methylphenol with potassium. [1 mark]

c) 1 mole of gas occupies 24 dm³ at room temperature and pressure. What mass of 2-methyl phenol would you need to produce 4.8 dm³ of hydrogen, at room temperature and pressure, by reaction with excess potassium? [3 mark]

2 a) Bromine water can be used to distinguish between benzene and phenol. Describe what you would observe in each case. [2 marks]

b) Name the product formed when phenol reacts with bromine water. [1 mark]

c) Explain why phenol reacts differently from benzene. [2 marks]

d) What type of reaction occurs between phenol and bromine? [1 mark]

Phenol Destination 4 — more chemicals, more equations, more horror...

You might not like this phenol stuff, but if you were a germ, you'd like it even less. If you're ever looking for TCP™ in the supermarket, try asking for a bottle of 2,4,6-trichlorophenol and see what you get — probably a funny look. Anyway, no time for shopping — you've got to get these pages learned. If you can do all the questions above, you're well on your way.

Aldehydes and Ketones

Aldehydes and ketones are both carbonyl compounds. They've got their carbonyl groups in different positions though.

Aldehydes and Ketones contain a Carbonyl Group

Aldehydes and ketones are **carbonyl compounds** — they contain the **carbonyl** functional group, **C=O**.

Aldehydes have their carbonyl group at the **end** of the carbon chain. Their names end in **–al**.

R and R' represent two (possibly different) carbon chains.

methanal   propanal

Ketones have their carbonyl group in the **middle** of the carbon chain. Their names end in **–one**, and often have a number to show which **carbon** the carbonyl group is on.

propanone   pentan-2-one

Aldehydes and Carboxylic Acids are made by Oxidising Primary Alcohols

You can use **acidified dichromate(VI) ions** ($Cr_2O_7^{2-}$) to **mildly** oxidise alcohols.
Acidified **potassium dichromate(VI)** ($K_2Cr_2O_7$ / H_2SO_4) is often used.

$$R-CH_2-OH + [O] \longrightarrow R-C{\overset{O}{\diagdown}}_H + [O] \xrightarrow{reflux} R-C{\overset{O}{\diagdown}}_{OH}$$

$$+ H_2O$$

primary alcohol   aldehyde   carboxylic acid

[O] = oxidising agent

The <u>orange</u> dichromate(VI) ion is reduced to the <u>green</u> chromium(III) ion, Cr^{3+}.

You can control how **far** the alcohol is oxidised by controlling the **reaction conditions**:

Oxidising Primary Alcohols

1) Gently heating ethanol with potassium dichromate(VI) solution and sulfuric acid in a test tube should produce "apple" smelling **ethanal** (an aldehyde). However, it's **really tricky** to control the amount of heat, and the aldehyde is usually oxidised to form "vinegar" smelling **ethanoic acid**.

2) To get just the **aldehyde**, you need to get it out of the oxidising solution **as soon** as it's formed. You can do this by gently heating excess alcohol with a **controlled** amount of oxidising agent in **distillation apparatus**, so the aldehyde (which boils at a lower temperature than the alcohol) is distilled off **immediately**.

Reflux Apparatus
water out
Liebig condenser
water in
round bottomed flask
anti-bumping granules (added to make boiling smoother)
heat

3) To produce the **carboxylic acid**, the alcohol has to be **vigorously oxidised**. The alcohol is mixed with excess oxidising agent and heated under **reflux**. Heating under reflux means you can increase the **temperature** of an organic reaction to boiling without losing **volatile** solvents, reactants or products. Any vaporised compounds are cooled, condense and drip back into the reaction mixture. Handy, hey.

Aldehydes and Ketones

Ketones are made by Oxidising Secondary Alcohols

1) Refluxing a secondary alcohol, e.g. propan-2-ol, with acidified dichromate(VI) will produce a **ketone**.

$$R_1 - \underset{\underset{R_2}{|}}{\overset{\overset{H}{|}}{C}} - OH + [O] \xrightarrow{\text{reflux}} \underset{R_2}{\overset{R_1}{>}}C=O \ + H_2O$$

2) Ketones can't be oxidised easily, so even prolonged refluxing won't produce anything more.

*Tertiary Alcohols **Can't** be Oxidised Easily*

Tertiary alcohols are **resistant** to oxidation. They **don't react** with potassium dichromate(VI) at all — the solution stays orange.

Have you heard the one about the chemist who tried to react an alcohol with potassium dichromate(VI)? He used... wait for it.... a tertiary alcohol.

*You can **Reduce** Aldehydes and Ketones Back to **Alcohols***

Using a **reducing agent** [H] you can:

1) reduce an **aldehyde** to a **primary alcohol**.

$$R - \overset{\overset{O}{\diagup}}{\underset{\diagdown H}{C}} + 2[H] \longrightarrow R - CH_2 - OH$$

2) reduce a **ketone** to a **secondary alcohol**.

$$R - \overset{\overset{O}{\diagup}}{\underset{\diagdown R'}{C}} + 2[H] \longrightarrow R - \underset{\underset{R'}{|}}{\overset{\overset{H}{|}}{C}} - OH$$

You'd usually use **NaBH₄** (sodium tetrahydridoborate(III) or sodium borohydride) dissolved in water with methanol as the reducing agent.

The **Reduction** of Aldehydes and Ketones is **Nucleophilic Addition**

The reducing agent, e.g. NaBH₄, supplies **hydride ions**, H⁻.
The extra pair of electrons on the H⁻ make this a **nucleophile**, which will attack the δ+ carbon on the **carbonyl group** of an aldehyde or ketone:

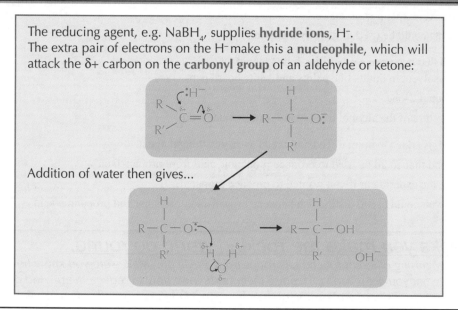

Addition of water then gives...

Aldehydes and Ketones

Knowing what aldehyde and ketone molecules look like won't help you decide which is which if you've got a test tube of each. There are chemical tests that will though. You can also just test for a carbonyl group.

Brady's Reagent Tests for a Carbonyl Group

Brady's reagent is **2,4-dinitrophenylhydrazine** (2,4-DNPH) dissolved in methanol and concentrated sulfuric acid.
The **2,4-dinitrophenylhydrazine** forms a **bright orange precipitate** if a carbonyl group is present.
This only happens with **C=O groups**, not with ones like COOH, so it only tests for **aldehydes** and **ketones**.

> The orange precipitate is a derivative of the carbonyl compound. Each different carbonyl compound produces a crystalline derivative with a different melting point.
>
> So if you measure the melting point of the crystals and compare it against the known melting points of the derivatives, you can identify the carbonyl compound.

Use Tollens' Reagent to Test for an Aldehyde

This test lets you distinguish between an aldehyde and a ketone. It uses the fact that an **aldehyde** can be **easily oxidised** to a carboxylic acid, but a ketone can't.

TOLLENS' REAGENT

Tollens' reagent is a **colourless** solution of **silver nitrate** dissolved in **aqueous ammonia**.

When heated together in a test tube, the aldehyde is **oxidised** and Tollens' reagent is **reduced** causing a silver mirror to form.

$$Ag(NH_3)_2^+{}_{(aq)} + e^- \rightarrow Ag_{(s)} + 2NH_{3(aq)}$$

The test tube should be heated in a beaker of hot water, rather than directly over a flame.

Practice Questions

Q1 What type of alcohol can be oxidised to a ketone?
Q2 Which oxidising agent is usually used to oxidise alcohols?
Q3 Draw the reaction mechanism for reducing a ketone or aldehyde to an alcohol.
Q4 What is Tollens' reagent used for?

Exam Questions

1 Compound X is an alcohol. When heated under reflux with acidified potassium dichromate(VI), compound Y is made. Compound Y does not give a silver mirror when heated with Tollens' reagent. Compound Y has a neutral pH.
   a) What type of compound is substance Y? Explain your answer. [3 marks]
   b) What type of alcohol is X? Explain your answer. [1 mark]
   c) Suggest a further test that could be used to identify compound Y. [2 marks]

2 Butan-2-one is a compound that occurs in some fruits, but is manufactured on a large scale for use as a solvent in things like paints and white board pens.
   a) Draw the structure of butan-2-one. [2 marks]
   b) Draw and name the structure of the alcohol that butan-2-one is made from. [2 marks]

3 Propanoic acid, C_2H_5COOH, is added to animal feed and bread as an anti-fungal agent.
   a) Briefly describe a method that could be used to produce propanoic acid from propan-1-ol. [1 mark]
   b) How would you change the experiment if you wanted to produce propanal? [1 mark]
   c) Describe two tests that you could use to distinguish between propan-1-ol, propanal and propanoic acid. [3 marks]

Round bottomed flasks you make the rocking world go round...

You've got to be a dab hand at recognising different functional groups from a mile off. Make sure you know how aldehydes differ from ketones and what you get when you oxidise them both. And how to reduce them. And don't forget all the details of those pesky tests. Phew, it's hard work some of this chemistry. Don't worry, it'll only make you stronger.

Carboxylic Acids and Esters

Carboxylic acids are much more interesting than cardboard boxes — as you're about to discover...

Carboxylic Acids contain –COOH

A <u>carboxyl</u> group contains a <u>carbonyl</u> group and a hydr<u>oxyl</u> group.

Carboxylic acids contain the **carboxyl** functional group **–COOH**.

To name them, you find and name the longest alkane chain, take off the 'e' and add **'–oic acid'**.

The carboxyl group is always at the **end** of the molecule and when naming it's more important than other functional groups — so all the other functional groups in the molecule are numbered starting from this carbon.

ethanoic acid   4-hydroxy-2-methylbutanoic acid   benzoic acid

Carboxylic Acids are Weak Acids

Carboxylic acids are **polar molecules**, since electrons are drawn towards the O atoms. This makes small carboxylic acids **very soluble** in water, as they form **hydrogen bonds** with the water molecules — $H^{\delta+}$ and $O^{\delta-}$ atoms on different molecules are attracted to each other.

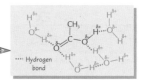

···· Hydrogen bond

Carboxylic acids are **weak acids** — in water they partially dissociate into **carboxylate ions** and **H^+ ions**.

carboxylic acid ⇌ carboxylate ion $+ H^+$

This equilibrium lies to the **left** because most of the molecules don't dissociate.

Carboxylic Acids React with Metals, Carbonates and Bases

1) Carboxylic acids react with the more **reactive metals** to form a **salt and hydrogen gas**.

ethanoic acid   magnesium ethanoate

$$2CH_3COOH_{(aq)} + Mg_{(s)} \rightarrow (CH_3COO)_2Mg_{(aq)} + H_{2(g)}$$

Salts of carboxylic acids are called carboxylates and their names end with –oate.

2) Carboxylic acids react with **carbonates CO_3^{2-}** to form a **salt, carbon dioxide** and **water**.

ethanoic acid   sodium ethanoate

$$2CH_3COOH_{(aq)} + Na_2CO_{3(s)} \rightarrow 2CH_3COONa_{(aq)} + H_2O_{(l)} + CO_{2(g)}$$

In reactions 1 and 2, the gas fizzes out of the solution.

3) Carboxylic acids are neutralised by **bases** to form **salts** and **water**

$$2CH_3COOH_{(aq)} + MgO_{(s)} \rightarrow (CH_3COO)_2Mg_{(aq)} + H_2O_{(l)}$$

Esters have the Functional Group –COO–

An **ester** is made by reacting an **alcohol** with a **carboxylic acid** (see next page). So the **name** of an **ester** is made up of **two parts** — the **first** bit comes from the **alcohol**, and the **second** bit from the **carboxylic acid**.

1) Look at the **alkyl group** that came from the **alcohol**. This is the first bit of the ester's name.

This is an **ethyl group**.

2) Now look at the part that came from the **carboxylic acid**. Swap its '-oic acid' ending for 'oate' to get the second bit of the name.

This came from **ethanoic acid**, so it is an **ethanoate**.

3) Put the two parts together.

It's **ethyl ethanoate**
$CH_3COOCH_2CH_3$

The name's written the opposite way round from the formula.

This goes for molecules with benzene rings too — react methanol with benzoic acid, and you get methyl benzoate, $C_6H_5COOCH_3$.

If either of the carbon chains is **branched** you need to name the attached groups too.

For an ester, number the carbons starting from the C atoms in the C–O–C bond.

1-methylpropyl methanoate
$HCOOCH(CH_3)CH_2CH_3$

ethyl 2-methylbutanoate
$CH_3CH_2CH(CH_3)COOCH_2CH_3$

Carboxylic Acids and Esters

You can make *Esters*...

1) From *Alcohols* and *Carboxylic Acids*

1) If you heat a **carboxylic acid** with an **alcohol** in the presence of an **acid catalyst**, you get an ester.
2) Concentrated sulfuric acid is usually used as the acid catalyst. It's called an **esterification** reaction.

This oxygen comes from the alcohol.

$$R-C \overset{O}{\underset{O-H}{}} + R-O-H \underset{\longleftarrow}{\overset{H^+}{\longrightarrow}} R-C \overset{O}{\underset{O-R}{}} + H \overset{O}{\underset{}{}} H$$

carboxylic acid · alcohol · ester · water

It's an example of a condensation reaction — where molecules combine by releasing a small molecule.

E.g.

$$H_3C-C \overset{O}{\underset{O-H}{}} + H-O-CH_2CH_3 \underset{\longleftarrow}{\overset{H^+}{\longrightarrow}} H_3C-C \overset{O}{\underset{O-CH_2CH_3}{}} + H \overset{O}{\underset{}{}} H$$

ethanoic acid · ethanol · ethyl ethanoate · water

3) The reaction is **reversible**, so you need to separate out the product **as it's formed**.
4) For small esters, you can warm the mixture and just **distil off** the ester, because it's more volatile than the other compounds.
5) Larger esters are harder to form so it's best to heat them under **reflux** and use **fractional distillation** to separate the ester from the other compounds.

2) From *Alcohols* and *Acid Anhydrides*

An **acid anhydride** is made from two identical carboxylic acid molecules. If you know the name of the carboxylic acid, they're easy to name — just take away 'acid' and add 'anhydride'.

$$CH_3-C\overset{O}{\underset{O-H}{}} \quad CH_3-C\overset{O}{} \\ CH_3-C\underset{O}{\overset{O-H}{}} \longrightarrow \overset{O}{\underset{CH_3-C}{}} + H_2O$$

ethanoic acid · ethanoic anhydride

Acid anhydrides can be reacted with alcohols to make **esters** too.

1) The acid anhydride is warmed with the **alcohol**. **No catalyst** is needed.
2) The products are an **ester** and a **carboxylic acid** which can then be separated by fractional distillation.

$$\overset{R^1}{\underset{R^2}{}}\overset{C\overset{O}{}}{\underset{C\overset{O}{}}{O}} + R-O-H \longrightarrow R^1-C\overset{O}{\underset{O-R}{}} + \overset{H}{\underset{O-C}{}}\overset{O}{\underset{R^2}{}}$$

acid anhydride · alcohol · ester · carboxylic acid

E.g.

$$\overset{CH_3-C\overset{O}{}}{\underset{CH_3-C\overset{O}{}}{O}} + CH_3CH_2-O-H \longrightarrow CH_3-C\overset{O}{\underset{O-CH_2CH_3}{}} + \overset{H}{\underset{O-C}{}}\overset{O}{\underset{CH_3}{}}$$

ethanoic anhydride · ethanol · ester · ethanoic acid

Esters are Used as *Food Flavourings* and *Perfumes*

1) Esters have a **sweet smell** — it varies from gluey sweet for smaller esters to a fruity 'pear drop' smell for the larger ones.
2) This makes them useful in **perfumes**.
3) The food industry uses esters to **flavour** things like drinks and sweets.
4) The **fragrances** and **flavours** of lots of flowers and fruits come from naturally occurring esters.

Jon enjoyed the naturally occurring fragrances and flavours of Esther.

Carboxylic Acids and Esters

Esters are *Hydrolysed* to Form *Alcohols*

There are two ways to hydrolyse esters — using **acid hydrolysis** or **base hydrolysis**.
With both types you get an **alcohol**, but the second product in each case is different.

ACID HYDROLYSIS

Acid hydrolysis splits the ester into a **carboxylic acid** and an **alcohol**.
You have to **reflux** the ester with a **dilute acid**, such as hydrochloric or sulfuric.

ethyl ethanoate   ethanoic acid   ethanol

As it's a reversible reaction, you need to use lots of water to push the equilibrium over to the right.

BASE HYDROLYSIS

This time you have to **reflux** the ester with a **dilute alkali**, such as sodium hydroxide.
You get a **carboxylate salt** and an **alcohol**.

ethyl ethanoate   sodium ethanoate   ethanol

Practice Questions

Q1 What is the functional group of: a) a carboxylic acid, b) an ester?

Q2 Explain why carboxylic acids dissolve in water.

Q3 What products are formed when carboxylic acids react with: a) metals,   b) carbonates,   c) bases?

Q4 Draw the structures of: a) propanoic acid,   b) 3-methylbutanoic acid,   c) benzoic acid.

Q5 Draw the structure of the ester 1-methylpropyl methanoate.

Exam Questions

1   Compound C, shown on the right, is found in raspberries.

a)   Name compound C.   [1 mark]

b)   Suggest a use for compound C.   [1 mark]

c)   Compound C is refluxed with dilute sulfuric acid.
     Name the products formed and draw their structures. What kind of reaction is this?   [5 marks]

d)   If compound C is refluxed with excess sodium hydroxide, a similar reaction occurs.
     Give a difference between this reaction and the reaction described in (c).   [1 mark]

2   Propyl ethanoate is a pear-scented oil. It is used as a solvent and as a flavouring.

a)   Name the alcohol that it can be made from.   [1 mark]

b)   Name two different substances that could be added to the alcohol to produce the propyl ethanoate.   [2 marks]

c)   Draw the structures of the two substances you have chosen in b).   [2 marks]

Carboxylic acid + alcohol produces ester — well, that's life...

I bet your apple flavoured sweets have never been near a nice rosy apple — it's all the work of esters. And for that matter, I reckon prawn cocktail crisps have never met a prawn, or a cocktail either. None of it's real. And as for potatoes...

Fatty Acids and Fats

OK, brace yourself, as you're about to experience three solid pages of pure, unadulterated lardfest.

Fatty Acids are **Carboxylic Acids**

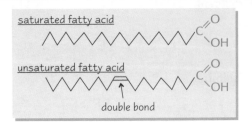

saturated fatty acid

unsaturated fatty acid

double bond

Fatty acids have a long hydrocarbon chain with a **carboxylic acid** group at the end. If the hydrocarbon chain contains **no double bonds** then the fatty acid is **saturated**, but if it contains one or more double bonds then it's **unsaturated**.

Fatty acids can also be written like this ⟹ where 'R' is a hydrocarbon chain.

A **Triglyceride** is a **Triester** of **Glycerol** and **Fatty Acids**

1) The **animal** and **vegetable fats** and **oils** we eat are mainly **triglycerides**.

2) Triglycerides contain the ester functional group –COO– three times — they are **triglyceryl esters**. They're made by reacting **glycerol (propane-1,2,3-triol)** with **fatty acids**.

3) The **three -OH groups** on the glycerol molecules link up to **fatty acids** to produce triglyceride molecules. Water is eliminated, so it's a type of **condensation** reaction.

$$\text{Glycerol} + 3 \times \text{Fatty Acid} \xrightarrow{\text{esterification / condensation}} \text{Triglyceride} + 3H_2O$$

Systematic Names are used for **Complex Molecules...**

...like **Fatty Acids**

Saturated and unsaturated fats and fatty acids are pretty **complex molecules**, which means describing their structure clearly without having to draw them can become slightly nightmarish. The best way is by using their **systematic names** which you need to know a few conventions for.

1) Fatty acids are long hydrocarbon chains with a COOH group at the end.

2) To name them systematically, you need to add numbers to say
   – **how many carbon atoms** there are.
   – **how many double bonds** there are.
   – **where** the double bonds are (count the carbons from the COOH group end).

3) A fatty acid with **14** carbon atoms and **0** double bonds (i.e. it's saturated) would be **tetradecanoic acid, 14, 0** (chemical formula $CH_3(CH_2)_{12}COOH$).

4) One with **16** carbon atoms and **1** double bond (i.e. unsaturated) between the **9th and 10th** carbon atoms, would be **hexadec-9-enoic acid, 16, 1(9)** (chemical formula $CH_3(CH_2)_5\mathbf{CH=CH}(CH_2)_7COOH$).

5) If it has **18** carbon atoms and **2** double bonds (i.e. unsaturated) in positions **9** and **12**, it'd be **octadec-9,12-enoic acid, 18, 2(9, 12)** (chemical formula $CH_3(CH_2)_4\mathbf{CH=CHCH_2CH=CH}(CH_2)_7COOH$).

tetra means 4
hexa means 6
octa means 8
deca means 10

Most of these chemicals also have a common name, e.g. 'oleic acid' but they're no help if you want to know about the structure.

Fatty Acids and Fats

...and *Triglycerides*

Triglycerides are named by showing **which carbon** from the glycerol molecule has **which fatty acid** attached. For example:

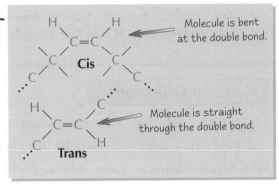

Octadecanoic acid, 18, 0 attached to carbon 1

Octadecanoic acid, 18, 0 attached to carbon 2

Hexadecanoic acid, 16, 0 attached to carbon 3

So this triglyceride could be named **propane-1,2-dioctadecanoic acid**, **18,0 -3-hexadecanoic acid**, **16,0**. (So that's simple enough.... NOT.) Don't panic though — you won't get anything this complicated in the exam.

Fatty acids come in *Cis* and *Trans* forms

Fatty acids can exist as **geometric isomers** — molecules with the same structural formula but different arrangements in space. This is because the C=C bond is **rigid** — the molecule can't rotate about this bond.

1) Almost all naturally-occurring fatty acids that are unsaturated have the **cis configuration**. This means that the hydrogens each side of the double bond are on the same side. This results in a **bent molecule**, or with several double bonds, a **curved molecule**.

2) In **trans fatty acids**, the **hydrogens** are on **opposite sides**. This gives long, straight molecules, similar to saturated fatty acids. They're almost always the product of human processing — hydrogen is added (**hydrogenation**) to unsaturated vegetable oils to saturate them, raising their melting point and creating solid fats.

Molecule is bent at the double bond.

Molecule is straight through the double bond.

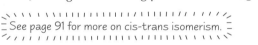
See page 91 for more on cis-trans isomerism.

Fats *Aren't Always* Bad (but they *Often Are*)

1) **Cholesterol** is a soft, waxy material found in cell membranes and transported in your blood stream. It is partly produced by your body and partly absorbed from animal products that you eat, e.g., eggs, meat, dairy products.

2) There are **two types** of cholesterol - 'good' cholesterol and 'bad' cholesterol.

3) **Bad cholesterol** can clog blood vessels, which increases the risk of heart attacks and strokes.

4) **Good cholesterol** removes bad cholesterol, taking it to the liver to be destroyed. So high levels of good cholesterol can give protection from heart disease.

5) Recent research has shown that **trans fats increase** the amount of bad cholesterol and decrease the amount of good cholesterol.

6) Trans fats are **triglycerides** made from trans fatty acids. They are almost all man-made and are used in many foods such as biscuits, cakes, chips and crisps. Because of recent health concerns, there have been moves to **reduce their use** and more **clearly label** foods that contain them.

7) Bad cholesterol is also increased by eating **saturated fats** (made from fatty acids with no double bonds). They occur in animal products but much less so in plants.

8) Plant oils such as olive and sunflower oils contain **unsaturated fats**. These can be **polyunsaturated** (several double bonds) or **monounsaturated** (one double bond per chain). Polyunsaturated oils have been shown to reduce "bad" cholesterol and are actually a good thing to eat in moderation to prevent heart disease. They can help counteract obesity if they're used instead of saturated fats.

'Good' cholesterol — good 'bad' cholesterol — bad.

Revision Bunny can help if you're struggling with the key point here.

Fatty Acids and Fats

Fats can be used to make Biodiesel

Biodiesel is a renewable fuel made from **vegetable oil** or **animal fats** that can be used in diesel engines. It is gaining popularity as a viable alternative to crude oil-based diesel.

1) Biodiesel is mainly a mixture of methyl and ethyl **esters of fatty acids**.

2) It's made by reacting **triglycerides** (oils or fats) with **methanol** or **ethanol**.

long carbon chain

Biodiesel is a mixture of methyl esters.

triglyceride + methanol → glycerol + methyl ester

3) The **vegetable oils** used in the process can be **new**, **low grade oil** or **waste oil** from chip shops and restaurants. **Animal fats** that can be used include chicken fat, waste fish oil and lard from meat processing.

4) At present, biodiesel is mainly used **mixed with conventional diesel**, rather than in pure form. **B20 fuel** contains 20% biodiesel and 80% conventional diesel. Diesel engines generally need converting before they're able to run **B100 fuel** (100% biodiesel).

5) There is debate about how feasible **large-scale use** of biodiesel is — to produce significant quantities would mean devoting **huge areas of land** to growing biodiesel crops (e.g. rapeseed and soy beans) rather than **food crops**.

Practice Questions

Q1 What is a fatty acid? How are saturated and unsaturated fatty acids different?

Q2 Give three examples of fatty acids using their systematic names and chemical formulas.

Q3 Write the systematic name of the triester that could be formed from these acids.

Q4 Explain how cis and trans fatty acids are different.

Q5 Give one advantage and one disadvantage of biodiesel over conventional diesel.

Exam Questions

1 Stearic acid is the common name for a fatty acid found in many animal fats.
Stearic acid is used in candle making. Its chemical name is octadecanoic acid,18,0.

 a) What is the chemical formula of stearic acid? [1 mark]

 b) Glycerol (propane-1,2,3-triol) forms a triester with stearic acid.
 This triester is widely used in shampoos and cosmetics to give a pearly effect.

 i) What name is given to triesters formed from glycerol and fatty acids? [1 mark]

 ii) Is the triester formed saturated or unsaturated? Explain how you know. [1 mark]

2 Cis fatty acids are considered to be more healthy than trans fatty acids.

 a) A major constituent of olive oil is a cis fatty acid called oleic acid.
 What does the term 'cis' tell you about its structure? [1 mark]

 b) Explain why trans fatty acids are harmful to human health. [2 marks]

Altogether now... 'Lard, lard, lard'... 'Lard, Lard, Lard'... 'Lard Lard Lard Lard'...

If you're struggling to remember everything, have a go at writing down the key facts like this: Fatty acid = carboxylic acid, triglyceride = triester = "fat". If you're still struggling, as a last resort you could summon Revision Bunny by standing on one leg and saying his name three times. Word of warning though, he's a bit loco ding dong. So don't blame me if things get ugly.

Amines

This is a-mean, fishy smelling topic...

Amines are Organic Derivatives of **Ammonia**

If one or more of the **hydrogens** in **ammonia** (NH_3) is replaced with an organic group, you get an **amine**.

methylamine
(primary amine)

dimethylamine
(secondary amine)

trimethylamine
(tertiary amine)

tetramethylamine ion
(quaternary
ammonium ion)

phenylamine
(primary amine)

aliphatic amines

aromatic amine

'Aliphatic' is a term for compounds without any benzene ring structures.

Small amines smell similar to **ammonia**, with a **slightly 'fishy'** twist. **Larger amines** smell very **'fishy'**. (Nice.)

Amines have a **Lone Pair of Electrons** that can Form **Dative Covalent Bonds**

1) Amines will **accept protons (H⁺ ions)**.

2) There's a **lone pair of electrons** on the **nitrogen** atom that forms a **dative (coordinate) bond** with an H⁺ ion. Dative bonds are covalent bonds where both electrons come from the **same atom**.

3) This means that amines are **bases** — bases can be defined as proton acceptors or electron donors.

Amines React with **Acids** to Form **Salts**

Amines are **neutralised** by **acids** to make an **ammonium salt**.
For example, **ethylamine** reacts with **hydrochloric** acid to form ethylammonium chloride:

$$CH_3CH_2NH_2 + HCl \rightarrow CH_3CH_2NH_3{}^+Cl^-$$

Aliphatic Amines can be Made From **Haloalkanes**

Amines can be made by heating a **haloalkane** with an excess of ethanolic **ammonia**.

You'll get a **mixture** of primary, secondary and tertiary amines, and quaternary ammonium salts, as more than one hydrogen is likely to be substituted. You can separate the products using **fractional distillation**.

E.g.

$$2 \; N + CH_3CH_2Br \longrightarrow CH_3CH_2N + NH_4Br$$

ammonia

ethylamine

Aromatic Amines are Made by **Reducing** a **Nitro Compound**

Nitro compounds, such as **nitrobenzene**, are reduced in two steps:

1) Heat a mixture of a **nitro compound**, **tin metal** and **conc. hydrochloric acid** under **reflux** — this makes a salt.

2) Then to get the **aromatic amine**, you have to add **sodium hydroxide**.

nitrobenzene

phenylamine

Amines

Aromatic Amines are Used to Make Azo Dyes

1) Azo dyes are man-made dyes that contain the **azo group**, –N=N–.

2) In most azo dyes, the azo group links **two aromatic groups**

3) Having two aromatic groups creates a very **stable molecule** — the azo group becomes part of the **delocalised electron system**.

4) The **colours** are the result of **light absorption** by the delocalised electron system. Different **colours** are made by combining different phenols and amines (see below).

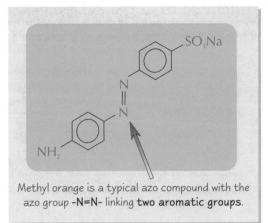

Methyl orange is a typical azo compound with the azo group **-N=N-** linking **two aromatic groups**.

Azo Dyes can be made in a Coupling Reaction

The first step in creating an azo dye is to make a **diazonium salt** — diazonium compounds contain the group $-\overset{+}{N}\equiv N-$. The **azo dye** is then made by **coupling** the diazonium salt with an **aromatic** compound that is susceptible to **electrophilic attack** — like a **phenol**.

Here's the method for creating a yellow-orange azo dye:

React Phenylamine with Nitrous Acid to make a Diazonium Salt

1) Nitrous acid (HNO$_2$) is **unstable**, so it has to be made *in situ* from sodium nitrite and hydrochloric acid.

   'in situ' means 'in the reaction'

   $$NaNO_2 + HCl \rightarrow HNO_2 + NaCl$$

2) **Nitrous acid** reacts with **phenylamine** and **hydrochloric acid** to form **benzenediazonium chloride**. The temperature **must** be below **10 °C** to prevent a phenol forming instead.

   ⬡— NH$_2$ + HNO$_2$ + HCl ⟶ ⬡— $\overset{+}{N}\equiv N$ Cl$^-$ + 2H$_2$O

Make the Azo Dye by Coupling the Diazonium Salt with a Phenol

1) First, the **phenol** has to be dissolved in **sodium hydroxide** solution to make **sodium phenoxide** solution.

2) It's then stood in **ice**, and chilled **benzenediazonium chloride** is added.

3) Here's the overall equation for the reaction:

   ⬡— $\overset{+}{N}\equiv N$ Cl$^-$ + ⬡—OH + NaOH ⟶ ⬡—N=N—⬡—OH + NaCl + H$_2$O

   yellow-orange azo compound

4) The azo dye **precipitates** out of the solution immediately.

5) Phenol is a **coupling agent**. The lone pairs on its oxygen increase the **electron density** of the benzene ring, especially around carbons 2, 4 and 6 (see page 8). This gives the diazonium ion (a **weak electrophile**) something to attack.

   Remember — electrophile means 'electron lover'.

Amines

Azo Dyes are used in Food, Textiles and Paints

1) Azo dyes produce **bright**, **vivid** colours, most of them in the **yellow** to **red spectrum**, though many other colours are possible too. Azo dyes make up about 70% of all dyes used in food and textiles.

2) Many azo dyes are used as **food colourings** (and have corresponding E numbers). Examples include tartrazine (E102), yellow 2G (E107), allura red (E129) and brilliant black BN (E151), but there are many, many more.

3) Because the molecules are very **stable**, azo dyes provide **lightfast** (i.e. strong light won't fade them), **permanent** colours for clothing.

4) They are added to materials like clay to produce **paint pigments**.

'Darn, I spilt my paint' on canvas, £2500

Some azo dyes have been linked to the condition "clown child".

5) Some azo dyes are used as **indicators**, e.g. methyl orange, because they change colour at different pHs.

6) In recent years there has been a lot of **concern** about the use of **artificial additives** in food. Some azo compounds that were previously used in foods have since been **banned** for health reasons — enzymes in the body can break some of them down to produce **toxic** or **carcinogenic** compounds. Others have been linked to **hyperactivity** in children.

Practice Questions

Q1 What are primary, secondary and tertiary amines? Draw and name an example of each.

Q2 Draw the structure of methyldiethylamine.

Q3 Why do amines act as bases?

Q4 Describe how you would make a diazonium salt.

Q5 What is formed when a diazonium salt reacts with a phenol?

Exam Questions

1 When 1-chloropropane is reacted with ammonia a mixture of different amines are produced.

   a) Name two of the amines produced in the reaction.   [2 marks]

   b) How would you separate the mixture?   [1 mark]

   c) Outline the steps needed to reduce nitrobenzene to make phenylamine.   [4 marks]

2 Sunset Yellow (E110) is a yellow dye used in orange squash and many foodstuffs.

$$OH$$
$$N=N$$
$$NaO_3S \qquad\qquad SO_3Na$$

It has been withdrawn from use in many countries as it has been connected to hyperactivity in children.

   a) Which class of dyes does it belong to?   [1 mark]

   b) Which part of its structure indicates this?   [1 mark]

   c) Draw the structures of two organic compounds that could be used to produce Sunset Yellow.   [2 marks]

You've got to learn it — amine it might come up in your exam...

Rotting fish smells so bad because the flesh releases diamines as it decomposes. Is it fish that smells of amines or amines that smell of fish — it's one of those chicken or egg things that no one can answer. Well, enough philosophical pondering — we all know the answer to the meaning of life. It's A2 chemistry. Now make sure you can do all the questions above.

Polymers

And the organic chemistry joy continues... you're going to be eased nice and gently into this section with a double page on polymers. Nothing too scary here, so you shouldn't feel a thing. Well, maybe a slight pinprick.

There are **Two Types** of Polymerisation — **Addition** and **Condensation**

Alkenes **Join Up** to form **Addition Polymers**

1) **Polymers** are long chain molecules formed when lots of small molecules, called **monomers**, join together as if they're holding hands.

2) Alkenes will form polymers — the **double bonds** open up and join together to make long chains. The individual, small alkenes are the monomers.

3) This is called **addition polymerisation**. For example, **poly(ethene)** is made by the **addition polymerisation** of **ethene**.

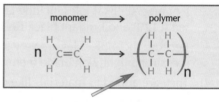

The bit in brackets is the 'repeating unit'. n is the number of repeating units.

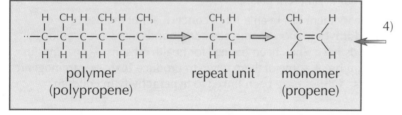

polymer
(polypropene)   repeat unit   monomer
(propene)

4) To find the **monomer** used to form an addition polymer, take the **repeating unit** and add a **double bond**.

5) Because of the loss of the double bond, poly(alkenes), like alkanes, are **unreactive**.

Condensation Polymers are formed as **Water** is **Removed**...

1) In **condensation** polymerisation, a small molecule, often **water**, is **lost** as the molecules link together.

2) Condensation polymers include **polyesters**, **polyamides** and **polypeptides**. Each of these is covered in more detail over the next few pages.

3) Each monomer in a condensation polymer has at least **two functional groups**. Each functional group reacts with a group on another monomer to form a **link**, creating the polymer **chain**.

4) In polyesters, an **ester link** (–COO–) is formed between the monomers.

5) In polyamides and polypeptides, **amide links** (–CONH–) are formed between the monomers. In polypeptides, these are usually called **peptide** bonds.

ester link   amide link

Terylene®   nylon 6,6

...and **Broken Down** by **Adding It**

1) The ester or amide link in polyesters and polyamides can be broken down by reaction with water in an acidic or alkaline solution. This is called **hydrolysis**. Even small amounts of acid will cause nylon to break down very quickly, so don't spill acids on your tights, boys...

2) The products of the hydrolysis are the **monomers** that were used to make the polymer — you're basically **reversing** the condensation reaction that was used to make them.

... + monomer + monomer + ...   ⇌ (Condensation / Hydrolysis)   polymer + water

Polymers

Polyesters and Polyamides are **Biodegradable**... kind of

1) Because **amide links** in polyamides and **ester links** in polyesters can be easily **hydrolysed**, they're **biodegradable**. These links are found in nature, so there are **fungi** and **bacteria** that are able to degrade them.

2) It's not all hunky-dory though. It takes **absolutely ages** for synthetic polyamides and polyesters to decompose — e.g. nylon takes around 40 years.

3) Nylon and polyester can be **recycled** — you can buy polyester fleece jackets made from recycled PET (Polyethylene terephthalate) bottles.

Easily **Biodegradable** Polymers from **Renewable Sources** are the Aim

1) Although condensation polymers will break down by hydrolysis, the huge time this takes to happen in nature means that they still create **waste problems**. **Addition polymers** are even more of a problem — they are very **stable** molecules and won't be broken down by hydrolysis.

2) Also, most polymers we use are made from monomers derived from **crude oil** which is **not** a **renewable resource**.

3) To tackle these problems, chemists are trying to produce alternative polymers, which are easily **biodegradable** and **renewable**.

> **Example:** The biodegradable polymer **poly(lactic acid)**
>
> 1) **Poly(lactic acid)**, or **PLA**, is a **polyester** made from **lactic acid**, which is produced by fermenting maize or sugar cane, which are both renewable crops — you can see it's structure on page 24.
>
> 2) PLA will **biodegrade** easily — it is hydrolysed by water if kept at a **high temperature** for **several days** in an industrial composter or more slowly at lower temperatures in **landfill** or home **compost heaps**.
>
> 3) PLA has many uses, including **rubbish bags**, food and electronic **packaging**, disposable **eating utensils** and internal **sutures** (stitches) that break down without having to open wounds to remove them.

Light can **Degrade** Some **Condensation Polymers**

Condensation polymers that contain **C=O (carbonyl) groups**, such as polyamides are **photodegradable** — they can be broken down by light as the C=O bond absorbs **ultra violet radiation**. This energy can cause bonds to break either side of the carbonyl group and the polymer breaks down into smaller units.

Practice Questions

Q1 What is the difference between addition and condensation polymerisation?

Q2 What type of bond do the monomers used to make addition polymers all have in their structure?

Q3 Give two environmental advantages of poly(lactic acid) over polythene.

Q4 What does photodegradable mean?

Exam Questions

1 Vinyl chloride is the monomer used in the manufacture of polyvinyl chloride (PVC), $\longrightarrow$ a polymer used to insulate electrical wires and in CD manufacture.

   vinyl chloride (chloroethene)

   a) What type of reaction is involved in the manufacture of PVC? [1 mark]

   b) Draw the repeating unit in PVC. [1 mark]

   c) Draw a three-unit section of the PVC molecule. [1 mark]

   d) Why is PVC not likely to be biodegradable? [2 marks]

2 Dissolving stitches used in operations are made from hydroxycarboxylic acid polyesters. Explain why the stitches dissolve in the human body. Why is it not possible to use a polymer like poly(propene) for this purpose? [3 marks]

<u>Wicked Witches are made of biodegradable polymers...</u>

...and Dorothy, being something of a chemistry whizz, figured this out and famously used it to her advantage...
A bucket of water, some alkaline cleaning fluid for good measure, and voila — witch is hydrolysed. Water is an excellent way to distinguish between good and bad witches. Just remember — only bad witches are biodegradable.

24

Polyesters and Polyamides

OK, so the fun intro is over, now it's time to get down and dirty with the details about dicarboxylic acids, diamines and de like. Did you like what I did dere wid dat allideration? Damn, I don't deem dable do durn idoff.

Reactions Between **Dicarboxylic Acids** and **Diamines** Make **Polyamides**

1) **Carboxyl** (–COOH) groups react with **amino** (–NH$_2$) groups to form **amide** (–CONH–) links.

2) A water molecule is lost each time an amide link is formed — it's a **condensation** reaction.

3) The condensation polymer formed is a **polyamide**.

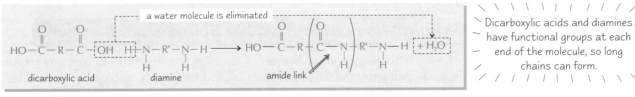

Dicarboxylic acids and diamines have functional groups at each end of the molecule, so long chains can form.

Example | **Nylon 6,6** — made from **1,6-diaminohexane** and **hexanedioic acid**.

Nylon fibre is very **strong, elastic** and quite **abrasion-resistant**.

Example | **Kevlar®** — made from **benzene-1,4-diamine** and **benzene-1,4-dicarboxylic acid**.

Kevlar® is really **strong** and **light** — five times stronger than steel. It's not stretchy, and is quite stiff. It's most famous for its use in bulletproof vests.

Reactions Between **Dicarboxylic Acids** and **Diols** Make **Polyesters**

Polyester fibres are also used in clothing — they are **strong** (but not as strong as nylon), **flexible** and **abrasion-resistant**.
Carboxyl groups (–COOH) react with **hydroxyl** (–OH) groups to form **ester links** (–COO–).
It's another **condensation** reaction.

Example | **Terylene®** (PET) — formed from **benzene-1,4-dicarboxylic acid** and **ethane-1,2-diol**.

Terylene® is used in **clothes** to keep them crease-free and make them last longer.

Example | **Poly(lactic acid)** — a biodegradable and renewable polymer (see page 23).

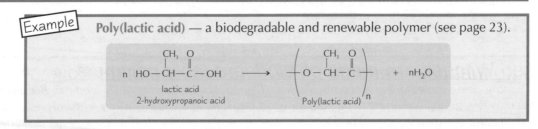

Polyesters and Polyamides

Hydrolysis Produces the Original Monomers

1) Condensation polymerisation can be reversed by **hydrolysis**
   — water molecules are added back in and the links are broken.

2) In practice, hydrolysis with just water is far too **slow**, so the reaction is done with an **acid** or **alkali**.

3) **Polyamides** will hydrolyse more easily with an **acid** than an alkali:

4) **Polyesters** will hydrolyse more easily with an **alkali**. A **metal salt** of the carboxylic acid is formed.

Practice Questions

Q1 What types of molecule can undergo condensation polymerisation?

Q2 Why is it called condensation polymerisation?

Q3 Which molecules are used to make a polyester?

Q4 What is a polyamide made from?

Exam Questions

1 a) Nylon 6,6 is the most commonly produced nylon. A section of the polymer is shown below:

   i) Draw the structural formulae of the monomers from which nylon 6,6 is formed.
      It is not necessary to draw the carbon chains out in full. [2 marks]
   ii) Give a name for the type of linkage between the monomers in this polymer. [1 mark]

   b) A polyester is formed by the reaction between the monomers hexane-1,6-dioic acid and hexane-1,6-diol.
   i) Draw the repeating unit for the polyester. [1 mark]
   ii) Explain why this is an example of condensation polymerisation. [1 mark]

2 Glycolic acid is produced from sugar cane, sugar beets and various fruit.
   It can be polymerised to produce a polymer used to make soluble sutures,
   which are used in surgery. The polymer is broken down by hydrolysis in
   the body and absorbed harmlessly.

   Glycolic acid

   a) Draw a section of this polymer made of three repeating units, and label the repeating unit. [2 marks]
   b) Which group of polymers does this polymer belong to? [1 mark]

I have no friends? Yes I do... Poly... Ester... the other Poly... Ami... Des...

...yeah and we have loads of fun together — cinema trips, bowling, sometimes just a few drinks down the pub. What do you mean, 'they're not real friends'? They so are — they're my special chemistry friends. And they're much more interesting than your dumb friends. Bet your friends can't hydrolyse and condense back again. No, your friends suck. Losers. LOOZERRRRS

Amino Acids and Proteins

Time for a bit of biochemistry action now. We're still on polymers, but these are ones that do pretty important jobs in our bodies, without which we'd be nothing more than blobs of luminescent purple pulsating ectojelly.

Amino Acids have an **Amino Group** and a **Carboxyl** Group

An amino acid has a **basic amino group** (NH_2) and an **acidic carboxyl group** (COOH). This makes amino acids **amphoteric** — they've got both acidic and basic properties.

a–amino acids have both groups attached to the same carbon atom – the 'a carbon'. The general formula of an α–amino acid is **RCH(NH_2)COOH**.

There are **four** different groups attached to the central (α) carbon — molecules like this are called **chiral** molecules. Chiral molecules have two **optical isomers** called **enantiomers** which have their functional groups **arranged differently** — how this all works is explained on p32.

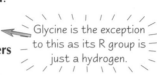
Glycine is the exception to this as its R group is just a hydrogen.

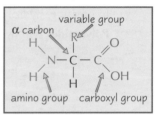

Amino Acids Can Exist As **Zwitterions**

A zwitterion is a **dipolar ion** — it has both a **positive** and a **negative charge** in different parts of the molecule.

Zwitterions only exist near an amino acid's **isoelectric point**. This is the **pH** where the **average overall charge** on the amino acid is zero. It's different for different acids — in α–amino acids it depends on the R-group.

In conditions more **acidic** than the isoelectric point, the $-NH_2$ group is likely to be **protonated**.	At the isoelectric point, both the carboxyl group and the amino group are likely to be ionised — forming an ion called a **zwitterion**.	In conditions more **basic** than the isoelectric point, the $-COOH$ group is likely to **lose** its proton.

low pH   zwitterion   high pH

Polypeptides are **Condensation Polymers** of Amino Acids

Amino acids join together in a **condensation** reaction. A **peptide bond** is made between the amino acids. Here's how two amino acids join together to make a **dipeptide**:

Peptide bonds are exactly the same as amide bonds, but they're called 'peptide' when you're linking amino acids.

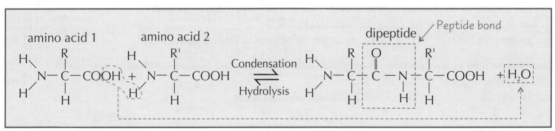

Polypeptides and **proteins** are made up of **lots** of amino acids joined together. A **water molecule is lost** each time an amino acid joins on.

amino acid   amino acid   polypeptides

Amino acids have both an amine group and a carboxylic acid group.

peptide bond (same as an amide link)

water's eliminated

Amino Acids and Proteins

Proteins and Other Peptides can be Taken Apart by Hydrolysis

When you eat proteins, **enzymes** in your digestive system break the proteins down to individual **amino acids** by **hydrolysis**. This process can be simulated in the lab by heating proteins with hydrochloric acid for 24 hours. A shorter reaction time will give a mixture of smaller peptides rather than individual acids. The reaction helps biochemists to work out the sequence of amino acids in a protein.

In the reaction, water molecules react with the **peptide links** and **break them apart**. The separate amino acids are then released.

water breaks the peptide bonds

Hydrolysis can also be carried out using alkalis, but in this case the hydrogen in the –COOH group is replaced by a metal to form a **carboxylate salt** of the amino acid, e.g. **RCH(NH$_2$)COO$^-$Na$^+$**.

Practice Questions

Q1 Which two groups do all amino acids contain?

Q2 What is a zwitterion?

Q3 What reaction joins amino acids together?

Q4 What reaction takes proteins apart?

Exam Questions

1   Alanine is an α-amino acid found in many foods. It has the molecular formula C$_3$H$_7$NO$_2$.
   a)   What is meant by an α-amino acid?   [1 mark]
   b)   Draw the structure of alanine.   [1 mark]
   c)   Which part of this molecule will be different in other α-amino acids?   [1 mark]
   d)   Alanine is a chiral molecule. What does this mean?   [1 mark]
   e)   Draw the structure of the zwitterion produced by alanine.   [1 mark]

2   A dipeptide X produces the amino acids glycine and phenylalanine when heated with hydrochloric acid overnight.

Glycine is:

Phenylalanine is:

   a)   What is meant by a dipeptide?   [1 mark]
   b)   Draw one of the two possible structures of dipeptide X.   [1 mark]
   c)   X is formed from glycine and phenylalanine in a condensation reaction.
        Explain what this means.   [1 mark]
   d)   What type of reaction occurs when X is heated with hydrochloric acid?   [1 mark]
   e)   Only one of these two amino acids is chiral. Explain why.   [1 mark]

Who killed the Zwittonians?

Zwitterions are actually the last physical remains of a race of highly advanced beings known as Zwittonians from the galaxy I Zwiky 19. It is thought that they lived approximately 9.75 billion years ago before evolving beyond the need for physical bodies, exploding in a ball of energy and emitting zwitterion particles throughout the cosmos.   Fascinating.... Also untrue.

Organic Synthesis

In your exam you may be asked to suggest a pathway for the synthesis of a particular molecule.
These pages contain a summary of some of the reactions you should know.

Chemists use **Synthesis Routes** to Get from One Compound to Another

Chemists have got to be able to make one compound from another. It's vital for things like **designing medicines**. It's also good for making imitations of **useful natural substances** when the real things are hard to extract.

> If you're asked how to make one compound from another in the exam, make sure you include:
>
> 1) any **special procedures**, such as refluxing.
> 2) the **conditions** needed, e.g. high temperature or pressure, or the presence of a catalyst.
> 3) any **safety** precautions, e.g. do it in a fume cupboard.
>
> If there are things like hydrogen chloride or hydrogen cyanide around, you really don't want to go breathing them in. Stuff like bromine and strong acids and alkalis are corrosive, so you don't want to splash them on your bare skin.

Most of these reactions are covered elsewhere in the book, so look back for extra details.

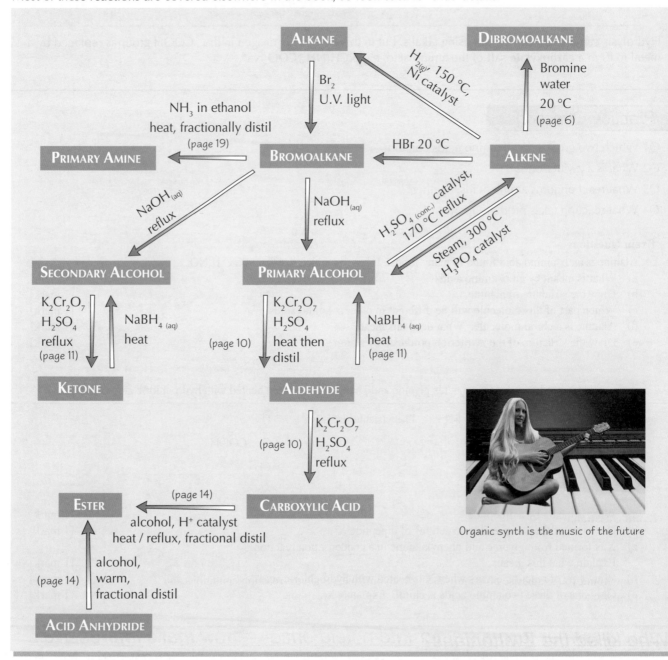

Organic synth is the music of the future

Organic Synthesis

Synthesis Route for Making Aromatic Compounds

There aren't so many of these reactions to learn — so make sure you know all the itty-bitty details.
If you can't remember any of the reactions, look back to the relevant pages and take a quick peek over them.

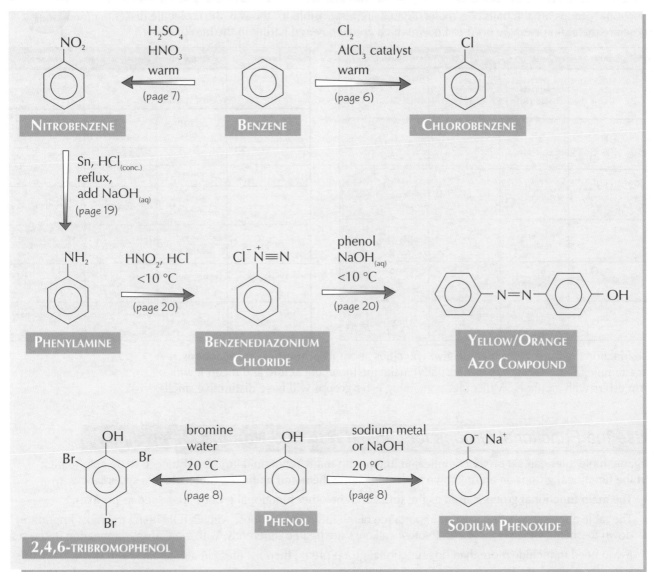

Practice Questions

Q1 How do you convert an alkane to a primary amine?

Q2 How do you make an alkene from an aldehyde?

Q3 How do you make phenylamine from benzene?

Exam Questions

1   Ethyl methanoate is one of the compounds responsible for the smell of raspberries.
     Outline, with reaction conditions, how it could be synthesised in the laboratory from methanol.   [7 marks]

2   How would you synthesise propanol starting with propane? State the reaction conditions and
     reagents needed for each step and any particular safety considerations.   [7 marks]

I saw a farmer turn a tractor into a field once — now that's impressive...

*There's loads of information here. Tons and tons of it. But you've covered pretty much all of it before, so it shouldn't be
too hard to make sure it's firmly embedded in your head. If it's not, you know what to do — go back over it again.
Then cover the diagrams up, and try to draw them out from memory. Keep going until you can do it perfectly.*

30

Functional Groups

It's been a bit of a hard slog of equations and reaction conditions and dubious puns to get this far. But with a bit of luck it should all be starting to come together now. If not, don't panic — there's always revision bunny.

Functional Groups are the Most Important Parts of a Molecule

Functional groups are the parts of a molecule that are responsible for the way the molecule reacts. These are the main ones you need to know (which are all covered earlier in the book)...

Group	Found in	Prefix / Suffix	Example
$-C{\begin{smallmatrix}O\\OH\end{smallmatrix}}$	carboxylic acids	carboxy– –oic acid	ethanoic acid
$-C{\begin{smallmatrix}O\\Cl\end{smallmatrix}}$	acid chlorides	–oyl chloride	ethanoyl chloride
$-C-O-C-$ (with O below each C)	acid anhydrides	–oic anhydide	ethanoic anhydride
$-C-O-$ (O above C)	esters, polyesters	–oate	ethyl methanoate
$-C{\begin{smallmatrix}O\\H\end{smallmatrix}}$	aldehydes	–al	propanal
$C=O$	ketones	–one	propanone

Group	Found in	Prefix / Suffix	Example
$-OH$	alcohols, phenols	hydroxy– –ol	propanol
$-NH_2$	primary amines	amino– –amine	methylamine
NH	secondary amines	–amine	dimethylamine
$N-$	tertiary amines	–amine	trimethylamine
$-NO_2$	nitro benzenes	nitro-	nitrobenzene
(benzene ring)	aromatic compounds	phenyl– –benzene	phenylamine
$C=C$	alkenes	-ene	butene

The functional groups in a molecule give you clues about its **properties** and **reactions**. For example, a **–COOH group** will (usually) make the molecule **acidic** and mean it will **form esters** with alcohols. Molecules containing **ester groups** will have **distinctive smells**.

Use the Functional Groups for Classifying and Naming Compounds

Organic molecules can get pretty complicated, often with many functional groups. You need to be able to **pick out** the functional groups on an unknown molecule, **name them** and **name the molecule** in a systematic way.

1) The **main functional group** is used as the **suffix** and the other functional groups are added as **prefixes**.

2) The table above shows the order of importance of the functional groups, with COOH being the most important, down to phenyl which is the least. (Note — alkenes are treated differently, with 'ene' always appearing in the suffix.)

3) If you need to include more than one functional group prefix, then list them in alphabetical order.

Example: Look at compound A, shown on the right.
a) What class of chemicals does compound A belong to?
b) Give the systematic name of compound A.

This is a skeletal formula where only the carbon bonds and functional groups are shown.

a) It's got a COOH group and an NH₂ group, so it must be an **amino acid** (see p.26)

b) COOH is the main functional group, so number the carbon atoms from this side. There's a 3-carbon chain, so it's a **propanoic acid**. The **phenyl** group is on the **2nd** carbon atom. The **amino** group is on the **3rd** carbon atom.

So the full name would be...
3-amino-2-phenylpropanoic acid.

UNIT 4: MODULE 2 — POLYMERS AND SYNTHESIS

Functional Groups

Example: Look at compounds B and C, shown on the right.
For each compound:
   a) circle and name the functional groups.
   b) work out the molecular formula.

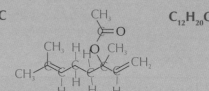

a) **B**

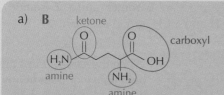

ketone
carboxyl
amine
(NH₂)
amine

C

ester
alkenyl   alkenyl

> In a molecular formula, you just need to say how many of each atom there are.

b) To work out the molecular formula from a skeletal formula, you need to work out how many C and H atoms there are. H atoms are the trickiest to find — remember, each C atom will have 4 bonds.

B $C_5H_{10}N_2O_3$

C $C_{12}H_{20}O_2$

Practice Questions

Q1 Name these functional groups and say what types of molecule they're found in:
   a) –COCl,   b) –COOCO–,   c) –COO–.

Q2 Draw the functional group of each of these families of compounds:
   a) acid anhydrides,   b) aromatic compounds,   c) secondary amines.

Exam Questions

1 a) Name the functional groups in molecules A–C.   [3 marks]
   b) Which molecule(s) are aromatic?   [1 mark]
   c) Which molecule(s) can be oxidised to an aldehyde?   [1 mark]
   d) Which molecule(s) will have a pH less than 7?   [1 mark]

   A $CH_3CH_2CH_2OH$

   B $CH_3-C=CH-CH_3$
            $|$
            OH

   C OH (on benzene ring)

2 This diagram shows the structure of urea, a compound excreted in urine as a product of protein metabolism.

   $H_2N-C-NH_2$ urea
        $\|$
        O

   a) Name the functional groups in this molecule.   [2 marks]
   b) Urea reacts with methanal, HCHO, to form a polymer resin.
      It contains the same bonds as those that link amino acids in proteins.
      i) Draw the functional group in methanal.   [1 mark]
      ii) Why is urea suitable for making into a polymer?   [2 marks]

3 Methyl salicylate is a compound produced by various plants that is used in deep heating liniments applied to sore muscles and joints. It is also used as flavouring in some confectionery.

   (benzene ring with)   methyl salicylate

   a) Identify the functional groups in this molecule.   [3 marks]
   b) From its name and structure what group of compounds does it belong to?   [1 mark]
   c) Deduce its molecular formula.   [1 mark]
   d) It is produced from salicylic acid and methanol. Draw the structure of salicylic acid.   [1 mark]

I used to be in a band — we played 2,4,6-tritechno hiphopnoic acid jazz...

As well as recognising functional groups, this page gives you practice of a few other useful skills you'll need for your exam, e.g. interpreting different types of formula. If you're rusty on the difference between structural, molecular and displayed formulae, have a look back at your AS book – it's fundamental stuff that could trip you up in the exam if you don't know it.

Stereoisomerism and Chirality

Stereoisomers have the same molecular formula and their atoms are arranged in the same way. The only difference is the orientation of the bonds in space. There are two types of stereoisomerism — E/Z and optical.

E/Z Isomerism is Stereoisomerism Caused by C=C Bonds

Alkenes can have stereoisomers because of the **lack of rotation** around the C=C double bond. If the two double-bonded carbon atoms each have **different atoms** or **groups** attached to them, then you get an '**E-isomer**' and a '**Z-isomer**'. For example, the double-bonded carbon atoms in but-2-ene each have an **H** and a **CH₃** group attached.

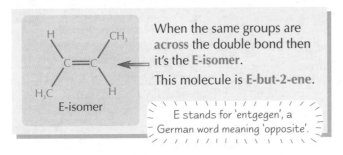

When the same groups are **across** the double bond then it's the **E-isomer**. This molecule is **E-but-2-ene**.

E stands for 'entgegen', a German word meaning 'opposite'.

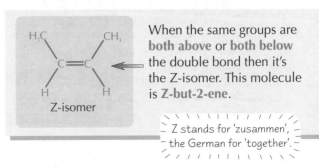

When the same groups are **both above** or **both below** the double bond then it's the **Z-isomer**. This molecule is **Z-but-2-ene**.

Z stands for 'zusammen', the German for 'together'.

Optical Isomers are Mirror Images of Each Other

A **chiral** (or **asymmetric**) carbon atom is one which has **four different** groups attached to it. It's possible to arrange the groups in two different ways around the carbon atom so that two different molecules are made — these molecules are called **enantiomers** or **optical isomers**.

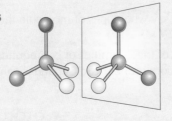

The enantiomers are **mirror images** and no matter which way you turn them, they can't be **superimposed**.

If the molecules can be superimposed, they're _achiral_ — and there's no optical isomerism.

One enantiomer is usually labelled **D** and the other **L** — luckily you don't have to worry about which is which.

Chiral compounds are very common in nature, but you usually only find **one** of the enantiomers — for example, all naturally occurring amino acids are **L–amino acids** (except glycine which isn't chiral) and most sugars are **D-isomers**.

Optical isomers are optically active — they **rotate plane-polarised light**. One enantiomer rotates it in a **clockwise** direction, the other rotates it in an **anticlockwise** direction.

Normal light vibrates in all directions, but plane-polarised light only vibrates in one direction.

Make Sure You Can Spot Chiral Centres

You have to be able to draw optical isomers. But first you have to identify the chiral centre...

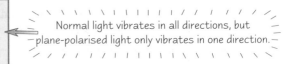

Example

Locating the chiral centre:
Look for the carbon atom with four different groups attached. Here it's the carbon with the four groups H, OH, CHO and CH₃ attached.

chiral centre

2-hydroxypropanoic acid

Drawing isomers:
Once you know the chiral carbon, draw one enantiomer in a tetrahedral shape. Don't try to draw the full structure of each group — it gets confusing. Then draw a mirror image beside it.

enantiomers of 2-hydroxypropanoic acid

Stereoisomerism and Chirality

Pharmaceutical Drugs Must Only Contain One Optical Isomer

1) Unlike naturally-occurring chiral molecules, those prepared in a lab tend to contain an **equal split** of enantiomers — this is called a **racemic** mixture. This creates problems when producing **pharmaceutical drugs**.

2) Drugs work by binding to **active sites** on **enzymes** or other **receptor molecules** in the body and **changing** chemical reactions. The drug must be the right **shape** to fit the active site — only **one enantiomer** will do. The other enantiomer might fit another active site, and may have **no effect** at all, or cause **harmful side**-effects.

3) So, usually, synthetic chiral drugs have to be made so that they only contain **one enantiomer**. This has the **benefit** that only half the dose is needed. It also reduces the risk of the drug companies being sued over side effects.

4) The problem is that optical isomers are very **tricky to separate** — producing single-enantiomer drugs is **expensive**.

> Ethambutol, a drug used to treat TB, is produced as a single enantiomer because the other causes blindness.

> The painkiller Ibuprofen is sold as a racemic mixture — the inactive enantiomer is harmless and the cost of separating the mixture is very high.

Methods for producing single-enantiomer drugs include (often in combination):

1) Using natural **enzymes** or **bacteria** in the process which tend to produce only one isomer.

2) Using **naturally-occuring** single optical isomer compounds as starting materials, e.g. sugars, amino acids.

3) Using **chemical chiral synthesis** — this basically involves using carefully chosen reagents and conditions which will ensure only one isomer is produced.

> Chemical chiral synthesis methods usually rely on chemically modifying the reagent molecule in a way that physically blocks most approaches to it, so that it can only be 'attacked' from one side. For example, you could turn your reagent into a cyclic molecule, or bond your reagent molecules to a polymer support and let the other reactants flow over them.

4) Using **chiral catalysts** — these basically do the same job of only producing only one isomer, but have the advantage that only a small amount is needed because they're reused in the reaction. (Getting large quantities of single-enantiomer compounds for these reactions is expensive.)

Practice Questions

Q1 Explain how molecules with C=C bonds can produce stereoisomers — what are the two types called?

Q2 What is a chiral carbon atom? Draw a diagram of a molecule that contains a chiral carbon atom.

Q3 Give four methods that could be used to produce a single optical isomer for use as a pharmaceutical drug.

Exam Questions

1 a) Identify the chiral carbon atom in each of the three molecules shown on the right. [3 marks]

b) Draw the two optical isomers of molecule B. [2 marks]

c) Explain why these two isomers are said to be optically active. [1 mark]

2 Parkinson's disease involves a deficiency of dopamine. It is treated by giving patients L-DOPA (dihydroxyphenylalanine), a naturally occurring amino acid, which is converted to dopamine in the brain.

a) DOPA is a chiral molecule. Its structure is shown above on the right. Mark the structure's chiral centre. [1 mark]

b) A D,L-DOPA racemic mixture was synthesised in 1911, but today natural L-DOPA is isolated from fava beans for use as a pharmaceutical.
   i) Suggest two reasons why L-DOPA is used in preference to the D,L-DOPA mixture. [2 marks]
   ii) Explain the meaning of the term 'racemic mixture'. [1 mark]
   iii) Why is it potentially dangerous to use the racemic mixture as a pharmaceutical drug? [1 mark]

I isolated it from some fava beans and a nice Chianti...

This isomer stuff's not all bad — you get to draw little pretty pictures of molecules. If you're having difficulty picturing them as 3D shapes, you could always make models with Blu-tack® and those matchsticks that're propping your eyelids open. Blu-tack®'s very therapeutic anyway and squishing it about'll help relieve all that revision stress. It's great stuff.

Chromatography

You've probably tried chromatography with a spot of ink on a piece of filter paper — it's a classic experiment.

Chromatography is Good for **Separating** and **Identifying** Things

Chromatography is used to **separate** stuff in a mixture — once it's separated out, you can often **identify** the components. There are quite a few different types of chromatography — you might have tried paper chromatography — but the ones you need to know about are **thin-layer chromatography** (TLC) and **gas chromatography** (GC).

They both have two phases:

> 1) A **mobile phase** — where the molecules can move. This is always a liquid or a gas.
>
> 2) A **stationary phase** — where the molecules can't move. This must be a solid, or a liquid on a solid support.

The mobile phase **moves through** the stationary phase. As this happens, the components in the mixture **separate out** between the phases.

Thin-Layer Chromatography Separates Components by **Adsorption**

In **thin-layer chromatography** (TLC):

> 1) The **mobile phase** is a **solvent**, such as ethanol, which passes over the stationary phase.
>
> 2) The **stationary phase** is a **thin layer of solid** (0.1-0.3 mm), e.g. silica gel or alumina powder, on a **glass or plastic plate**.

Here's the method:

1) Draw a **pencil line** near the bottom of the plate and put a **spot** of the mixture to be separated on the line.

2) Dip the bottom of the plate (not the spot) into a **solvent**.

3) As the solvent spreads up the plate, the different substances in the mixture move with it, but at **different rates** — so they separate out.

4) When the solvent's **nearly** reached the top, take the plate out and **mark** the distance that the solvent has moved (**solvent front**) in pencil.

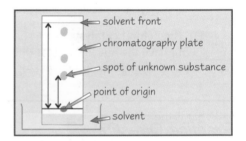
solvent front
chromatography plate
spot of unknown substance
point of origin
solvent

5) You can work out what was in the mixture by calculating an **R$_f$ value** for each spot and looking them up in a **table of known values**.

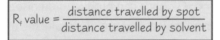

$$R_f \text{ value} = \frac{\text{distance travelled by spot}}{\text{distance travelled by solvent}}$$

The stationary phase and solvent used will affect the R$_f$ value.

How far each part of the mixture travels depends on **how strongly** it's **attracted** to the stationary phase. The **attraction** between a substance and the surface of the stationary phase is called **adsorption**. A substance that is **strongly adsorbed** will move **slowly**, so it **won't travel as far** as one that's only **weakly adsorbed**. This means it will have a **different R$_f$ value**.

Gas Chromatography is a Bit More **High-Tech**

1) In **gas chromatography** (GC) the stationary phase is a **viscous liquid**, such as an oil, or a **solid**, which coats the inside of a long tube. The tube's **coiled** to save space, and built into an oven.

2) The mobile phase is an **unreactive carrier gas** such as nitrogen or helium.

3) The **sample** to be analysed is **injected** into the stream of carrier gas, which carries it through the **tube** and over the stationary phase.

sample injected here
detector and recorder
carrier gas enters here
retention time
temperature-controlled oven
Recorder response
2 4 6 8 10 12 14
Time/min

4) The components of the mixture constantly **dissolve in the stationary phase**, **evaporate** into the mobile phase and then **redissolve** as they travel through the tube.

5) The **solubility** of each component of the mixture determines **how long** it spends **dissolved in the stationary phase** and how long it spends **moving along** the tube in the **mobile phase**. A substance with a high solubility will spend more time dissolved, so will take longer to travel through the tube to the detector than one with a lower solubility. The time taken to reach the detector is called the **retention time**. It can be used to help **identify** the substances.

Chromatography

GC Chromatograms Show the Proportions of the Components in a Mixture

A **gas chromatogram** shows a **series of peaks** at the times when the **detector** senses something other than the carrier gas **leaving the tube**. They can be used to **identify the substances** within a sample and their **relative proportions**.

1) Each **peak** on a chromatogram corresponds to a substance with a particular **retention time**.

2) **Retention times** are measured from **zero** to the **centre** of each peak, and can be looked up in a **reference table** to **identify** the **substances** present.

3) The **area** under each peak is proportional to the relative **amount of each substance** in the original mixture. Remember, it's **area**, not height, that's important — the **tallest** peak on the chromatogram **won't always** represent the **most abundant substance**.

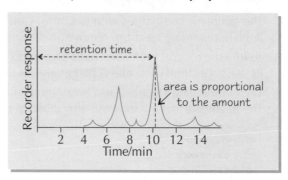

Gas Chromatography has Limitations

Although a very useful and widely used technique, GC does have **limitations** when it comes to identifying chemicals.

1) **Compounds** which are **similar** often have **very similar retention times**, so they're difficult to identify accurately. A mixture of **two similar substances** may only produce **one peak** so you **can't tell how much** of each one there is. Handily, you can combine GC with mass spectrometry to make a much more powerful identification tool — there's more on this on page 37.

2) You can only use GC to identify substances that you already have **reliable reference retention times** for. (That means someone must have run a sample of the same pure substance under exactly the same conditions before.)

Practice Questions

Q1 Explain the terms 'stationary phase' and 'mobile phase' in the context of chromatography.

Q2 What is the stationary phase in TLC?

Q3 What is the mobile phase in GC?

Q4 Describe how you would calculate the R_f value of a substance on a TLC plate.

Exam Questions

1 Look at this diagram of a chromatogram produced using TLC on a mixture of substances A and B.

   a) Calculate the R_f value of spot A. [2 marks]

   b) Explain why substance A has moved further up the plate than substance B. [3 marks]

2 A scientist has a mixture of several organic chemicals. He wants to know if it contains any hexene. He runs a sample of pure hexene through a GC machine and finds that its retention time is 5 minutes. Then he runs a sample of his mixture through the same machine, under the same conditions, and produces the chromatogram shown on the right.

   a) What feature of the chromatogram suggests that the sample contains hexene? [1 mark]

   b) Give a reason why the researcher may still not be absolutely certain that his mixture contains hexene. [1 mark]

3 A mixture of 25% ethanol and 75% benzene is run through a GC apparatus.

   a) Describe what happens to the mixture in the apparatus. [4 marks]

   b) Explain why the substances separate. [2 marks]

   c) How will the resulting chromatogram show the proportions of ethanol and benzene present in the mixture? [1 mark]

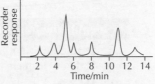

A little bit of TLC is what you need...

If you only remember one thing about chromatography, remember that it's really good at separating mixtures, but not so reliable at identifying the substances that make up the mixture. Or does that count as two things? Hmm... well it's probably not the best idea to only learn one thing from each page anyway. Learn lots of stuff, that's my advice.

Mass Spectrometry and Chromatography

Mass spectrometry is an analysis technique that can be used with chromatography to positively identify compounds.

Mass Spectrometry Can Help to Identify Compounds

1) A mass spectrum is produced when a sample of a **gaseous compound** is analysed in a mass spectrometer.

2) The sample is bombarded with electrons, causing other electrons to break off from the molecules. If the bombarding electrons remove a single electron from a molecule, the **molecular ion**, $M^+_{(g)}$, is formed.

3) To find the relative molecular mass of a compound you can look at the **molecular ion peak** (the **M peak**) on its mass spectrum. The mass/charge value of the molecular ion peak is the **molecular mass** of the compound.

4) The bombarding electrons also break some of the molecules up into **fragments**. The fragments that are **ions** will also show up on the mass spectrum, giving a **fragmentation pattern**.

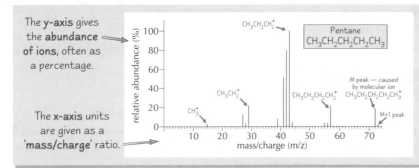

The **y-axis** gives the **abundance** of ions, often as a percentage.

The **x-axis** units are given as a 'mass/charge' ratio.

Here's the mass spectrum of **pentane**.

Each **peak** on the mass spectrum is caused by a different **fragment** ion. The M peak is at 72 — so the compound's M_r must be 72.

For most **organic compounds** the M peak is the one with the second highest mass/charge ratio. (The smaller peak to the right of the M peak is the **M+1 peak** — it's caused by the presence of the carbon isotope ^{13}C.)

You Can Join the Fragments Together to Find the Molecule's Structure

Fragmentation patterns are really useful — you can use them to identify **molecules** and work out their **structures**.

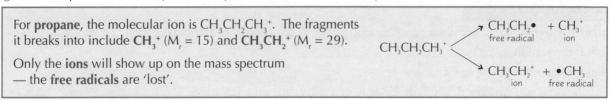

For **propane**, the molecular ion is $CH_3CH_2CH_3^+$. The fragments it breaks into include CH_3^+ (M_r = 15) and $CH_3CH_2^+$ (M_r = 29).

Only the **ions** will show up on the mass spectrum — the **free radicals** are 'lost'.

To work out the structural formula, you've got to work out what **ion** could have made each peak from its **m/z value**. (You assume that the m/z value of a peak matches the **mass** of the ion that made it.)

Example: Use this mass spectrum to work out the structure of the molecule:

It's only the m/z values you're interested in — ignore the heights of the bars.

Fragment	Molecular Mass
CH_3	15
C_2H_5	29
C_3H_7	43
OH	17
CH_2NH_2	30

1. Identify the fragments

This molecule's got a peak at 15 m/z, so it's likely to have a CH_3 group.

It's also got a peak at 17 m/z, so it's likely to have an **OH** group.

Other ions are matched to the peaks here:

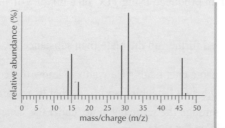

2. Piece them together to form a molecule with the correct M_r

Ethanol has all the fragments on this spectrum.

Ethanol's **molecular mass** is 46. This should be the same as the m/z value of the M peak — and it is.

Mass Spectrometry and Chromatography

Mass Spectrometry is Used to **Differentiate** Between **Similar Molecules**

Even if two **different compounds** contain **the same atoms**, you can still tell them apart with mass spectrometry because they won't produce exactly the same set of fragments.

> **Example:** The mass spectra of **propanal** and **propanone**:
> 1) **Propanal** and **propanone** have the same empirical formula — C_3H_6O. So they also have the **same M$_r$ (58)**.
> 2) But they have different molecular **structures** — one is an **aldehyde,** ⟹ and the other's a **ketone**.
> 3) Because their structures are different, they'll break up into **different fragments** in a mass spectrometer. So the **mass spectrum** of propanal is different from the mass spectrum of propanone.

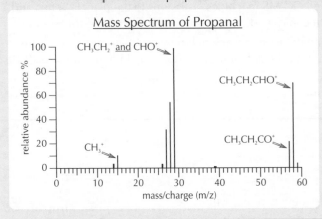

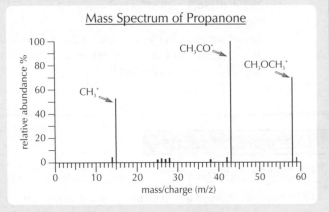

Every compound produces a different mass spectrum — so the spectrum is like a **fingerprint** for that compound. Large computer **databases** of mass spectra can be used to identify a sample of a compound from its spectrum.

Mass Spectrometry can be **Combined** with **Gas Chromatography**

Gas chromatography (see pages 34-35) is very good at **separating** a mixture into its individual components, but not so good at identifying those components. **Mass spectrometry**, on the other hand, is very good at **identifying** unknown compounds, but would give confusing results from a mixture of substances.

If you put these **two techniques together**, you get an **extremely useful** analytical tool.

> **Gas chromatography-mass spectrometry** (or GC-MS for short) **combines the benefits** of gas chromatography and mass spectrometry to make a super analysis tool.
>
> The sample is **separated** using **gas chromatography**, but instead of going to a detector, the separated components are fed into a **mass spectrometer**.
>
> The spectrometer produces a **mass spectrum** for each **component**, which can be used to **identify** each one and show what the original **sample** consisted of.

Oh, excuse me — chemistry always sends me to sleep, I'm afraid

The **advantage** of this method over normal GC is that the components separated out by the chromatography can be **positively identified**, which can be impossible from a chromatogram alone.

Computers can be used to match up the **mass spectrum** for each component of the mixture against a **database**, so the whole process can be **automated**.

You can also combine **high pressure liquid chromatography**, or **HPLC**, with **mass spectrometry** to get **HPLC-MS**.

> 1) In **HPLC**, the **stationary phase** is a **solid** that is packed into a glass **column**, like tiny silica beads.
> 2) The **mobile phase** (a solvent) and the **mixture** are **pushed** through the column under **high pressure**. This allows the separation to happen much **faster** than if the solvent just dripped through.
> 3) As with GC, HPLC is more useful for **separating** mixtures of substances than **identifying** them — **combining it** with **mass spectrometry** gives a better **identification** tool than either method alone.

Mass Spectrometry and Chromatography

GC-MS is used in Forensics and Security

GC-MS is a really **important analytical tool**, and not just in chemistry labs — check out the four uses below.

1) **Forensics** — GC-MS can be used to **identify unknown substances** found on **victims** or **suspects** or at **crime scenes**. For example, if GC-MS shows that a substance found at a crime scene is **identical** to one found on a suspect, then it is evidence that the suspect was at the crime scene. Or **fire investigators** can use the method to detect whether fires were started **deliberately** using substances such as petrol or paraffin.

2) **Airport security** — GC-MS can be used to look for **specific substances** — e.g. **explosives** or **illegal drugs**. The MS can be set to only look at a substance produced at a particular retention time on the GC to find out if it is present or not. The whole process is quick — it takes just a few minutes — and is accurate enough to be used in **court** as evidence.

3) **Space probes** — several space probes have carried GC-MS machines. Missions to the planets Venus and Mars, and to Saturn's moon Titan, have used the technique to examine the **atmosphere** and **rocks**.

4) **Environmental analysis** — the technique is used to **detect and track pollutants** such as pesticides in the environment. **Foods** can be tested in the same way to check that they do not contain harmful levels of substances such as **pesticides**.

Practice Questions

Q1 What is a molecular ion?

Q2 How can you use the M+1 peak on a mass spectrum to identify a molecule?

Q3 What pattern of peaks on a mass spectrum tell you that chlorine is present?

Q4 Give two uses of GC-MS.

Exam Questions

1 Below is the mass spectrum of a carboxylic acid. Use the spectrum to answer this question.

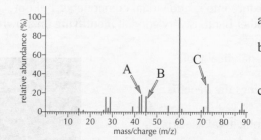

a) What is the molecular mass of this acid? [1 mark]

b) Suggest the formulae of the fragment ions that are responsible for the peaks labelled A, B and C. [3 marks]

c) Use your answers from parts (a) and (b) to draw the structure of the acid, and give its name. [2 marks]

2 The Huygens probe sent to Titan, the giant moon of Saturn, carried a GC-MS machine to examine the atmosphere. The atmosphere surrounding Titan consists of 98.4% nitrogen with the rest mainly methane, and trace amounts of many other gases including several hydrocarbons.

a) One of the gases found in the atmosphere is ethane.
Why is a GC-MS machine necessary to verify the presence of ethane, rather than just GC? [2 marks]

b) Give the formula and the mass of the molecular ion that ethane produces. [2 marks]

c) The mass spectrum of ethane also has peaks at m/z = 29 and m/z = 15.
i) Which fragment ion produces the peak at m/z = 29? [1 mark]
ii) Which fragment ion produces the peak at m/z = 15? [1 mark]

Mass spectrometry — weight watching for molecules...

So mass spectrometry's a bit like weighing yourself, then taking bits off your body, weighing them separately, then trying to work out how they all fit together. Luckily you won't get anything as complicated as a body, and you won't need to cut yourself up either. Good news all round then. Just learn this page and watch out for the M peak in the exam.

NMR Spectroscopy

NMR isn't the easiest of things, so ingest this information one piece at a time — a bit like eating a bar of chocolate.

NMR *Gives You* Information *about the* Structure of Molecules

Nuclear magnetic resonance (**NMR**) **spectroscopy** is an analysis technique that you can use to work out the **structure** of an organic molecule. The way that NMR works is pretty **complicated**, but you only need to know the **basics**:

1) A sample of a compound is placed in a **strong magnetic field** and exposed to a range of different **frequencies** of **low-energy radio waves**.

2) The **nuclei** of certain atoms within the molecule **absorb energy** from the radio waves.

3) The amount of energy that a nucleus absorbs at each frequency will depend on the **environment** that it's in — there's more about this further down the page.

4) The **pattern** of these absorptions gives you information about the **positions** of certain atoms within the molecule, and about **how many** atoms of that type the molecule contains.

5) You can piece these bits of information together to work out the **structure of the molecule**.

The two types of NMR spectroscopy you need to know about are **carbon-13** (or **¹³C**) **NMR** and **high resolution proton NMR**.

Carbon-13 NMR gives you information about the **number of carbon atoms** that are in a molecule, and the **environments** that they are in.

High resolution proton NMR gives you information about the **number of hydrogen atoms** that are in a molecule, and the **environments** that they're in.

Nuclei in Different Environments *Absorb* Different Amounts of Energy

1) A nucleus is partly **shielded** from the effects of external magnetic fields by its **surrounding electrons**.

2) Any **other atoms** and **groups of atoms** that are around a nucleus will also affect its amount of electron shielding.
   E.g. If a carbon atom bonds to a more electronegative atom (like oxygen) the amount of electron shielding around its nucleus will decrease.

3) This means that the nuclei in a molecule feel different magnetic fields depending on their **environments**. This means that they will absorb **different amounts** of energy at **different frequencies**.

4) It's these **differences in absorption** of energy between environments that you're looking for in **NMR spectroscopy**.

5) An atom's **environment** depends on **all** the groups that it's connected to, going **right along the molecule** — not just the atoms it's actually bonded to. To be in the **same environment**, two atoms must be joined to **exactly the same things**.

H H | | H–C–C–Cl | | H H	H Cl H | | | H–C–C–C–H | | | H H H	H H H H | | | | H–C–C–C–C–Cl | | | | H H H H
Chloroethane has 2 carbon environments — its carbons are bonded to different atoms.	2-chloropropane has 2 carbon environments: • 1 C in a CHCl group, bonded to (CH₃)₂ • 2 Cs in CH₃ groups, bonded to CHCl(CH₃)	1-chlorobutane has 4 carbon environments. (The two carbons in CH₂ groups are different distances from the electronegative Cl atom — so their environments are different.)

Tetramethylsilane *is Used as a* Standard

The diagram below shows a typical **carbon-13 NMR spectrum**. The **peaks** show the **frequencies** at which **energy was absorbed** by the carbon nuclei. **Each peak** represents one **carbon environment** — so this molecule has two.

1) The **differences in absorption** are measured relative to a **standard substance** — **tetramethylsilane** (**TMS**).

2) TMS produces a **single absorption peak** in both types of NMR because all its carbon and hydrogen nuclei are in the **same environment**.

3) It's chosen as a standard because the **absorption peak** is at a **lower frequency** than just about everything else.

4) This peak is given a value of **0** and all the peaks in other substances are measured as **chemical shifts** relative to this.

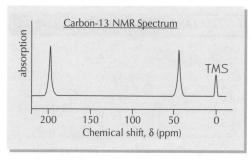

Chemical shift is the **difference in the radio frequency** absorbed by the nuclei (hydrogen or carbon) in the molecule being analysed and that absorbed by the same nuclei in **TMS**. They're given the symbol δ and are measured in **parts per million**, or **ppm**. A small amount of TMS is often added to samples to give a **reference peak** on the spectrum.

NMR Spectroscopy

¹³C NMR Spectra Tell You About Carbon Environments

It's very likely that you'll be given an **NMR spectrum** to **interpret** in your exam. It might be a **carbon-13 NMR spectrum** or a **proton NMR spectrum** (you might even see both if you're really lucky), so you need to have both kinds sussed. First, here's a **step-by-step guide** to interpreting carbon-13 spectra.

1) Count the Number of Carbon Environments

First, count the **number of peaks** in the spectrum — this is the **number of carbon environments** in the molecule. If there's a peak at δ = 0, **don't count it** — it's the reference peak from **TMS**.

The spectrum on the right has **three peaks** — so the molecule must have **three different carbon environments**. This **doesn't** necessarily mean it only has **three carbons**, as it could have **more than one** in the **same environment**. In fact the molecular formula of this molecule is $C_5H_{10}O$, so it must have **several carbons** in the **same environment**.

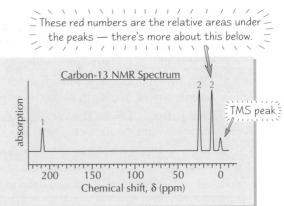

These red numbers are the relative areas under the peaks — there's more about this below.

Carbon-13 NMR Spectrum

TMS peak

2) Look Up the Chemical Shifts in a Data Table

¹³C NMR Chemical Shifts Relative to TMS	
Chemical shift, δ (ppm)	Type of Carbon
5 – 55	C – C
30 – 70	C – Cl or C – Br
35 – 60	C – N (amines)
50 – 70	C – O
115 – 140	C = C (alkenes)
110 – 165	aromatic
160 – 185	carbonyl (ester, amide, or carboxylic acid)
190 – 220	carbonyl (ketone or aldehyde)

In your exam you'll get a **data sheet** that will include a **table** like this one. The table shows the **chemical shifts** experienced by **carbon nuclei** in **different environments**.

You need to **match up** the **peaks** in the spectrum with the **chemical shifts** in the table to work out which **carbon environments** they could represent.

For example, the peak at δ ≈ 10 in the spectrum above represents a **C–C** bond. The peak at δ ≈ 25 is also due to a **C–C** bond. The carbons causing this peak have a different chemical shift to those causing the first peak — so they must be in a slightly different environment.

Matching peaks to the groups that cause them isn't always straightforward, because the chemical shifts can **overlap**. For example, a peak at δ ≈ 30 might be caused by **C–C**, **C–Cl** or **C–Br**.

The peak at δ ≈ 210, is due to a **C=O** group in an **aldehyde** or a **ketone** — but you **don't** know which.

3) Compare the Area Under Each Peak

To work out **how many** carbon nuclei are in **each environment**, you look at the **area under each peak**. In the spectrum above, the **ratio of the areas** under the peaks is shown by the numbers above them, i.e. **2 : 2 : 1**. This means there are **two carbons** in the first **C–C** environment, to every **two** in the second **C–C** environment, to every one in an **aldehyde or ketone C=O** group.

4) Try Out Possible Structures

An **aldehyde** with 5 carbons:

This doesn't work — it does have the right molecular formula ($C_5H_{10}O$), but it also has five carbon environments.

A **ketone** with five carbons:

This works. **Pentan-3-one** has **three** carbon environments — two CH_3 carbons, each bonded to $CH_2COCH_2CH_3$, two CH_2 carbons, each bonded to CH_3 and $COCH_2CH_3$, and one **CO** carbon bonded to $(CH_2CH_3)_2$. It has the right **molecular formula** ($C_5H_{10}O$) too.

It can't be pentan-2-one — that has 5 carbon environments.

So, the molecule analysed was **pentan-3-one**.

NMR Spectroscopy

Interpreting NMR Spectra Gets Easier with Practice

EXAMPLE

The diagram shows the carbon-13 NMR spectrum of an alcohol with the molecular formula $C_4H_{10}O$. Analyse and interpret the spectrum to identify the structure of the alcohol.

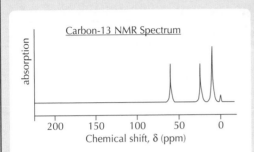

Carbon-13 NMR Spectrum

absorption

Chemical shift, δ (ppm)
200   150   100   50   0

1) The spectrum has **three peaks** and there are **four carbons** in the alcohol, so two carbons must be in the **same environment**.

2) Looking at the **table** on the **previous page**, the peak with a **chemical shift** of $\delta \approx 65$ is likely to be due to a **C–O** bond.

3) The two peaks around $\delta \approx 20$ probably both represent carbons in **C–C** bonds, but with slightly different environments. Remember the alcohol doesn't contain any **chlorine**, **bromine** or **nitrogen** so you can **ignore** those entries in the table.

4) The peak with the **lowest chemical shift** has the **largest area**, so **two** of the carbons in C–C groups must be in the **same environment**.

5) Put together all the **information** you've got so far, and try out some **structures**:

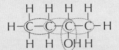

$$H\text{–}\overset{\displaystyle H}{\underset{\displaystyle H}{C}}\text{–}\overset{\displaystyle H}{\underset{\displaystyle H}{C}}\text{–}\overset{\displaystyle H}{\underset{\displaystyle H}{C}}\text{–}\overset{\displaystyle H}{\underset{\displaystyle H}{C}}\text{–}OH$$

This has one C–O bond, and three C–C bonds, which is right. But, all four carbons are in different environments.

$$H\text{–}\overset{\displaystyle H}{\underset{\displaystyle H}{C}}\text{–}\overset{\displaystyle H}{\underset{\displaystyle H}{C}}\text{–}\overset{\displaystyle H}{\underset{\displaystyle OH}{C}}\text{–}\overset{\displaystyle H}{\underset{\displaystyle H}{C}}\text{–}H$$

Again, this has one the right groups. But, the carbons are still all in different environments.

This time two of the carbons in the C–C groups are in exactly the same environment, so this must be the correct structure.

MRI Scanners Use NMR Technology

Magnetic resonance imaging (**MRI**) is a **scanning** technique that's used in **hospitals** to study the **internal structures** of the body. MRI uses the **same technology** as NMR spectroscopy — the patient is placed inside a very **large magnet** and **radio waves** are directed at the area of the body being investigated. **Hydrogen nuclei** in **water molecules** in the body **absorb** energy from the radio waves at certain frequencies. The **frequency** depends on the kind of **tissue** that the water is in, so an **image** of the different tissues can be built up.

The **benefit** of MRI is that it **doesn't** use **damaging radiation** like **X-rays** or gamma rays, but does give **high quality images** of soft tissue like the **brain**. The technique is used to diagnose and monitor **cancerous tumours**, examine **bones** and **joints** for signs of injury, and to study the **brain** and **cardiovascular system**.

Never stick your head into a giant washing machine.

Practice Questions

Q1 What part of the electromagnetic spectrum does NMR spectroscopy use?

Q2 What is meant by chemical shift? What compound is used as a reference for chemical shifts?

Q3 How can you tell from a carbon-13 NMR spectrum how many carbon environments a molecule contains?

Q4 What is the medical scanning technique that uses the same technology as NMR?

Exam Question

1 The carbon-13 NMR spectrum shown on the right was produced by a compound with the molecular formula C_3H_9N.

a) Explain why there is a peak at $\delta = 0$. [1 mark]

b) The compound does not have the formula $CH_3CH_2CH_2NH_2$. Explain how the spectrum shows this. [2 marks]

c) Suggest and explain a possible structure for the compound. [2 marks]

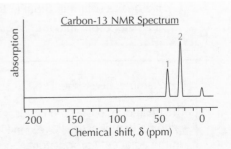

Carbon-13 NMR Spectrum

absorption

Chemical shift, δ (ppm)
200   150   100   50   0

Why did the carbon peak? Because it saw the radio wave...

The ideas behind NMR are difficult, but don't worry too much if you don't really understand them. The important thing is to make sure you know how to interpret a spectrum — that's what will get you marks in the exam. If you're having trouble, go over the examples and practice questions a few more times. You should have the "ahh... I get it" moment sooner or later.

More NMR Spectroscopy

So, you know how to interpret carbon-13 NMR spectra — now it's time to get your teeth into some proton NMR spectra.

¹H NMR Spectra Tell You About Hydrogen Environments

Interpreting **proton NMR spectra** starts off in exactly the **same way** as interpreting carbon-13 NMR spectra:

1) Count the **number of hydrogen environments**.

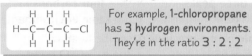

For example, 1-chloropropane has 3 hydrogen environments. They're in the ratio 3 : 2 : 2.

2) Look up the **chemical shifts** in a **data table** to → identify possible environments. The shifts are different from carbon-13 NMR, so make sure you look at the **correct table** on the data sheet.

3) Compare the **area under each peak** — this is sometimes given with ratio numbers (like the ¹³C spectrum on page 40) and sometimes with an **integration trace**.

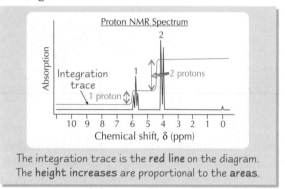

The integration trace is the **red line** on the diagram. The **height increases** are proportional to the **areas**.

¹H NMR Chemical Shifts Relative to TMS	
Chemical shift, δ (ppm)	**Type of Proton**
0.7 – 1.6	R – CH₃
1.0 – 5.5	N – H R – OH
1.2 – 1.4	R – CH₂ – R
1.6 – 2.0	R₃CH
2.0 – 2.9	H₃C – C(=O) RCH₂ – C(=O) R₂CH – C(=O)
2.3 – 2.7	⬡– CH₃ ⬡– CH₂R ⬡– CHR₂
2.3 – 2.9	N – CH₃ N – CH₂R N – CHR₂
3.3 – 4.3	O – CH₃ O – CH₂R O – CHR₂
3.0 – 4.2	Br/Cl – CH₃ Br/Cl – CH₂R Br/Cl – CHR₂
4.5 – 10.0	⬡– OH
4.5 – 6.0	– CH = CH –
5.0 – 12.0	– C(=O)NH₂ – C(=O)NH –
6.5 – 8.0	⬡– H
9.0 – 10.0	– C(=O)H
11.0 – 12.0	– C(=O)O – H

The big difference between carbon-13 and proton NMR spectra is that the peaks in a proton NMR spectrum **split** according to how the **hydrogen environments are arranged**. Putting all this info together should let you work out the structure.

Spin-Spin Coupling Splits the Peaks in a Proton NMR Spectrum

In a proton NMR spectrum, a peak that represents a hydrogen environment can be **split**. The splitting is caused by the influence of hydrogen atoms that are bonded to **neighbouring carbons**. This effect is called **spin-spin coupling**. Only hydrogen nuclei on **adjacent** carbon atoms affect each other.

These **split peaks** are called **multiplets**. They always split into one more than the number of hydrogens on the neighbouring carbon atoms — it's called the **n + 1 rule**. For example, if there are **2 hydrogens** on the adjacent carbon atoms, the peak will be split into 2 + 1 = 3.

You can work out the **number** of **neighbouring hydrogens** by looking at how many the peak splits into:

If a peak's split into **two** (a **doublet**) then there's **one hydrogen** on the neighbouring carbon atoms.

If a peak's split into **three** (a **triplet**) then there are **two hydrogens** on the neighbouring carbon atoms.

If a peak's split into **four** (a **quartet**) then there are **three hydrogens** on the neighbouring carbon atoms.

For example, here's the ¹H NMR spectrum of **1,1,2-trichloroethane**:

The peak due to the green hydrogens is split into **two** because there's **one hydrogen** on the adjacent carbon atom.

The peak due to the red hydrogen is split into **three** because there are **two hydrogens** on the adjacent carbon atom.

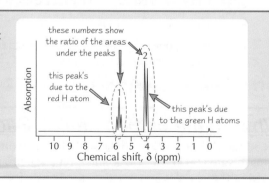

More NMR Spectroscopy

Deuterated Solvents are used in Proton NMR Spectroscopy

NMR spectra are recorded with the molecule that is being analysed in **solution**. But if you used a ordinary solvent like water or ethanol, the **hydrogen nuclei** in the solvent would **add peaks** to the spectrum and confuse things. To overcome this, the **hydrogen nuclei** in the solvent are **replaced** with **deuterium** (D) — an **isotope** of hydrogen with **one proton** and **one neutron**. Deuterium nuclei don't absorb the radio wave energy, so they don't add peaks to the spectrum. A commonly used example of a 'deuterated solvent' is **deuterated chloroform**, $CDCl_3$.

OH and NH Protons can be Identified by Proton Exchange Using D_2O

The **chemical shift** due to protons attached to oxygen (OH) or nitrogen (NH) is very **variable** — check out the huge **ranges** given in the **table** on the previous page. They make quite a **broad** peak that isn't usually split.

Don't panic, though, as there's a clever little trick chemists use to identify OH and NH protons:

1) Run **two** spectra of the molecule — one with a little **deuterium oxide**, D_2O, added.

2) If an OH or NH proton is present it'll swap with deuterium and, hey presto, the peak will **disappear**. (This is because deuterium doesn't absorb the radio wave energy).

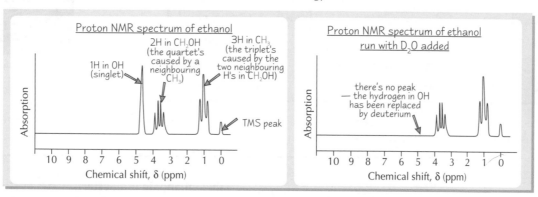

Practice Questions

Q1 What causes the peaks on a high resolution proton NMR spectrum to split?
Q2 What causes a triplet of peaks on a high resolution proton NMR spectrum?
Q3 What are deuterated solvents? Why are they needed?
Q4 How can you get rid of a peak caused by an OH group?

Exam Question

1   The proton NMR spectrum below is for an alkyl halide. Use the table of chemical shifts on page 42 to answer this question.

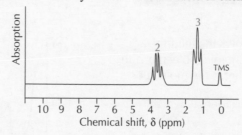

a) What is the likely environment of the two protons with a shift of 3.6 p.p.m.? [1 mark]

b) What is the likely environment of the three protons with a shift of 1.3 p.p.m.? [1 mark]

c) The molecular mass of the molecule is 64. Suggest a possible structure and explain your suggestion. [2 marks]

d) Explain the shapes of the two peaks. [4 marks]

Never mind splitting peaks — this stuff's likely to cause splitting headaches...

Is your head spinning yet? I know mine is. Round and round like a merry-go-round. It's a hard life when you're tied to a desk trying to get NMR spectroscopy firmly fixed in your head. You must be looking quite peaky by now... so go on, learn this stuff, take the dog around the block, then come back and see if you can still remember it all.

Infrared Spectroscopy

Eeek... more spectroscopy. Infrared (IR to its friends) radiation has less energy than visible light, and a longer wavelength.

Infrared Spectroscopy Lets You Identify Organic Molecules

1) In infrared (IR) spectroscopy, a beam of **IR radiation** is passed through a sample of a chemical.

2) The IR radiation is absorbed by the **covalent bonds** in the molecules, increasing their **vibrational** energy.

3) **Bonds between different atoms** absorb **different frequencies** of IR radiation. Bonds in different **places** in a molecule absorb different frequencies too — so the O–H group in an **alcohol** and the O–H in a **carboxylic acid** absorb different frequencies.

This table shows what **frequencies** different bonds absorb:

Bond	Where it's found	Frequency/Wavenumber (cm^{-1})
C–O	alcohols, carboxylic acids and esters	1000 – 1300
C=O	aldehydes, ketones, carboxylic acids, esters and amides	1640 – 1750
O–H	carboxylic acids	2500 – 3300 (very broad)
C–H	organic compounds	2850 – 3100
N–H	amines and amides	3200 – 3500
O–H	alcohols, phenols	3200 – 3550 (broad)

This data will be on the data sheet in the exam, so you don't need to learn it. BUT you do need to understand how to use it.

Clark began to regret having an infrared mechanism installed in his glasses.

4) An infrared spectrometer produces a **graph** that shows you what frequencies of radiation the molecules are absorbing. You can use it to identify the **functional groups** in a molecule:

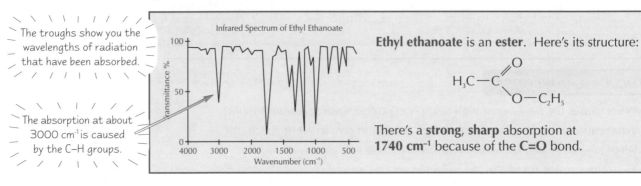

The troughs show you the wavelengths of radiation that have been absorbed.

The absorption at about 3000 cm^{-1} is caused by the C–H groups.

Ethyl ethanoate is an **ester**. Here's its structure:

There's a **strong**, **sharp** absorption at **1740 cm^{-1}** because of the **C=O** bond.

First Identify the Type of Molecule...

Example: The diagram on the right shows the infrared absorption spectrum of an organic molecule with a molecular mass of 46. What is the molecule?

Start off by looking at the troughs to try to identify which **functional groups** the molecule has:

a) A trough at around **1200 cm^{-1}**. This could be due to the **C–O bond** in an **alcohol**, **carboxylic acid** or **ester**.

b) A trough at around **1700 cm^{-1}**, which is the characteristic place for a **C=O bond** in an aldehyde, ketone, carboxylic acid, ester or amide.

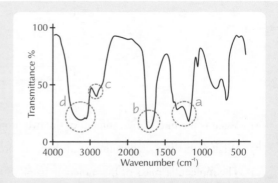

c) A small trough just below **3000 cm^{-1}**, which is characteristic of **C–H bonds** in an organic molecule.

d) A very broad trough at around **3100 cm^{-1}**. This is due to the **O–H bond** in a **carboxylic acid**.

So the only type of molecule that could create this pattern of absorptions is a **carboxylic acid**.

Infrared Spectroscopy

...Then Use the **Molecular Mass** to **Work Out Which One It Is**

Now you know that the molecule is a **carboxylic acid**. But you'd need a **database** of **all possible carboxylic acids** to work out which one it is just from the spectrum. Instead, you can use the **molecular mass** to work out its **molecular formula**.

First look at the **general formula** of a **carboxylic acid**:

The mass of the whole molecule is **46**.
So by **subtracting** the mass of the **functional group**, you can find the mass of the **rest of the molecule**.

$46 - [12 + (2 \times 16) + 1] = 46 - 45 = 1$.

To have a **mass of 1**, the rest of the molecule must just be **H**, so the molecule is **HCOOH** — or **methanoic acid**.

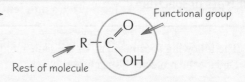

Functional group

Rest of molecule

Practice Questions

Q1 What happens when bonds absorb infrared radiation?

Q2 What do the troughs on a spectrum show?

Q3 Which bond absorbs strongly at 1700 cm^{-1}?

Q4 What extra information can help you identify a molecule?

Exam Questions

1   A molecule with a molecular mass of 74 gives the following IR spectrum.

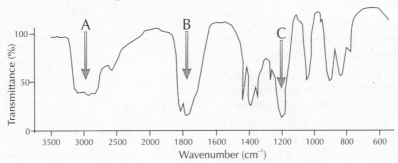

a)   What type of bonds are likely to have produced the troughs labelled A, B and C?   [3 marks]

b)   Suggest a molecular formula and name for this molecule. Explain your suggestion.   [3 marks]

2   Substance A gives this IR spectrum. It has a molecular mass of 46.

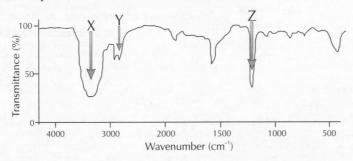

a)   Suggest what type of bonds could have caused the troughs labelled X, Y and Z.   [3 marks]

b)   Suggest a molecular formula and explain your reasoning.   [3 marks]

Ooooh — I'm picking up some good vibrations...

Now, I've warned you — infrared glasses are not for fun. They're highly advanced pieces of technology which if placed in the wrong hands could cause havoc and destruction across the universe. There's not much to learn on these pages — so make sure you can apply it. You'll be given a data table, so you don't have to bother learning all the wavenumber ranges.

More on Spectra

Yes, I know, it's yet another page on spectra — but it's the last one (alright, two) I promise.

You Can Use **Data From Several Spectra** to **Work Out a Structure**

All the **spectroscopy techniques** in this section will **give clues** to the **identity of a mystery molecule**, but you can be more **certain** about a structure (and avoid jumping to wrong conclusions) if you look at **data from several different types of spectrum**.

EXAMPLE

The following spectra are all of the same molecule. Deduce the molecule's structure.

The **mass spectrum** tells you the molecule's got a **mass of 44** and it's likely to contain a **CH₃ group**.

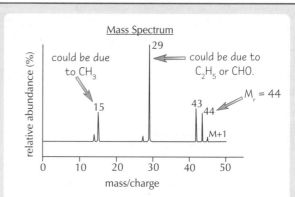
Mass Spectrum

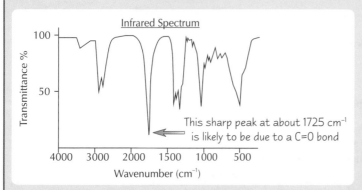
Infrared Spectrum

This sharp peak at about 1725 cm⁻¹ is likely to be due to a C=O bond

The **IR spectrum** strongly suggests a **C=O** bond in an aldehyde, ketone, ester or carboxylic acid.

But since it **doesn't** also have a broad absorption between 2500 and 3300, the molecule **can't** be a carboxylic acid.

The **high resolution proton NMR spectrum** shows that there are **hydrogen nuclei in 2 environments**.

The peak at δ ≈ **9.5** is due to a **CHO group** and the one at δ ≈ **2.5** is probably the hydrogen atoms in **COCH₃**. (You know that these can't be any other groups with similar chemical shifts thanks to the mass spectrum and IR spectrum.)

The **area** under the peaks is in the ratio **1 : 3**, which makes sense as there's **1 hydrogen in CHO** and **3 in COCH₃**.

The **splitting pattern** shows that the protons are on **adjacent carbon atoms**, so the group must be **HCOCH₃**.

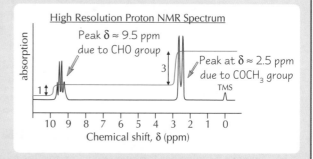
High Resolution Proton NMR Spectrum

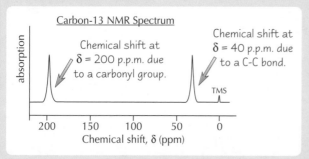
Carbon-13 NMR Spectrum

The **carbon-13 NMR spectrum** shows that the molecule has carbon nuclei in **2 different environments**.

The peak at δ = **200** corresponds to a carbon in a **carbonyl group** and the other peak is due to a **C–C bond**.

Putting all this together we have a molecule with a **mass of 44**, which contains a **CH₃** group, a **C=O** bond, and an **HCOCH₃** group.

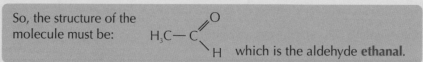
So, the structure of the molecule must be: which is the aldehyde **ethanal**.

You probably could have worked the molecule's structure out **without** using all the spectra, but in more **complex examples** you might well need all of them, so it's good practice. And while we're on the subject, there are a couple **more examples** for you to practise on the next page — enjoy.

More on Spectra

Practice Questions

Q1 Which type of spectrum gives you the mass of a molecule?

Q2 Which spectrum can tell you how many carbon environments are in a molecule?

Q3 Which spectrum can tell you how many different hydrogen environments there are in a molecule?

Q4 Which spectrum involves radio wave radiation?

Exam Questions

1 The four spectra below were produced by running different tests on samples of the same pure organic compound.

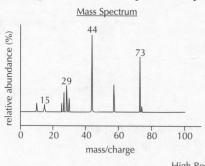
Mass Spectrum

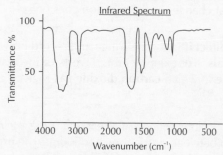
Infrared Spectrum

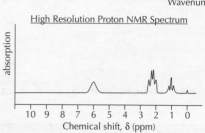
High Resolution Proton NMR Spectrum

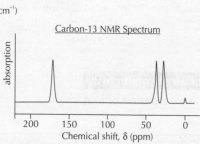
Carbon-13 NMR Spectrum

Use them to work out:

a) The molecular mass of the compound. [1 mark]

b) The probable structure of the molecule. Explain your reasoning. [6 marks]

2 The four spectra below were produced by running different tests on samples of the same pure organic compound.

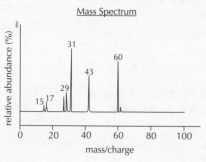
Mass Spectrum

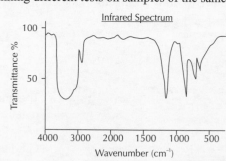
Infrared Spectrum

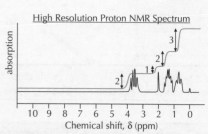
High Resolution Proton NMR Spectrum

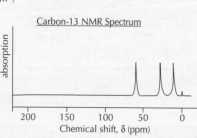
Carbon-13 NMR Spectrum

Use them to work out:

a) The molecular mass of the compound. [1 mark]

b) The probable structure of the molecule. Explain your reasoning. [6 marks]

Spectral analysis — psychology for ghosts...

So that's analysis done and dusted, you'll be pleased to hear. But before you rush off to learn about rates, take a moment to check that you really know how to interpret all the different spectra. You might want to go back and have a look at page 30 too if you're having trouble remembering what all the different functional groups look like.

UNIT 4: MODULE 3 — ANALYSIS

Rate Graphs and Orders

This section's a whole lot of fun. Well, it is if you like learning about speed of reactions anyway, and who doesn't...

The **Reaction Rate** tells you How Fast **Reactants** are Converted to **Products**

The **reaction rate** is the **change in the amount** of reactants or products **per unit time** (normally per second).

If the reactants are in **solution**, the rate'll be **change in concentration per second** and the units will be **mol dm^{-3} s^{-1}**.

There are **Loads** of Ways to **Follow the Rate of a Reaction**

Although there are quite a few ways to follow reactions, not every method works for every reaction. You've got to **pick a property** that **changes** as the reaction goes on.

Gas volume

If a **gas** is given off, you could **collect it** in a gas syringe and record how much you've got at **regular time intervals**. For example, this'd work for the reaction between an **acid** and a **carbonate** in which **carbon dioxide gas** is given off.

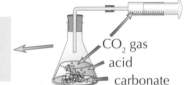

CO_2 gas
acid
carbonate

Colour change

You can sometimes track the colour change of a reaction using a gadget called a **colorimeter**. For example, in the reaction between propanone and iodine, the **brown** colour fades.

$$CH_3COCH_{3(aq)} + I_{2(aq)} \rightarrow CH_3COCH_2I_{(aq)} + H^+_{(aq)} + I^-_{(aq)}$$

colourless   brown   colourless

Electrical conductivity

If the **number of ions** changes, so will the **electrical conductivity**.

This also happens in the reaction between propanone and iodine.

Work Out **Reaction Rate** from a **Concentration-Time Graph**

1) By repeatedly taking **measurements** during a reaction you can plot a **concentration-time** graph.

2) The rate at any point in the reaction is given by the **gradient** (slope) at that point on the graph.

3) If the graph is a curve, you'll have to draw a **tangent** to the curve and find the gradient of that.

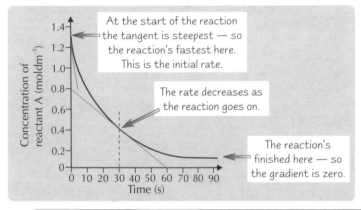

At the start of the reaction the tangent is steepest — so the reaction's fastest here. This is the initial rate.

The rate decreases as the reaction goes on.

The reaction's finished here — so the gradient is zero.

A tangent is a line that just touches a curve and has the same gradient as the curve does at that point.

The gradient of the blue tangent is the rate of the reaction after **30 seconds**.

$$\text{Gradient} = \frac{-0.8}{60} = \textbf{-0.013 mol dm}^{-3}\textbf{ s}^{-1}$$

So, the rate after 30 seconds is **0.013 mol dm^{-3} s^{-1}**

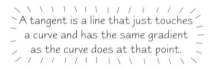

The sign of the gradient doesn't really matter — it's a negative gradient when you're measuring reactant concentration because the reactant decreases. If you measured the product concentration, it'd be a positive gradient.

Orders Tell You How a Reactant's **Concentration** Affects the **Rate**

1) The **order of reaction** with respect to a particular reactant tells you how the **reactant's concentration** affects the **rate**.

If you double the reactant's concentration and the rate **stays the same**, the order with respect to that reactant is **0**.
If you double the reactant's concentration and the rate **also doubles**, the order with respect to that reactant is **1**.
If you double the reactant's concentration and the rate **quadruples**, the order with respect to that reactant is **2**.

2) You can only find **orders of reaction** from **experiments**. You **can't** work them out from chemical equations.

Rate Graphs and Orders

The **Shape** of a **Rate-Concentration Graph** Tells You the **Order**

You can use your concentration-time graph to construct a **rate-concentration graph**, which you can then use to work out the order of the reaction. Here's how:

1) Find the **gradient** (which is the rate, remember) at various points along the concentration-time graph. This gives you a **set of points** for the rate-concentration graph.

2) Just **plot the points** and then **join them up** with a line or smooth curve, and you're done. The **shape** of the new graph tells you the **order**...

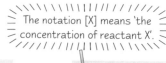

The notation [X] means 'the concentration of reactant X'.

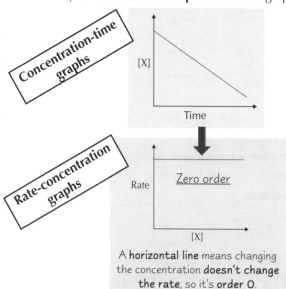

Concentration-time graphs

Rate-concentration graphs

A **horizontal line** means changing the concentration **doesn't change the rate**, so it's order 0.

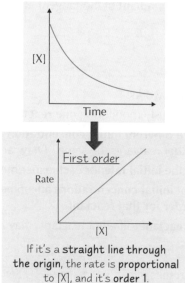

If it's a **straight line through the origin**, the rate is **proportional** to [X], and it's **order 1**.

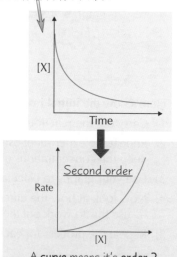

A **curve** means it's **order 2**. The rate will be proportional to [X]² (In theory, a curve could mean a higher order than 2 but you won't be asked about them.)

Practice Questions

Q1 Give two things that could be measured to follow the rate of a reaction.

Q2 What does the gradient of a concentration-time graph measure?

Q3 If you double the concentration of a reactant and the rate doubles, what is the order of reaction with respect to that reactant?

Q4 Sketch a typical rate-concentration graph for a second order reaction.

Exam Questions

1   It takes 200 seconds to completely dissolve a 0.4 g piece of magnesium in 25 ml of dilute hydrochloric acid. It takes 100 seconds if the concentration of the acid is doubled.

a)   What is the order of the reaction with respect to the concentration of the acid?   [1 mark]

b)   Sketch a graph to show the relationship between the concentration of the acid and the overall rate of the reaction.   [2 marks]

c)   What could be measured to follow the rate of this reaction in more detail?   [2 marks]

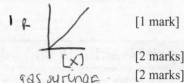

gas syringe

2   The rate of decomposition of hydrogen peroxide was followed by monitoring the concentration of hydrogen peroxide.

$$2H_2O_{2(aq)} \rightarrow 2H_2O_{(l)} + O_{2(g)}$$

Time (minutes)	0	20	40	60	80	100
$[H_2O_2]$ (mol dm^{-3})	2.00	1.00	0.50	0.25	0.125	0.0625

a)   Suggest an alternative method that could have been used to follow the rate of this reaction.   [2 marks]

b)   Using the data above, plot a graph and determine the rate of the reaction after 30 minutes.   [6 marks]

Mmmm, look at those seductive curves...

..sorry, chemistry gets me a bit over-excited sometimes. I think I'm OK now. Remember — the [X]-time graphs on this page slope downwards, i.e. have negative gradients, because they're showing the concentration of reactants. If you measure concentration of products instead the graph would be flipped the other way up — it'd slope upwards instead, but still level off in the same way.

Initial Rates and Half-Life

This is where it starts getting a bit mathsy. But don't panic, just take a deep breath and dive in... And don't bash your head on the bottom. Oh, and don't start sentences with 'And' or 'But' — English teachers hate it. 'Butt' is fine though.

The **Initial Rates Method** can be used to work out **Orders** too

On the previous page, reaction order was found by turning a concentration-time graph into a rate-concentration graph. Another way to find order is by looking at **initial reaction rates**.

> The **initial rate of a reaction** is the rate right at the **start** of the reaction. You can find this from a **concentration-time** graph by calculating the **gradient** of the **tangent** at **time = 0**.
>
>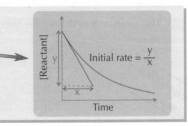

Here's how the **initial rates method** works:

1) Carry out the reaction, continuously monitoring **one reactant**. Use this to draw a **concentration-time graph**.

2) Repeat the experiment using a **different initial concentration** of the reactant.
   Keep the concentrations of other reactants the same. Draw another **concentration-time graph**.

3) Use your graphs to calculate the **initial rate** for each experiment using the method above.

4) Now look at how the different **initial concentrations** affect the **initial rate**
   — use this to work out the **order for that reactant**.

5) Repeat the process for **each reactant** (different reactants may have different orders).

Example:
The table on the right shows the results of a series of initial rate experiments for the reaction:

$$NO_{(g)} + CO_{(g)} + O_{2(g)} \rightarrow NO_{2(g)} + CO_{2(g)}$$

Write down the order with respect to each reactant.

Experiment number	$[NO_{(g)}]$ (mol dm^{-3})	$[CO_{(g)}]$ (mol dm^{-3})	$[O_{2(g)}]$ (mol dm^{-3})	Initial rate (mol dm^{-3} s^{-1})
1	2.0×10^{-2}	1.0×10^{-2}	1.0×10^{-2}	0.176
2	4.0×10^{-2}	1.0×10^{-2}	1.0×10^{-2}	0.704
3	2.0×10^{-2}	2.0×10^{-2}	1.0×10^{-2}	0.176
4	2.0×10^{-2}	1.0×10^{-2}	2.0×10^{-2}	0.176

1) Look at experiments 1 and 2 — when $[NO_{(g)}]$ doubles (but all the other concentrations stay constant), the rate **quadruples**. So the reaction is **second order** with respect to NO.

2) Look at experiments 1 and 3 — when $[CO_{(g)}]$ doubles (but all the other concentrations stay constant), the rate **stays the same**. So the reaction is **zero order** with respect to CO.

3) Look at experiments 1 and 4 — when $[O_{2(g)}]$ doubles (but all the other concentrations stay constant), the rate **stays the same**. So the reaction is **zero order** with respect to O_2.

Clock Reactions can be used to **Simplify** the Initial Rate Method

The method described above is a bit faffy — lots of measuring and drawing graphs.
In clock reactions, the initial rate can be **easily estimated**.

1) In a **clock reaction**, you can easily **measure the time** it takes for a given amount of product to form
   — usually there's a sudden colour change. The **shorter** the time, the faster the **initial rate**.

2) It's a much easier way to find **initial rates** than drawing lots of **concentration-time graphs**.

> The most famous clock reaction is the **iodine-clock** reaction.
> - sodium thiosulfate solution and starch are added to hydrogen peroxide and iodide ions in acid solution.
> - the important product is **iodine** — after a certain amount of time, the solution **suddenly** turns dark blue.
> - varying iodide or hydrogen peroxide concentration while keeping the others constant will give **different times** for the colour change. These can be used to work out the **reaction order**.

Initial Rates and Half-Life

Half-life is the Time for Half the Reactant to Disappear

The **half-life** of a reaction is the time it takes for **half of the reactant** to be used up.
The **half-life** of a first order reaction is **independent of the concentration**.

Example:
This graph shows the decomposition of hydrogen peroxide, H_2O_2.

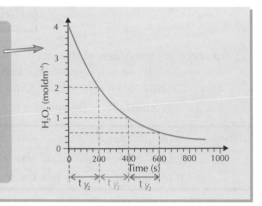

- Use the graph to measure the half-life at various points:
  $[H_2O_2]$ from **4 to 2** mol dm^{-3} = **200 s**,
  $[H_2O_2]$ from **2 to 1** mol dm^{-3} = **200 s**,
  $[H_2O_2]$ from **1 to 0.5** mol dm^{-3} = **200 s**.

- The half-life is constant, regardless of the concentration,
  so it's a **first order reaction** with respect to $[H_2O_2]$.

Practice Questions

Q1 What is meant by the initial rate of a reaction?

Q2 Describe how to calculate the initial rate of a reaction.

Q3 What is a clock reaction?

Q4 What does the term 'half-life' mean?

Exam Questions

1   The table below shows the results of a series of initial rate experiments for the reaction between substances D and E.

Experiment	[D] (mol dm^{-3})	[E] (mol dm^{-3})	Initial rate × 10^{-3} (mol dm^{-3} s^{-1})
1	0.2	0.2	1.30
2	0.4	0.2	5.19
3	0.2	0.4	2.61

Find the order of the reaction with respect to reactants D and E. Explain your reasoning.   [4 marks]

2   The table shows the results of an experiment on the decomposition of nitrogen(V) oxide at constant temperature.

$$2N_2O_5 \rightarrow 4NO_2 + O_2$$

Time (s)	0	50	100	150	200	250	300
$[N_2O_5]$ (mol dm^{-3})	2.50	1.66	1.14	0.76	0.50	0.32	0.22

a) Plot a graph of these results.   [3 marks]
b) From the graph, find the times for the concentration of N_2O_5 to decrease:
    i)   to half its original concentration.   [2 marks]
    ii) from 2.0 mol dm^{-3} to 1.0 mol dm^{-3}.   [2 marks]
c) Giving a reason, deduce the order of this reaction.   [2 marks]

If you thought this was fun, just wait till you get a load of...

...page 52. That's even better. It's got a proper maths equation. It's also got shape-shifters, dogs and industrial men.
And speaking of other things that are fun, can I recommend... flying kites, peeling bananas, making models of your friends
out of apples, the literary works of Virginia Woolf, counting spots on the carpet, eating all the pies and cuddling with a boy.

Rate Equations

Now you're going to take all the stuff you've learned from the previous pages and make a maths equation. Yay!?

The **Rate Equation** Links **Reaction Rate** to **Reactant Concentrations**

Rate equations look mean, but all they're really telling you is how the **rate** is affected by the **concentrations of reactants**. For a general reaction: **A + B → C + D**, the **rate equation** is:

The units of rate are mol $dm^{-3} s^{-1}$.

$$\text{Rate} = k[A]^m[B]^n$$

Remember — square brackets mean the concentration of whatever's inside them.

1) **m** and **n** are the **orders of the reaction** with respect to reactant A and reactant B. **m** tells you how the **concentration of reactant A** affects the **rate** and **n** tells you the same for **reactant B**.

2) **k** is the **rate constant** — the bigger it is, the **faster** the reaction.

Rate constants are shape-shifters. Here is one in its true form.

> Remember — If [A] doubles and the rate **stays the same**, the order with respect to A is **0**.
> If [A] doubles and the rate **also doubles**, the order with respect to A is **1**.
> If [A] doubles and the rate **quadruples**, the order with respect to A is **2**.

Example:
The chemical equation below shows the acid-catalysed reaction between propanone and iodine.

$$CH_3COCH_{3(aq)} + I_{2(aq)} \xrightarrow{H^+_{(aq)}} CH_3COCH_2I_{(aq)} + H^+_{(aq)} + I^-_{(aq)}$$

This reaction is **first order** with respect to propanone and $H^+_{(aq)}$ and **zero order** with respect to iodine. Write down the rate equation.

Even though $H^+_{(aq)}$ is a catalyst, rather than a reactant, it can still be in the rate equation.

The **rate equation** is: rate $= k[CH_3COCH_{3(aq)}]^1[H^+_{(aq)}]^1[I_{2(aq)}]^0$

But $[X]^1$ is usually written as **[X]**, and $[X]^0$ equals **1** so is usually **left out** of the rate equation.

So you can **simplify** the rate equation to: **rate $= k[CH_3COCH_{3(aq)}][H^+_{(aq)}]$**

Think about the powers laws from maths.

You can Calculate the **Rate Constant** from the **Orders** and **Rate of Reaction**

Once the rate and the orders of the reaction have been found by experiment, you can work out the **rate constant**, **k**. The **units** of the rate constant vary, so you have to **work them out**.

Example:
The reaction below was found to be second order with respect to NO and zero order with respect to CO and O_2. The rate is 1.76×10^{-3} mol $dm^{-3} s^{-1}$, when $[NO_{(g)}] = [CO_{(g)}] = [O_{2(g)}] = 2.00 \times 10^{-3}$ mol dm^{-3}.

$$NO_{(g)} + CO_{(g)} + O_{2(g)} \rightarrow NO_{2(g)} + CO_{2(g)}$$

Find the value of the rate constant.

First write out the **rate equation**: Rate $= k[NO_{(g)}]^2[CO_{(g)}]^0[O_{2(g)}]^0 = k[NO_{(g)}]^2$

Next insert the **concentration** and the **rate**. **Rearrange** the equation and calculate the value of **k**:

$$\text{Rate} = k[NO_{(g)}]^2, \text{ so, } 1.76 \times 10^{-3} = k \times (2.00 \times 10^{-3})^2 \Rightarrow k = \frac{1.76 \times 10^{-3}}{\left(2.00 \times 10^{-3}\right)^2} = 440$$

Find the **units for k** by putting the other units in the rate equation:

$$\text{Rate} = k[NO_{(g)}]^2, \text{ so mol } dm^{-3} s^{-1} = k \times (\text{mol } dm^{-3})^2 \Rightarrow k = \frac{\text{mol } dm^{-3} s^{-1}}{\left(\text{mol } dm^{-3}\right)^2} = \frac{s^{-1}}{\text{mol } dm^{-3}} = dm^3 \text{ mol}^{-1} s^{-1}$$

So the answer is: **$k = 440$ dm³ mol⁻¹ s⁻¹**

Rate Equations

Temperature Changes Affect the Rate Constant

1) Reactions happen when the reactant particles **collide** and have enough energy to **break** the existing bonds.

2) Increasing the temperature **speeds up** the reactant particles, so that they collide **more often**. It also increases the chances of the particles reacting when they do hit each other, as they have more energy.

3) In other words, **increasing temperature** increases the **reaction rate**.

4) According to the rate equation, reaction rate depends **only** on the rate constant and reactant concentrations. Since temperature **does** increase the reaction rate, it must **change the rate constant**.

> The **rate constant** applies to a **particular reaction** at a **certain temperature**.
> At a **higher** temperature, the reaction will have a **higher** rate constant.

Practice Questions

Q1 Write down a general rate equation for a reaction with reactants A, B and C.

Q2 How do you work out the units of k?

Q3 How does temperature affect the value of k?

Exam Questions

1 The following reaction is second order with respect to NO and first order with respect to H_2.

$$2NO_{(g)} + 2H_{2(g)} \rightarrow 2H_2O_{(g)} + N_{2(g)}$$

   a) Write a rate equation for the reaction. [2 marks]

   b) The rate of the reaction at 800 °C was determined to be 0.00267 mol dm^{-3} s^{-1} when $[H_{2(g)}] = 0.0020$ mol dm^{-3} and $[NO_{(g)}] = 0.0040$ mol dm^{-3}.

      i)   Calculate a value for the rate constant at 800 °C, including units. [3 marks]

      ii)   Predict the effect on the rate constant of decreasing the temperature of the reaction to 600 °C. [1 mark]

2 The ester ethyl ethanoate, $CH_3COOC_2H_5$, is hydrolysed by heating with dilute acid to give ethanol and ethanoic acid. The reaction is first order with respect to the concentration of H^+ and the ester.

   a) Write the rate equation for the reaction. [1 mark]

   b) When the initial concentration of the acid is 2.0 mol dm^{-3} and the ester is 0.25 mol dm^{-3}, the initial rate is 2.2×10^{-3} mol dm^{-3} s^{-1}. Calculate a value for the rate constant at this temperature and give its units. [3 marks]

   c) The temperature is kept constant and more solvent is added to the initial mixture so that the volume doubles. Calculate the new initial rate. [2 marks]

3 A reaction between substances X and Y, which is first order with respect to X and Y, has an initial rate of 1.6×10^{-3} mol dm^{-3} s^{-1} at 300 K. The reaction rate is doubled when the temperature rises by 10 K (a 3.33% increase).

Which of the following changes has a greater effect on the reaction rate?

     Increasing the temperature by 10 K

OR Increasing the concentration of X from 2.00 mol dm^{-3} to 2.06 mol dm^{-3} (a 3.33% increase)? [4 marks]

Rate constants are masters of disguise...

Here's some of their most common disguises. If you think you've spotted one, heating it will transform it back.

pumpkins → recycling bins

folding chairs

small dogs

real dog   rate constant

Rates and Reaction Mechanisms

It's a cold, miserable grey day outside, but on the plus side I just had a really nice slice of carrot and ginger cake. Anyway, this page is about the connection between rate equations and reaction mechanisms.

The **Rate-Determining Step** is the **Slowest Step** in a Multi-Step Reaction

Mechanisms can have **one step** or a **series of steps**. In a series of steps, each step can have a **different rate**.
The **overall rate** is decided by the step with the **slowest** rate — the **rate-determining step**. ⟵ *Otherwise known as the rate-limiting step.*

Reactants in the **Rate Equation** Affect the **Rate**

The rate equation is handy for helping you work out the **mechanism** of a chemical reaction.

You need to be able to pick out which reactants from the chemical equation are involved in the **rate-determining step**. Here are the **rules** for doing this:

> If a reactant appears in the **rate equation**, it must be affecting the **rate**. So this reactant, or something derived from it, must be in the **rate-determining step**.
>
> If a reactant **doesn't** appear in the **rate equation**, then it **won't** be involved in the **rate-determining step** (and neither will anything derived from it).

Catalysts can appear in rate equations, so they can be in rate-determining steps too.

Some **important points** to remember about rate-determining steps and mechanisms are:
1) The rate-determining step **doesn't** have to be the first step in a mechanism.
2) The reaction mechanism **can't** usually be predicted from **just** the chemical equation.

You Can Predict the **Rate Equation** from the **Rate-Determining Step**...

> The **order of a reaction** with respect to a reactant shows the **number of molecules** of that reactant which are involved in the **rate-determining step**.

So, if a reaction's second order with respect to X, there'll be two molecules of X in the rate-determining step.

For example, the mechanism for the reaction between **chlorine free radicals** and **ozone**, O_3, consists of **two steps**:

$$Cl\bullet_{(g)} + O_{3(g)} \rightarrow ClO\bullet_{(g)} + O_{2(g)} \text{ — slow (rate-determining step)}$$
$$ClO\bullet_{(g)} + O\bullet_{(g)} \rightarrow Cl\bullet_{(g)} + O_{2(g)} \text{ — fast}$$

$Cl\bullet$ and O_3 must both be in the rate equation, so the rate equation is of the form: **rate = $k[Cl\bullet]^m[O_3]^n$**.
There's only **one** $Cl\bullet$ radical and **one** O_3 molecule in the rate-determining step, so the **orders**, m and n, are both **1**.
So the rate equation is **rate = $k[Cl\bullet][O_3]$**.

...And You Can Predict the **Mechanism** from the **Rate Equation**

Knowing exactly which reactants are in the **rate-determining step** gives you an idea of the reaction **mechanism**.

For example, here are two possible mechanisms for the reaction $(CH_3)_3CBr + OH^- \rightarrow (CH_3)_3COH + Br^-$

The actual **rate equation** was worked out by rate experiments: **rate = $k[(CH_3)_3CBr]$**
OH^- isn't in the **rate equation**, so it **can't** be involved in the rate-determining step.
The **second mechanism** is most likely to be correct because OH^- **isn't** in the rate-determining step.

Rates and Reaction Mechanisms

You have to **Take Care** when Suggesting a **Mechanism**

If you're suggesting a mechanism, **watch out** — things might not always be what they seem.
For example, when nitrogen(V) oxide, N_2O_5, decomposes, it forms nitrogen(IV) oxide and oxygen:

$$2N_2O_{5(g)} \rightarrow 4NO_{2(g)} + O_{2(g)}$$

From the chemical equation, it looks like **two** N_2O_5 molecules react with each other. So you might predict that the reaction is **second order** with respect to N_2O_5... but you'd be wrong.

Experimentally, it's been found that the reaction is **first order** with respect to N_2O_5 — the rate equation is: **rate = $k[N_2O_5]$**. This shows that there's only one molecule of N_2O_5 in the rate-determining step.

One **possible mechanism** that fits the rate equation is:

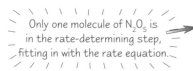
Only one molecule of N_2O_5 is in the rate-determining step, fitting in with the rate equation.

$N_2O_{5(g)} \rightarrow NO_{2(g)} + NO_{3(g)}$ — slow (rate-determining step)
$NO_{3(g)} + N_2O_{5(g)} \rightarrow 3NO_{2(g)} + O_{2(g)}$ — fast

The two steps add up to the overall chemical equation.
You can cancel the $NO_{3(g)}$ as it appears on both sides.

Practice Questions

Q1 What is meant by the rate-determining step?

Q2 Is the rate-determining step the first step in the reaction?

Q3 What is the connection between the rate equation and the rate-determining step?

Q4 How can the rate-determining step help you to understand the mechanism?

Exam Questions

1   The following reaction is first order with respect to H_2 and first order with respect to ICl.

$$H_{2(g)} + 2ICl_{(g)} \rightarrow I_{2(g)} + 2HCl_{(g)}$$

a) Write the rate equation for this reaction.   [1 mark]

b) The mechanism for this reaction consists of two steps.
    i)   Identify the molecules that are in the rate-determining step. Justify your answer.   [2 marks]
    ii)   A chemist suggested the following mechanism for the reaction.

$$2ICl_{(g)} \rightarrow I_{2(g)} + Cl_{2(g)} \quad \text{slow}$$
$$H_{2(g)} + Cl_{2(g)} \rightarrow 2HCl_{(g)} \quad \text{fast}$$

    Suggest, with reasons, whether this mechanism is likely to be correct.   [2 marks]

2   The reaction between HBr and oxygen gas occurs rapidly at 700 K.

    It can be represented by the equation $4HBr_{(g)} + O_{2(g)} \rightarrow 2H_2O_{(g)} + 2Br_{2(g)}$

    The rate equation found by experiment is Rate = $k[HBr][O_2]$

a) Explain why the reaction cannot be a one-step reaction.   [3 marks]

b) Each of the 4 steps of this reaction involves the reaction of 1 molecule of HBr.
    Two of the steps are the same. The rate-determining step is the first one and results
    in the formation of $HBrO_2$. Write equations for the full set of 4 reactions.   [4 marks]

I found rate-determining step aerobics a bit on the slow side...

These pages show you how rate equations, orders of reaction and reaction mechanisms all tie together and how each actually means something in the grand scheme of A2 Chemistry. It's all very profound. So get it all learnt and answer the questions and then you'll have plenty of time to practise the quickstep for your Strictly Come Dancing routine.

The Equilibrium Constant

'Oh no, not another page on equilibria', I hear you cry. Well actually it's the first one, so quit moaning.

At **Equilibrium** the Amounts of Reactants and Products **Stay the Same**

1) Lots of changes are **reversible** — they can go **both ways**. To show a change is reversible, you stick in a $\rightleftharpoons$.

2) As the **reactants** get used up, the **forward** reaction **slows down** — and as more **product** is formed, the **reverse** reaction **speeds up**. After a while, the forward reaction will be going at exactly the **same rate** as the backward reaction.

    The amounts of reactants and products **won't be changing** any more, so it'll seem like **nothing's happening**.
    It's a bit like you're **digging a hole** while someone else is **filling it in** at exactly the **same speed**.
    This is called a **dynamic equilibrium**.

3) Equilibria can be set up in **physical** systems, e.g.:

    > When **liquid bromine** is shaken in a closed flask, some of it changes to orange **bromine gas**.
    > After a while, **equilibrium** is reached — bromine liquid is **still** changing to bromine gas and
    > bromine gas is still changing to bromine liquid, but they are changing at the **same rate**.
    >
    > $Br_{2(l)} \rightleftharpoons Br_{2(g)}$

    ...and **chemical** systems, e.g.:

    > If **hydrogen gas** and **iodine gas** are mixed together in a closed flask, **hydrogen iodide** is formed.
    >
    > $$H_{2(g)} + I_{2(g)} \rightleftharpoons 2HI_{(g)}$$
    >
    > Imagine that **1.0 mole** of hydrogen gas is mixed with **1.0 mole** of iodine gas at a constant temperature of **640 K**.
    > When this mixture reaches equilibrium, there will be **1.6 moles** of hydrogen iodide and **0.2 moles** of both
    > hydrogen gas and iodine gas. No matter how long you leave them at this temperature, the **equilibrium** amounts
    > **never change**. As with the physical system, it's all a matter of the forward and backward rates **being equal**.

4) A **dynamic equilibrium** can only happen in a **closed system** at a **constant temperature**. *A closed system just means nothing can get in or out.*

K_c is the **Equilibrium Constant**

If you know the **molar concentration** of each substance at equilibrium, you can work out the **equilibrium constant**, K_c.
Your value of K_c will only be true for that particular **temperature**.
Before you can calculate K_c, you have to write an **expression** for it. Here's how:

> For the general reaction $aA + bB \rightleftharpoons dD + eE$, $K_c = \dfrac{[D]^d [E]^e}{[A]^a [B]^b}$

The products go on the top line. The square brackets, [ ], mean concentration in mol dm⁻³.

The lower-case letters a, b, d and e are the number of moles of each substance.

So for the reaction $H_{2(g)} + I_{2(g)} \rightleftharpoons 2HI_{(g)}$, $K_c = \dfrac{[HI]^2}{[H_2]^1 [I_2]^1}$. This simplifies to $K_c = \dfrac{[HI]^2}{[H_2][I_2]}$.

Calculate K_c by **Sticking Numbers** into the Expression

If you know the **equilibrium concentrations**, just bung them in your expression. Then, using a handy calculator, you can
work out the **value** of K_c. The **units** are trickier though — they **vary**, so you have to work them out after each calculation.

> **Example:**   If the volume of the closed flask in the hydrogen iodide example above is 2.0 dm³, what is the equilibrium
> constant for the reaction at 640 K? The equilibrium concentrations are:
>
> $[HI] = 0.8$ mol dm⁻³, $[H_2] = 0.1$ mol dm⁻³, and $[I_2] = 0.1$ mol dm⁻³ .
>
> Just stick the concentrations into the **expression** for K_c: $K_c = \dfrac{[HI]^2}{[H_2][I_2]} = \dfrac{0.8^2}{0.1 \times 0.1} = 64$ ← This is the value of K_c.
>
> To work out the **units** of K_c put the units in the expression instead of the numbers:
>
> $$K_c = \frac{(\text{mol dm}^{-3})^2}{(\text{mol dm}^{-3})(\text{mol dm}^{-3})} = 0,$$ so there are **no units** for K_c because the concentration units cancel.
>
> So K_c is just **64**.

The Equilibrium Constant

You Might Need to Work Out the Equilibrium Concentrations

You might have to figure out some of the **equilibrium concentrations** before you can find K_c:

Example: 0.20 moles of phosphorus(V) chloride decomposes at 600 K in a vessel of 5.00 dm^3. The equilibrium mixture is found to contain 0.08 moles of chlorine. Write the expression for K_c and calculate its value, including units.

$$PCl_{5(g)} \rightleftharpoons PCl_{3(g)} + Cl_{2(g)}$$

First find out how many moles of PCl_5 and PCl_3 there are at equilibrium:

The **equation** tells you that when **1 mole of PCl_5** decomposes, **1 mole of PCl_3** and **1 mole of Cl_2** are formed.
So if 0.08 moles of chlorine are produced at equilibrium, then there will be **0.08 moles** of PCl_3 as well.
0.08 mol of PCl_5 must have decomposed, so there will be **0.12 moles** left (0.2 – 0.08).

Divide each number of moles by the volume of the flask to give the molar concentrations:

$$[PCl_3] = [Cl_2] = 0.08 \div 5.00 = \textbf{0.016 mol dm}^{-3} \qquad [PCl_5] = 0.12 \div 5.00 = \textbf{0.024 mol dm}^{-3}$$

Put the concentrations in the expression for K_c and calculate it: $\quad K_C = \dfrac{[PCl_3][Cl_2]}{[PCl_5]} = \dfrac{[0.016][0.016]}{[0.024]} = \textbf{0.011}$

Now find the units of K_c: $\quad K_c = \dfrac{(\text{mol dm}^{-3})(\text{mol dm}^{-3})}{\text{mol dm}^{-3}} = \textbf{mol dm}^{-3}$ $\qquad$ So $K_c = \textbf{0.011 mol dm}^{-3}$

Practice Questions

Q1 Describe what a dynamic equilibrium is.

Q2 Write the expression for K_c for the following reaction: $2NO_{(g)} + O_{2(g)} \rightleftharpoons 2NO_{2(g)}$

Q3 Explain why you need to work out the units for K_c.

Q4 What are the units for K_c in the reaction in question 2?

Exam Questions

1   In the Haber process to make ammonia, nitrogen and hydrogen are reacted over an iron catalyst.

$$N_{2\,(g)} + 3H_{2\,(g)} \rightleftharpoons 2NH_{3\,(g)}$$

At 900 K, the equilibrium concentrations are $[N_2] = 1.06$ mol dm^{-3}, $[H_2] = 1.41$ mol dm^{-3} and $[NH_3] = 0.150$ mol dm^{-3}

a)   Write an expression for the equilibrium constant for this reaction. [2 marks]

b)   Calculate a value for K_c at this temperature and give its units. [3 marks]

2   Nitrogen dioxide dissociates according to the equation $2NO_{2(g)} \rightleftharpoons 2NO_{(g)} + O_{2(g)}$.

When 42.5 g of nitrogen dioxide were heated in a vessel of volume 22.8 dm^3 at 500 °C, 14.1 g of oxygen were found in the equilibrium mixture.

a)   Calculate   i)   the number of moles of nitrogen dioxide originally. [1 mark]
               ii)   the number of moles of each gas in the equilibrium mixture. [3 marks]

b)   Write an expression for K_c for this reaction. Calculate the value for K_c at 500 °C and give its units. [5 marks]

A big K_c means heaps of product...

Most organic reactions and plenty of inorganic reactions are reversible. Sometimes the backwards reaction's about as speedy as a dead snail though, so some reactions might be thought of as only going one way. It's like if you're walking forwards, continental drift could be moving you backwards at the same time, just reeeeally slowly.

More on the Equilibrium Constant

You didn't think it was going to be that easy, did you? No, there's lots more to learn about the equilibrium constant...
Did you know his friends call him Reggie, he's a fan of hardcore hip hop and he's a sworn enemy of the rate constant?

K_c can be used to Find Concentrations in an Equilibrium Mixture

Example: When ethanoic acid was allowed to reach equilibrium with ethanol at 25 °C, it was found that the equilibrium mixture contained 2.0 mol dm^{-3} ethanoic acid and 3.5 mol dm^{-3} ethanol. The K_c of the equilibrium is 4.0 at 25 °C. What are the concentrations of the other components?

$$CH_3COOH_{(l)} + C_2H_5OH_{(l)} \rightleftharpoons CH_3COOC_2H_{5(l)} + H_2O_{(l)}$$

Put all the values you know in the K_c expression:
$$K_c = \frac{[CH_3COOC_2H_5][H_2O]}{[CH_3COOH][C_2H_5OH]} \Rightarrow 4.0 = \frac{[CH_3COOC_2H_5][H_2O]}{2.0 \times 3.5}$$

Rearranging this gives: $[CH_3COOC_2H_5][H_2O] = 4.0 \times 2.0 \times 3.5 = 28.0$

But from the equation, $[CH_3COOC_2H_5] = [H_2O]$. ← This step might take a while to get your head around — the equation tells you that for every mole of $CH_3COOC_2H_5$ produced, one mole of H_2O is also produced, so their concentrations will always be equal. (The reactant concentrations aren't the same since they were different at the start).

So: $[CH_3COOC_2H_5] = [H_2O] = \sqrt{28} = 5.3$ mol dm^{-3}

The concentration of $CH_3COOC_2H_5$ and H_2O is 5.3 mol dm^{-3}

If Conditions Change the Position of Equilibrium Will Move

If you **change** the **concentration**, **pressure** or **temperature** of a reversible reaction, you're going to **alter** the **position of equilibrium**. This just means you'll end up with **different amounts** of reactants and products at equilibrium.

If the position of equilibrium moves to the **left**, you'll get more **reactants**. $\textbf{H}_{2(g)} + \textbf{I}_{2(g)} \rightleftharpoons 2HI_{(g)}$

If the position of equilibrium moves to the **right**, you'll get more **products**. $H_{2(g)} + I_{2(g)} \rightleftharpoons \textbf{2HI}_{(g)}$

There's a rule that lets you predict how the **position of equilibrium** will change if a **condition changes**. Here it is:

If there's a change in **concentration**, **pressure** or **temperature**, the equilibrium will move to help **counteract** the change.

So, basically, if you **raise the temperature**, the position of equilibrium will shift to try to **cool things down**.
And if you **raise the pressure or concentration**, the position of equilibrium will shift to try to **reduce it again**.

Temperature Changes Alter K_c

TEMPERATURE

1) If you **increase** the temperature of a reaction, the equilibrium will shift in the **endothermic direction** to absorb the extra heat.

2) **Decreasing** the reaction temperature will shift the equilibrium in the **exothermic direction** to replace the lost heat.

3) If the change means **more product** is formed, K_c will **increase**. If it means **less product** is formed, then K_c will **decrease**.

An exothermic reaction releases heat and has a negative ΔH.
An endothermic reaction absorbs heat and has a positive ΔH.

The reaction below is exothermic in the forward direction. If you increase the temperature, the equilibrium shifts to the left to absorb the extra heat. This means that less product is formed.

Exothermic ⟶
$$2SO_{2(g)} + O_{2(g)} \rightleftharpoons 2SO_{3(g)} \quad \Delta H = -197 \text{ kJ mol}^{-1}$$
⟵ Endothermic

$$K_c = \frac{[SO_3]^2}{[SO_2]^2[O_2]}$$

There's less product, so K_c decreases.

If the forward direction of a reversible reaction is endothermic, the reverse direction will be exothermic, and vice versa.

More on the Equilibrium Constant

Concentration and Pressure Changes Don't Affect K_c

CONCENTRATION

The value of the **equilibrium constant, K_c**, is **fixed** at a given temperature. So if the concentration of one thing in the equilibrium mixture **changes** then the concentrations of the others must change to keep the value of K_c the same.

$$CH_3COOH_{(l)} + C_2H_5OH_{(l)} \rightleftharpoons CH_3COOC_2H_{5(l)} + H_2O_{(l)}$$

If you increase the concentration of CH_3COOH then the equilibrium will move to the right to get rid of the extra CH_3COOH — so more $CH_3COOC_2H_5$ and H_2O are produced. This keeps the equilibrium constant the same.

PRESSURE (changing this only really affects **equilibria involving gases**)

Increasing the pressure shifts the equilibrium to the side with **fewer** gas molecules — this **reduces** the pressure. **Decreasing** the pressure shifts the equilibrium to the side with **more** gas molecules. This **raises** the pressure again. K_c stays the **same**, no matter what you do to the pressure.

There are 3 moles on the left, but only 2 on the right. So an increase in pressure would shift the equilibrium to the right. $\longrightarrow$ $$2SO_{2(g)} + O_{2(g)} \rightleftharpoons 2SO_{3(g)}$$

The removal of his dummy was a change that Maxwell always opposed.

> **Catalysts** have **NO EFFECT** on the **position of equilibrium**.
> They **can't** increase **yield** — but they **do** mean equilibrium is approached **faster**.

Practice Questions

Q1 If you raise the temperature of a reversible reaction, in which direction will the reaction move?

Q2 Does temperature change affect K_c?

Q3 Why does concentration not affect K_c?

Q4 What effect do catalysts have on the equilibrium of a reaction?

Exam Questions

1   The following equilibrium was established at temperature T_1:

$$2SO_{2(g)} + O_{2(g)} \rightleftharpoons 2SO_{3(g)} \quad \Delta H = -196 \text{ kJmol}^{-1}.$$

K_c at T_1 was found to be 0.67 $\text{mol}^{-1}\text{dm}^3$.

a) When equilibrium was established at a different temperature, T_2, the value of K_c was found to have increased. State which of T_1 or T_2 is the lower temperature and explain why. [3 marks]

b) The experiment was repeated exactly the same in all respects at T_1, except a flask of smaller volume was used. How would this change affect the yield of sulfur trioxide and the value of K_c? [2 marks]

2   The reaction between methane and steam is used to produce hydrogen. The forward reaction is endothermic.

$$CH_{4\,(g)} + H_2O_{\,(g)} \rightleftharpoons CO_{\,(g)} + 3H_{2\,(g)}$$

a) Write an equation for K_c for this reaction. [2 marks]

b) How will the value of K_c be affected by:
    i) increasing the temperature,
    ii) using a catalyst. [2 marks]

c) How will the composition of the equilibrium mixture be affected by increasing the pressure? [2 marks]

Shift to the left, and then jump to the right...

Hmm, sounds like there's a song in there somewhere. I'm getting an image now of chemists in lab coats dancing at a Xmas party... Let's not go there. Instead just make sure you really get your head round this concept of changing conditions and the equilibrium shifting to compensate. Reread until you've definitely got it — it makes this topic much easier to learn.

Acids and Bases

Remember this stuff? Well, it's all down to Brønsted and Lowry — they've got a lot to answer for.

An Acid **Releases** Protons — a Base **Accepts** Protons

Brønsted-Lowry acids are **proton donors** — they release **hydrogen ions** (H^+) when they're mixed with water. You never get H^+ ions by themselves in water though — they're always combined with H_2O to form **hydroxonium ions, H_3O^+**.

HA is just any old acid. $\longrightarrow$ $HA_{(aq)} + H_2O_{(l)} \rightarrow H_3O^+_{(aq)} + A^-_{(aq)}$

Brønsted-Lowry bases do the opposite — they're **proton acceptors**. When they're in solution, they grab **hydrogen ions** from water molecules.

B is just a random base. $\longrightarrow$ $B_{(aq)} + H_2O_{(l)} \rightarrow BH^+_{(aq)} + OH^-_{(aq)}$

Acids React with **Metals** and **Carbonates**

1) **Reactive metals** react with acids releasing **hydrogen gas**.
2) The metal atoms **donate electrons** to the **H^+ ions** in the acid solution. The metal atoms are **oxidised** and the H^+ ions are **reduced**.

E.g. $Mg_{(s)} + 2H^+_{(aq)} \rightarrow Mg^{2+}_{(aq)} + H_{2(g)}$ $\longleftarrow$ Oxidation Is Loss, Reduction Is Gain.

3) **Carbonates** react with acids to produce **carbon dioxide** and **water**.

$CO_3^{2-}_{(aq)} + 2H^+_{(aq)} \rightarrow H_2O_{(l)} + CO_{2(g)}$

Acids React with **Bases** and **Alkalis** Too

1) Acids produce H^+ ions when dissolved in water and bases produce OH^- ions.
2) Acids and bases **neutralise** each other to form water.
   E.g. acids and **alkalis** react like this...

$H^+_{(aq)} + OH^-_{(aq)} \rightarrow H_2O_{(l)}$

Remember — alkalis are bases that dissolve in water.

Most insoluble bases are **metal oxides** and they're neutralised in a similar way.

$2H^+_{(aq)} + O^{2-}_{(s)} \rightarrow H_2O_{(l)}$

Acids and Bases can be **Strong** or **Weak**

1) **Strong acids** dissociate (or ionise) almost completely in water — **nearly all** the H^+ ions will be released. E.g. hydrochloric acid is a strong acid:

$HCl_{(g)} + water \rightarrow H^+_{(aq)} + Cl^-_{(aq)}$

These are really all reversible reactions, but the equilibrium lies extremely far to the right.

2) **Strong bases** ionise almost completely in water too.
   E.g. sodium hydroxide is a strong base:

$NaOH_{(s)} + water \rightarrow Na^+_{(aq)} + OH^-_{(aq)}$

3) **Weak acids** (e.g. ethanoic or citric) dissociate only very **slightly** in water — so only small numbers of H^+ ions are formed. An **equilibrium** is set up which lies well over to the **left**.

E.g. $CH_3COOH_{(aq)} \rightleftharpoons CH_3COO^-_{(aq)} + H^+_{(aq)}$

4) **Weak bases** (e.g. ammonia) only slightly ionise in water.
   Just like with weak acids, the **equilibrium** lies well over to the **left**.

E.g. $NH_{3(aq)} + H_2O_{(l)} \rightleftharpoons NH_4^+_{(aq)} + OH^-_{(aq)}$

Acids and Bases

Acids and Bases form **Conjugate Pairs** in Water

When an acid is added to water, the equilibrium below is set up.

Don't forget — protons and H^+ ions are the same thing.

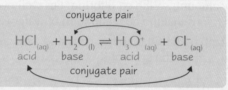

conjugate pair

$$HA + H_2O \rightleftharpoons H_3O^+ + A^-$$
acid   base   acid   base

conjugate pair

- In the **forward reaction**, HA acts as an **acid** as it **donates** a proton.
- In the **reverse reaction**, A^- acts as a **base** and **accepts** a proton from the H_3O^+ ion to form HA.

HA and A^- are called a **conjugate pair** — HA is the **conjugate acid** of A^- and A^- is the **conjugate base** of the acid, HA. H_2O and H_3O^+ are a conjugate pair too.

The acid and base of a conjugate pair can be linked by an **H^+**, like this: $HA \rightleftharpoons H^+ + A^-$ or this: $H^+ + H_2O \rightleftharpoons H_3O^+$

Here's the equilibrium for aqueous HCl.
Cl^- is the conjugate base of $HCl_{(aq)}$.

conjugate pair

$$HCl_{(aq)} + H_2O_{(l)} \rightleftharpoons H_3O^+_{(aq)} + Cl^-_{(aq)}$$
acid   base   acid   base

conjugate pair

An equilibrium with **conjugate pairs** is also set up when a **base** dissolves in water. The base B takes a proton from the water to form **BH^+** — so B is the **conjugate base** of BH^+, and BH^+ is the **conjugate acid** of B. H_2O and OH^- also form a **conjugate pair**.

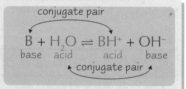

conjugate pair

$$B + H_2O \rightleftharpoons BH^+ + OH^-$$
base   acid   acid   base

conjugate pair

Practice Questions

Q1 Give the Brønsted-Lowry definitions of an acid and a base.

Q2 Describe, in terms of equilibrium, how strong and weak acids differ in the way they dissolve in water.

Q3 What is the conjugate base of nitric acid, HNO_3?

Q4 Write an ionic equation to show the reaction between copper(II) oxide and hydrochloric acid.

Exam Questions

1   Magnesium completely dissolves in aqueous sulfuric acid, $H_2SO_{4 (aq)}$.

   a) Which ions are present in a solution of sulfuric acid?   [1 mark]

   b) Write an ionic equation for the reaction of the acid and magnesium.   [1 mark]

   c) What is the conjugate base of sulfuric acid?   [1 mark]

   d) Explain in equilibrium terms why sulfuric acid is considered a strong acid.   [2 marks]

2   Hydrocyanic acid, HCN, is a weak acid.

   a) Write an equation to show the equilibrium set up when it is added to water.   [1 mark]

   b) Use your equation to explain why HCN is a weak acid.   [1 mark]

   c) From your equation, identify the two conjugate pairs formed.   [2 marks]

   d) Which ion links conjugate pairs?   [1 mark]

3   Dry ammonia gas is neutral but when it is added to water, a weakly alkaline solution forms.

   a) Write an equation to show the equilibrium set up when ammonia is dissolved into water.   [1 mark]

   b) Is water behaving as an acid or a base in this equilibrium? Give a reason for your answer.   [2 marks]

   c) What species forms a conjugate pair with water in this reaction?   [1 mark]

Alsatians and Bassets — keep them apart or they'll neuterise each other...

Don't confuse strong acids with concentrated acids, or weak acids with dilute acids. Strong and weak are to do with how much an acid ionises, whereas concentrated and dilute are to do with the number of moles of acid you've got per dm^3. You can have a dilute strong acid, or a concentrated weak acid. It works just the same way with bases too.

pH

Just when you thought it was safe to turn the page — it's even more about acids and bases.
This page is positively swarming with calculations and constants...

The Ionic Product of Water, K_w, is Always the Same at a Certain Temperature

Water dissociates into **hydroxonium ions** and **hydroxide ions**.

So this equilibrium exists in water:

$$H_2O_{(l)} + H_2O_{(l)} \rightleftharpoons H_3O^+_{(aq)} + OH^-_{(aq)}$$ or more simply $$H_2O_{(l)} \rightleftharpoons H^+_{(aq)} + OH^-_{(aq)}$$

And, just like for any other equilibrium reaction, you can apply the equilibrium law and write an expression for the **equilibrium constant**:
(If you need a quick reminder on equilibrium constants, flick back to page 56.)

$$K_c = \frac{[H^+][OH^-]}{[H_2O]}$$

Water only dissociates a **tiny amount**, so the equilibrium lies well over to the **left**. There's so much water compared to the amounts of H^+ and OH^- ions that the concentration of water is considered to have a **constant** value.

So if you multiply K_c (a constant) by $[H_2O]$ (another constant), you get a **constant**. This new constant is called the **ionic product of water** and it is given the symbol K_w.

$$K_w = K_c \times [H_2O] = [H^+][OH^-] \Rightarrow \boxed{K_w = [H^+][OH^-]}$$

The units of K_w are always mol^2dm^{-6}.

K_w always has the **same value** for an aqueous solution at a **given temperature**. You'll see in a bit how this is useful...

The pH Scale is a Measure of Hydrogen Ion Concentration

Concentration of hydrogen ions can vary enormously, so it's given on a **logarithmic scale** — the **pH scale**, with pH defined by this equation:

$$pH = -\log_{10}[H^+]$$

The pH scale goes from **0** (very acidic) to **14** (very alkaline). **pH 7** is **neutral**.

1) If you know the **hydrogen ion concentration** of a solution, you can calculate its **pH** by sticking the numbers into the **formula**.

Example: A solution of hydrochloric acid has a hydrogen ion concentration of 0.01 mol dm^{-3}. What is the pH of the solution?

$$pH = -\log_{10}[H^+] = -\log_{10}[0.01] = 2$$

Use the 'log' button on your calculator for this.

2) If you've got the **pH** of a solution, and you want to know its **hydrogen ion concentration**, then you need the **inverse** of the pH formula: $$[H^+] = 10^{-pH}$$

Example: A solution of sulfuric acid has a pH of 1.52. What is the hydrogen ion concentration of this solution?

$$[H^+] = 10^{-pH} = 10^{-1.52} = 0.03 \text{ mol dm}^{-3} = 3 \times 10^{-2} \text{ mol dm}^{-3}$$

For Strong Monobasic Acids, [H+] = [Acid]

1) Hydrochloric acid and nitric acid ($HNO_{3(aq)}$) are **strong acids** so they ionise fully.
2) They're also **monobasic**, which means **one mole of acid** produces **one mole of hydrogen ions**. So the H^+ concentration is the **same** as the acid concentration.

So for **0.1 mol dm^{-3} HCl**, $[H^+]$ is also 0.1 mol dm^{-3}. So the pH $= -\log_{10}[H^+] = -\log_{10} 0.1 = $ **1.0**.
Or for **0.05 mol dm^{-3} HNO$_3$**, $[H^+]$ is also 0.05 mol dm^{-3}, giving pH $= -\log_{10} 0.05 = $ **1.30**

pH

Use K_w to Find the pH of a Strong Base

1) Sodium hydroxide (NaOH) and potassium hydroxide (KOH) are **strong bases** that **fully ionise** in water.
2) They donate **one mole of OH⁻ ions** per mole of base.
   This means that the concentration of OH⁻ ions is the **same** as the **concentration of the base**.
   So for 0.02 mol dm⁻³ sodium hydroxide solution, [OH⁻] is also **0.02 mol dm⁻³**.
3) But to work out the **pH** you need to know **[H⁺]**
   — luckily this is linked to **[OH⁻]** through the **ionic product of water**, K_w: $K_w = [H^+][OH^-]$
4) So if you know K_w and [OH⁻] for a **strong aqueous base** at a certain temperature,
   you can work out **[H⁺]** and then the **pH**.

Example: The value of K_w at 298 K is 1.0×10^{-14}. Find the pH of 0.1 mol dm⁻³ NaOH at 298 K.

$$[OH^-] = 0.1 \text{ mol dm}^{-3} \Rightarrow [H^+] = \frac{K_w}{[OH^-]} = \frac{1.0 \times 10^{-14}}{0.1} = 1.0 \times 10^{-13} \text{ mol dm}^{-3}$$

So pH = $-\log_{10} 1.0 \times 10^{-13}$ = **13.0**

Get off the page, rate constant! You're not relevant here.

Practice Questions

Q1 Write down the formula of the ionic product of water. What are its units?

Q2 Write the formula for calculating the pH of a solution.

Q3 What is a monobasic acid? What can you assume about [H⁺] for a strong monobasic acid?

Q4 Explain how you'd find the pH of a strong base.

Q5 Should the rate constant be allowed to stay on this page or should he make like a tree?

Exam Questions

1 a) Explain the relationship between K_c and K_w for water. [2 marks]
   b) A solution of the strong acid hydrobromic acid, HBr, has a concentration of 0.32 mol dm⁻³.
      Calculate its pH. [2 marks]
   c) Hydrobromic acid is a stronger acid than hydrochloric acid.
      Explain what that means in terms of hydrogen ions and pH. [2 marks]

2 A solution of sodium hydroxide contains 2.5 g dm⁻³. The value of K_w at 298 K is 1.0×10^{-14}.
   a) What is the molar concentration of the hydroxide ions in this solution? [2 marks]
   b) Calculate the pH of this solution. [3 marks]
   c) Why is this value temperature dependent? [1 mark]

3 The value of K_w, the ionic product of water, is 1.0×10^{-14} at 298 K.
   Calculate the pH of a 0.0370 mol dm⁻³ solution of sodium hydroxide at 298 K. [4 marks]

All I want for Christmas is a chemistry question requiring the use of logs...

You know things are getting serious when maths stuff like logs start appearing. It's fine really though, just practise a few questions and make sure you know how to use the log button on your calculator. And make sure you've learned the equation for K_w and both pH equations. And while you're up, go and make me a nice cup of coffee, lots of milk, no sugar.

More pH Calculations

More acid calculations to come, so you'll need to get that calculator warmed up... Either hold it for a couple of minutes in your armpit, or even better, warm it between your clenched buttocks. OK done that? Good stuff...

To Find the pH of a Weak Acid you use K_a (the Acid Dissociation Constant)

Weak acids **don't** ionise fully in solution, so the $[H^+]$ **isn't** the same as the acid concentration.
This makes it a **bit trickier** to find their pH. You have to use yet another **equilibrium constant**, K_a.

For a weak aqueous acid, HA, you get the following equilibrium: $HA_{(aq)} \rightleftharpoons H^+_{(aq)} + A^-_{(aq)}$

As only a **tiny amount** of HA dissociates, you can assume that $[HA_{(aq)}]_{start} = [HA_{(aq)}]_{equilibrium}$.

So if you apply the equilibrium law, you get: $K_a = \dfrac{[H^+][A^-]}{[HA]}$

You can also assume that **all the H^+ ions** come from the **acid**, so $[H^+_{(aq)}] = [A^-_{(aq)}]$.

So $K_a = \dfrac{[H^+]^2}{[HA]}$ ← The units of K_a are mol dm^{-3}.

Here's an example of how to use K_a to find the **pH** of a weak acid:

> **Example:**
> Calculate the hydrogen ion concentration and the pH of a
> 0.02 mol dm^{-3} solution of propanoic acid (CH_3CH_2COOH).
> K_a for propanoic acid at this temperature is 1.30×10^{-5} mol dm^{-3}.
>
> $K_a = \dfrac{[H^+]^2}{[CH_3CH_2COOH]} \Rightarrow [H^+]^2 = K_a[CH_3CH_2COOH] = 1.30 \times 10^{-5} \times 0.02 = 2.60 \times 10^{-7}$
>
> $\Rightarrow [H^+] = \sqrt{2.60 \times 10^{-7}} = \textbf{5.10} \times \textbf{10}^{-4}$ **mol dm**$^{-3}$
>
> So pH $= -\log_{10} 5.10 \times 10^{-4} = \textbf{3.29}$

You Might Have to Find the Concentration or K_a of a Weak Acid

You don't need to know anything new for this type of calculation. You usually just have to find $[H^+]$ from the pH, then fiddle around with the K_a **expression** to find the missing bit of information.

> **Example:**
> The pH of an ethanoic acid (CH_3COOH) solution was 3.02 at 298 K.
> Calculate the molar concentration of this solution.
> The K_a of ethanoic acid is 1.75×10^{-5} mol dm^{-3} at 298 K.
>
> $[H^+] = 10^{-pH} = 10^{-3.02} = 9.55 \times 10^{-4}$ mol dm^{-3}
> $K_a = \dfrac{[H^+]^2}{[CH_3COOH]} \Rightarrow [CH_3COOH] = \dfrac{[H^+]^2}{K_a} = \dfrac{(9.55 \times 10^{-4})^2}{1.75 \times 10^{-5}}$
> $= \textbf{0.0521 mol dm}^{-3}$

This bunny may look cute, but he can't help Horace with his revision.

Mmmm, that does looks like a tasty bone, Rex, but I don't think it'll help with K_a calculations.

> **Example:**
> A solution of 0.162 mol dm^{-3} HCN has a pH of 5.05 at 298 K. What is the value of K_a for HCN at 298 K?
>
> $[H^+] = 10^{-pH} = 10^{-5.05} = 8.91 \times 10^{-6}$ mol dm^{-3}
>
> $K_a = \dfrac{[H^+]^2}{[HCN]} = \dfrac{(8.91 \times 10^{-6})^2}{0.162} = \textbf{4.90} \times \textbf{10}^{-10}$ **mol dm**$^{-3}$

More pH Calculations

pK_a is calculated from K_a in exactly the same way as pH is calculated from $[H^+]$ — and vice versa.
So if an acid has a K_a value of 1.50×10^{-7} mol dm^{-3}, its $pK_a = -log_{10}(1.50 \times 10^{-7}) = 6.82$.
And if an acid has a pK_a value of 4.32, its $K_a = 10^{-4.32} = 4.79 \times 10^{-5}$ mol dm^{-3}.

Notice how pK_a values aren't annoyingly tiny like K_a values.

Just to make things that bit more complicated, there might be a pK_a value in a question.
If so, you need to convert it to K_a so that you can use the K_a expression.

Example:
Calculate the pH of 0.050 mol dm^{-3} methanoic acid (HCOOH).
Methanoic acid has a pK_a of 3.75 at this temperature.

$K_a = 10^{-pK_a} = 10^{-3.75} = 1.78 \times 10^{-4}$ mol dm^{-3} $\Longleftarrow$ First you have to convert the pK_a to K_a.

$K_a = \dfrac{[H^+]^2}{[HCOOH]}$ $\Rightarrow [H^+]^2 = K_a[HCOOH] = 1.78 \times 10^{-4} \times 0.050 = 8.9 \times 10^{-6}$

$\Rightarrow [H^+] = \sqrt{8.9 \times 10^{-6}} = 2.98 \times 10^{-3}$ mol dm^{-3}

$pH = -log_{10} 2.98 \times 10^{-3} = 2.53$

Sometimes you have to give your answer as a pK_a value.
In this case, you just work out the K_a value as usual and
then convert it to pK_a — and Bob's a revision goat.

Bob the revision goat

Practice Questions

Q1 What are the units of K_a?

Q2 Describe how you would calculate the pH of a weak acid from its acid dissociation constant.

Q3 How is pK_a defined?

Q4 Would you expect strong acids to have higher or lower K_a values than weak acids?

Exam Questions

1   The value of K_a for the weak acid HA, at 298 K, is 5.60×10^{-4} mol dm^{-3}.
    a) Write an expression for K_a for HA.   [1 mark]
    b) Calculate the pH of a 0.280 mol dm^{-3} solution of HA at 298 K.   [3 marks]

2   The pH of a 0.150 mol dm^{-3} solution of a weak monobasic acid, HX, is 2.65 at 298 K.
    a) Calculate the value of K_a for the acid HX at 298 K.   [4 marks]
    b) Calculate pK_a for this acid.   [2 marks]

3   Benzoic acid is a weak acid that is used as a food preservative. It has a pK_a of 4.2 at 298 K.
    Find the pH of a 1.6×10^{-4} mol dm^{-3} solution of benzoic acid at 298 K.   [4 marks]

Fluffy revision animals... aaawwwww...

*Strong acids have high K_a values and weak acids have low K_a values. For pK_a values, it's the other way round — the
stronger the acid, the lower the pK_a. If something's got p in front of it, like pH, pK_w or pK_a, it'll mean $-log_{10}$ of whatever.
Oh and did you like all the cute animals on this page? Did it really make your day? Good, I'm really pleased about that.*

Buffer Action

I always found buffers a bit mind-boggling. How can a solution resist becoming more acidic if you add acid to it? And why would it want to? Here's where you find out...

Buffers Resist Changes in pH

> A **buffer** is a solution that **resists** changes in pH when **small** amounts of acid or alkali are added.

A buffer **doesn't** stop the pH from changing completely — it does make the changes **very slight** though.
Buffers only work for small amounts of acid or alkali — put too much in and they'll go "Waah" and not be able to cope.
You can get **acidic buffers** and **basic buffers** — but you only need to know about acidic ones.

Acidic Buffers are Made from a Weak Acid and one of its Salts

Acidic buffers have a pH of less than 7 — they're made by mixing a **weak acid** with one of its **salts**.
Ethanoic acid and **sodium ethanoate** is a good example:

The salt **fully** dissociates into its ions when it dissolves: $CH_3COO^-Na^+_{(aq)} \rightarrow CH_3COO^-_{(aq)} + Na^+_{(aq)}$.
$\qquad\qquad$ Sodium ethanoate $\qquad$ Ethanoate ions

The ethanoic acid is a **weak acid**, so it only **slightly** dissociates: $CH_3COOH_{(aq)} \rightleftharpoons H^+_{(aq)} + CH_3COO^-_{(aq)}$

So in the solution you've got heaps of **ethanoate ions** from the salt, and heaps of **undissociated ethanoic acid molecules**.

Buffers work because of shifts in equilibrium (look back at p58 for more on this):

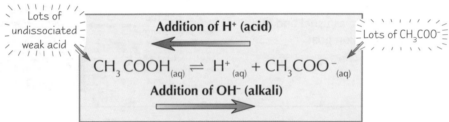

Lots of undissociated weak acid

Addition of H⁺ (acid)

Lots of CH_3COO^-

$$CH_3COOH_{(aq)} \rightleftharpoons H^+_{(aq)} + CH_3COO^-_{(aq)}$$

Addition of OH⁻ (alkali)

If you add a **small** amount of **acid** the **H⁺ concentration** increases. Most of the extra H⁺ ions combine with CH_3COO^- ions to form CH_3COOH. This shifts the equilibrium to the **left**, reducing the H⁺ concentration to close to its original value. So the **pH** doesn't change much.

The large number of CH_3COO^- ions make sure that the buffer can cope with the addition of acid.

There's no problem doing this as there's absolutely loads of spare CH_3COOH molecules.

If a **small** amount of **alkali** (e.g. NaOH) is added, the **OH⁻ concentration** increases. Most of the extra OH⁻ ions react with H⁺ ions to form water — removing H⁺ ions from the solution. This causes more CH_3COOH to **dissociate** to form H⁺ ions — shifting the equilibrium to the **right**. The H⁺ concentration increases until it's close to its original value, so the **pH** doesn't change much.

Buffer Solutions are Important in Biological Environments

1) **Cells** need a constant pH to allow the **biochemical reactions** to take place. The pH is controlled by a buffer based on the equilibrium between **dihydrogen phosphate** ions and **hydrogen phosphate** ions.
$$H_2PO_4^- \rightleftharpoons H^+ + HPO_4^{2-}$$

2) **Blood** needs to be kept at pH 7.4. It is buffered using carbonic acid. The levels of H_2CO_3 are controlled by **respiration**.
and $\quad H_2CO_{3(aq)} \rightleftharpoons H^+_{(aq)} + HCO_3^-_{(aq)}$
$\qquad\quad H_2CO_{3(aq)} \rightleftharpoons H_2O_{(l)} + CO_{2(aq)}$
By **breathing out CO₂** the level of H_2CO_3 is reduced as it moves this **equilibrium** to the **right**. The levels of HCO_3^- are controlled by the **kidneys** with excess being **excreted** in the urine.

3) Buffers are used in **food products** to control the pH. Changes in pH can be caused by **bacteria** and **fungi** and cause food to **deteriorate**. A common buffer is **citric acid** and **sodium citrate**. **Phosphoric acid/phosphate ions** and **benzoic acid/benzoate** ions are also used as buffers.

Buffer Action

Here's How to Calculate the pH of a Buffer Solution

Calculating the **pH** of an acidic buffer isn't too tricky. You just need to know the K_a of the weak acid and the **concentrations** of the weak acid and its salt. Here's how to go about it:

> **Example:** A buffer solution contains 0.40 mol dm^{-3} methanoic acid, HCOOH, and 0.60 mol dm^{-3} sodium methanoate, HCOO$^-$Na$^+$.
> For methanoic acid, $K_a = 1.8 \times 10^{-4}$ mol dm^{-3}. What is the pH of this buffer?
>
> Firstly, write the expression for K_a of the weak acid:
>
> $$HCOOH_{(aq)} \rightleftharpoons H^+_{(aq)} + HCOO^-_{(aq)} \quad \Rightarrow \quad K_a = \frac{[H^+_{(aq)}] \times [HCOO^-_{(aq)}]}{[HCOOH_{(aq)}]}$$
>
> Remember — these all have to be equilibrium concentrations.
>
> Then rearrange the expression and stick in the data to calculate [H$^+_{(aq)}$]:
>
> $$[H^+_{(aq)}] = K_a \times \frac{[HCOOH_{(aq)}]}{[HCOO^-_{(aq)}]}$$
>
> $$\Rightarrow \quad [H^+_{(aq)}] = 1.8 \times 10^{-4} \times \frac{0.4}{0.6} = 1.20 \times 10^{-4} \text{ moldm}^{-3}$$
>
>
>
> Nobody's gonna change my pH.
>
> You have to make a **few assumptions** here:
> - HCOO$^-$Na$^+$ is fully dissociated, so assume that the equilibrium concentration of HCOO$^-$ is the same as the initial concentration of HCOO$^-$Na$^+$.
> - HCOOH is only slightly dissociated, so assume that its equilibrium concentration is the same as its initial concentration.
>
> Acids and alkalis didn't mess with Jeff after he became buffer.
>
> Finally, convert [H$^+_{(aq)}$] to pH: $\quad$ pH $= -\log_{10}[H^+_{(aq)}] = -\log_{10}(1.20 \times 10^{-4}) = \mathbf{3.92}$ $\quad$ And that's your answer.

Practice Questions

Q1 What's a buffer solution?

Q2 Describe how a mixture of ethanoic acid and sodium ethanoate act as a buffer.

Q3 Describe how the pH of the blood is buffered.

Exam Questions

1 A buffer solution contains 0.40 mol dm^{-3} benzoic acid, C$_6$H$_5$COOH, and 0.20 mol dm^{-3} sodium benzoate, C$_6$H$_5$COO$^-$Na$^+$. At 25 °C, K$_a$ for benzoic acid is 6.4×10^{-5} mol dm^{-3}.

   a) Calculate the pH of the buffer solution. $\hfill$ [3 marks]

   b) Explain the effect on the buffer of adding a small quantity of dilute sulfuric acid. $\hfill$ [3 marks]

2 A buffer was prepared by mixing solutions of butanoic acid, CH$_3$(CH$_2$)$_2$COOH, and sodium butanoate, CH$_3$(CH$_2$)$_2$COO$^-$Na$^+$, so that they had the same concentration.

   a) Write a balanced chemical equation to show butanoic acid acting as a weak acid. $\hfill$ [1 mark]

   b) Given that K$_a$ for butanoic acid is 1.5×10^{-5} mol dm^{-3}, calculate the pH of the buffer solution. $\hfill$ [3 marks]

Old buffers are often resistant to change...

So that's how buffers work. There's a pleasing simplicity and neatness about it that I find rather elegant.
Like a fine wine with a nose of berry and undertones of... OK, I'll shut up now.

pH Curves, Titrations and Indicators

If you add alkali to an acid, the pH changes in a squiggly sort of way.

Use **Titration** to Find the **Concentration** of an **Acid** or **Alkali**

Titrations let you find out **exactly** how much alkali is needed to **neutralise** a quantity of acid.

1) You measure out some **acid** of known concentration using a pipette and put it in a flask, along with some **appropriate indicator** (see below).

2) First do a rough titration — add the **alkali** to the acid using a **burette** fairly quickly to get an approximate idea of where the solution changes colour (the **end point**). Give the flask a regular **swirl**.

3) Now do an **accurate** titration. Run the alkali in to within 2 cm^3 of the end point, then add it **drop by drop**. If you don't notice exactly when the solution changes colour you've **overshot** and your result won't be accurate.

4) **Record** the amount of alkali needed to **neutralise** the acid. It's best to **repeat** this process a few times, making sure you get very similar answers each time (within about 0.2 cm^3 of each other).

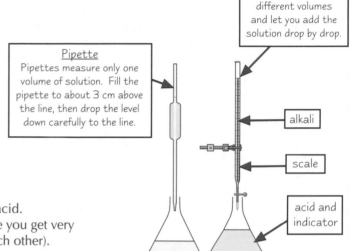

Burette
Burettes measure different volumes and let you add the solution drop by drop.

Pipette
Pipettes measure only one volume of solution. Fill the pipette to about 3 cm above the line, then drop the level down carefully to the line.

alkali

scale

acid and indicator

You can also find out how much **acid** is needed to neutralise a quantity of **alkali**. It's exactly the same as above, but you add **acid to alkali** instead.

pH Curves Plot pH Against Volume of Acid or Alkali Added

The graphs below show pH curves for the **different combinations** of **strong and weak** monobasic acids and alkalis.

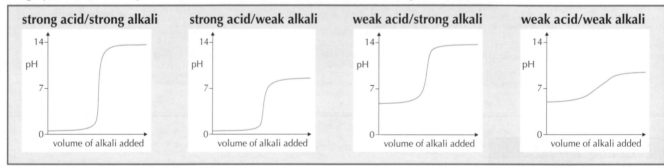

All the graphs apart from the weak acid/weak alkali graph have a bit that's almost vertical — this is the **equivalence point** or **end point**. At this point, a tiny amount of alkali causes a sudden, big change in pH — it's here that all the acid is just **neutralised**.

You don't get such a sharp change in a **weak acid/weak alkali** titration. The indicator colour changes **gradually** and it's tricky to see the exact end point. You're usually better off using a **pH meter** for this type of titration.

pH Curves can Help you Decide which Indicator to Use

Methyl orange and **phenolphthalein** are **indicators** that are often used for acid-base titrations. They each change colour over a **different pH range**:

Name of indicator	Colour at low pH	Approx. pH of colour change	Colour at high pH
Methyl orange	red	3.1 – 4.4	yellow
Phenolphthalein	colourless	8.3 – 10	pink

For a **strong acid/strong alkali** titration, you can use **either** of these indicators — there's a rapid pH change over the range for **both** indicators.

For a **strong acid/weak alkali** only **methyl orange** will do. The pH changes rapidly across the range for methyl orange, but not for phenolphthalein.

For a **weak acid/strong alkali**, **phenolphthalein** is the stuff to use. The pH changes rapidly over phenolphthalein's range, but not over methyl orange's.

For **weak acid/weak alkali** titrations there's no sharp pH change, so **neither** of these indicators will work.

pH Curves, Titrations and Indicators

You can Calculate **Concentrations** from Titration Data

If you're doing an acid-base titration using an **indicator**, you can use the **volume of acid** added when the **indicator changes colour** to calculate how much acid is needed to neutralise the alkali (or vice versa). Once you know this, you can use it to work out the **concentration** of the alkali.

If you use a **pH meter** rather than an indicator, you can draw a pH curve of the titration and use it to work out how much acid or base is needed for neutralisation. You do this by finding the **equivalence point** (the mid-point of the line of rapid pH change) and drawing a **vertical line downwards** until it meets the x-axis. The value at this point on the x-axis is the volume of acid or base needed.

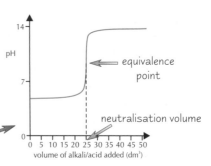

Here's an example of how you can use the neutralisation volume to calculate the concentration of the acid or base:

Example: 25 cm³ of 0.5 mol dm⁻³ HCl was needed to neutralise 35 cm³ of NaOH solution. Calculate the concentration of the sodium hydroxide solution.

First write a **balanced equation** and decide what you know and what you **need to know**:

$$HCl + NaOH \rightarrow NaCl + H_2O$$
$$25 \text{ cm}^3 \quad 35 \text{ cm}^3$$
$$0.5 \text{ mol dm}^{-3} \quad ?$$

Now work out how many **moles of HCl** you have:

$$\text{Number of moles of HCl} = \frac{\text{concentration} \times \text{volume (cm}^3)}{1000} = \frac{0.5 \times 25}{1000} = 0.0125 \text{ moles}$$

You should remember this formula from AS — you divide by 1000 to get the volume from cm³ to dm³.

From the equation, you know 1 mole of HCl neutralises 1 mole of NaOH. So 0.0125 moles of HCl must neutralise **0.0125** moles of NaOH.

Now it's a doddle to work out the **concentration of NaOH**.

This is just the formula above, rearranged.

$$\text{Concentration of NaOH}_{(aq)} = \frac{\text{moles of NaOH} \times 1000}{\text{volume (cm}^3)} = \frac{0.0125 \times 1000}{35} = \textbf{0.36 mol dm}^{-3}$$

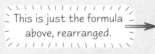

Q1 Sketch the pH curve for a weak acid/strong alkali titration.

Q2 What indicator should you use for a strong acid/weak alkali titration — methyl orange or phenolphthalein?

Q3 What colour is methyl orange at pH 2?

Exam Questions

1   1.0 mol dm⁻³ NaOH is added separately to 25 cm³ samples of 1.0 mol dm⁻³ nitric acid and 1.0 mol dm⁻³ ethanoic acid. Describe two differences between the pH curves of the titrations. [2 marks]

2   A sample of 0.350 mol dm⁻³ ethanoic acid was titrated against potassium hydroxide.

a)   Calculate the volume of 0.285 mol dm⁻³ potassium hydroxide required to just neutralise 25.0 cm³ of the ethanoic acid. [3 marks]

b)   From the table on the right, select the best indicator for this titration, and explain your choice. [2 marks]

Name of indicator	pH range
bromophenol blue	3.0 – 4.6
methyl red	4.2 – 6.3
bromothymol blue	6.0 – 7.6
thymol blue	8.0 – 9.6

Try learning this stuff drop by drop...

Titrations involve playing with big bits of glassware that you're told not to break as they're really expensive — so you instantly become really clumsy. If you manage not to smash the burette, you'll find it easier to get accurate results if you use a dilute acid or alkali — drops of dilute acid and alkali contain fewer particles so you're less likely to overshoot.

Neutralisation and Enthalpy

I love the smell of a new section in the morning, but this one kinda merges with the last one. Never mind. Before you continue with neutralisation I'm sure you remember enthalpies from AS... well here's a quick reminder just in case...

First — **A Few Definitions** You Should Remember

ΔH is the symbol for **enthalpy change**. Enthalpy change is the **heat** energy transferred in a reaction at **constant pressure**. $\Delta H^{\ominus}$ means that the enthalpy change was measured under **standard conditions** (**100 kPa and 298 K**).

Exothermic reactions have a **negative** ΔH value, because heat energy is given out.
Endothermic reactions have a **positive** ΔH value, because heat energy is absorbed.

You can work out ΔH from a calorimeter experiment, which basically involves measuring the temperature change in some water as a result of the reaction. The formulas you use are:

$$q = mc\Delta T$$
$$\Delta H = -mc\Delta T$$

where, q = enthalpy change of the water (in kJ)
ΔH = enthalpy change of the reactants (in kJ)
m = mass of the water (in kg)
c = specific heat capacity (for water it's 4.18 kJ kg^{-1} K^{-1})
ΔT = the change in temperature of the water (K)

The change of sign is because ΔH is looking at the reactants (the water in this case), not the surroundings.

Learn These Definitions for the Different types of **Enthalpy Changes**

There's lots of different enthalpy terms you need to **know** on the next few pages.
So spend some time looking at them now and it'll make everything coming up a bit easier.

Enthalpy change of formation, ΔH_f, is the enthalpy change when **1 mole** of a **compound** is formed from its **elements** in their standard states under standard conditions, e.g. $2C_{(s)} + 3H_{2(g)} + \frac{1}{2}O_{2(g)} \rightarrow C_2H_5OH_{(l)}$
It's used on pages 72 and 73.

The enthalpy change of neutralisation ($\Delta H_{neutralisation}$) is the enthalpy change when **1 mole** of water is formed by the reaction between an acid and a base under **standard conditions**. It's an **exothermic** process.
It's used on page 71

Enthalpy change of atomisation of an element, ΔH_{at}, is the enthalpy change when **1 mole** of **gaseous atoms** is formed from an element in its **standard state**, e.g. $\frac{1}{2}Cl_{2(g)} \rightarrow Cl_{(g)}$
It's used on pages 72 and 73.

Enthalpy change of atomisation of a compound, ΔH_{at}, is the enthalpy change when **1 mole** of **gaseous atoms** is formed from a compound in its **standard state**, e.g. $NaCl_{(s)} \rightarrow Na_{(g)} + Cl_{(g)}$
It's used on pages 72 and 73.

The first ionisation enthalpy, ΔH_{ie1}, is the enthalpy change when **1 mole** of gaseous 1+ ions is formed from **1 mole** of gaseous atoms, e.g. $Mg_{(g)} \rightarrow Mg^+_{(g)} + e^-$
It's used on pages 72 and 73.

The second ionisation enthalpy, ΔH_{ie2}, is the enthalpy change when **1 mole** of gaseous 2+ ions is formed from **1 mole** of gaseous 1+ ions, e.g. $Mg^+_{(g)} \rightarrow Mg^{2+}_{(g)} + e^-$
It's used on page 73.

First electron affinity, ΔH_{e1}, is the enthalpy change when **1 mole** of gaseous 1– ions is made from **1 mole** of gaseous **atoms**, e.g. $O_{(g)} + e^- \rightarrow O^-_{(g)}$
It's used on pages 72 and 73.

Second electron affinity, ΔH_{e2}, is the enthalpy change when **1 mole** of gaseous 2– ions is made from **1 mole** of gaseous 1– ions, e.g. $O^-_{(g)} + e^- \rightarrow O^{2-}_{(g)}$
It's used on page 73.

The enthalpy change of hydration, ΔH_{hyd}, is the enthalpy change when **1 mole** of **aqueous ions** is formed from **gaseous ions**, e.g. $Na^+_{(g)} \rightarrow Na^+_{(aq)}$
It's used on page 74.

The enthalpy change of solution, $\Delta H_{solution}$, is the enthalpy change when **1 mole** of **solute** is dissolved in **sufficient solvent** that no further enthalpy change occurs on further dilution, e.g. $NaCl_{(s)} \rightarrow NaCl_{(aq)}$
It's used on page 74.

Neutralisation and Enthalpy

The *Enthalpy* of *Neutralisation* can be *Calculated* From *Experimental Data*

Neutralisation always involves the reaction of **hydrogen ions** (H^+) with **hydroxide ions** (OH^-) to make **water** (H_2O). The change in energy when this happens is called the **enthalpy change of neutralisation** ($\Delta H_{neutralisation}$).

Example: 150 ml of hydrochloric acid (concentration 0.25 mol dm^{-3}) was neutralised by 150 ml of potassium hydroxide. The temperature increased by 1.71 °C. Calculate $\Delta H_{neutralisation}$.

1 The first thing to do is calculate the enthalpy change, ΔH, by plugging the numbers into $\Delta H = -mc\Delta T$.
$\Delta H = -mc\Delta T = -0.3 \times 4.18 \times 1.71 = -2.144$ kJ
The 0.3 comes from the mass of the solution — assume the solution has the same specific heat capacity and density (1 g/ml) as water.
But this is only the ΔH and **not** the $\Delta H_{neutralisation}$.

2 To find the enthalpy of **neutralisation**, you need to calculate ΔH for **1 mole** of H_2O produced. To find out how many moles of water the reaction makes you can look at the **equation** for it.
$$HCl + KOH \rightarrow KCl + H_2O$$

3 The number of moles of H_2O **made** is **equal** to the number of moles of acid used. And to work that out you can look back at the question.
150 ml of 0.25 mol dm^{-3} hydrochloric acid has $0.25 \times 0.15 = 0.0375$ moles
So, to make **1 mole** of H_2O: *Don't forget to convert ml to dm^3*
$$\Delta H_{neutralisation} = -2.144 \div 0.0375 = -57.2 \text{ kJ mol}^{-1}$$
The minus sign shows the reaction is exothermic

Weirdly, the value for **any strong acid** is about **–57 kJ mol^{-1}**. This is because all strong acids and bases completely ionise in water so essentially the reaction for each of them is the same ($H^+ + OH^- \rightarrow H_2O$).

For **weaker acids** and **alkalis** the value is **less negative** because energy is used to fully dissociate the acid or alkali meaning there's less energy released.

Practice Questions

Q1 What are the units of any enthalpy change?

Q2 What are standard conditions?

Q3 What is defined as "the enthalpy change when 1 mole of gaseous atoms is formed from a compound in its standard state"?

Q4 Why is the enthalpy change of neutralisation the same for all strong acids?

Exam Questions

1 In an experiment, 200 ml of 2.75 mol dm^{-3} H_2SO_4 was reacted with 200 ml of NaOH solution. The temperature rose by 38 °C. Assume the density of the resulting solution is 1 g ml^{-1}.
a) Write an equation for the reaction. [1 mark]
b) The specific heat capacity of water is 4.18 kJ kg^{-1} K^{-1}.
   Use this to calculate the enthalpy change of neutralisation for this reaction. [3 marks]

2 100 ml of 1 mol dm^{-3} HCl was added to 100 ml of 4 mol dm^{-3} KOH solution. The experiment was then repeated, replacing the acid with 100 ml of 1 mol dm^{-3} H_2SO_4 and again with 100 ml of 1 mol dm^{-3} H_3PO_4. Assume all three acids are equally strong.
a) Write equations for the three reactions. [3 marks]
b) The enthalpy change of neutralisation for any strong acid is about –57 kJ mol^{-1}.
   Explain which of the three experiments would give the largest temperature rise. [2 marks]

3 100 ml of a solution of hydrochloric acid with a concentration of X mol dm^{-3} was reacted with 100 ml of a solution of sodium hydroxide. The change in temperature was 3.4 K. The enthalpy change of neutralisation was –57 kJ mol^{-1}. Calculate the value of X. [4 marks]

My eyes, MY EYES — the definitions make them hurt...

The worst thing about this page is all the definitions. What's worse is it's not enough to just have a vague idea what each one means; you have to know the ins and outs — like whether it applies to gases, or to elements in their standard states. If you've forgotten, standard conditions are 298 K (otherwise known as 25 °C) and 100 kPa pressure.

Lattice Enthalpy and Born-Haber Cycles

On this page you can learn about lattice enthalpy, not lettuce enthalpy, which is the enthalpy change when 1 mole consumes salad from a veggie patch. Bu–dum cha... (that was meant to be a drum — work with me here).

Lattice Enthalpy is a Measure of Ionic Bond Strength

Remember how **ionic compounds** form regular structures called **giant ionic lattices** — and how the positive and negative ions are held together by **electrostatic attraction**. Well, when **gaseous ions** combine to make a solid lattice, energy is given out — this is called the **lattice enthalpy**. It's quite handy as it tells you how **strong** the ionic bonding is.

Here's the definition of **standard lattice enthalpy** that you need to know:

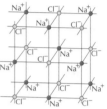

Part of the sodium chloride lattice

> The **standard lattice enthalpy**, $\Delta H^{\ominus}_{latt}$, is the enthalpy change when **1 mole** of a **solid ionic compound** is formed from its **gaseous ions** under standard conditions.
> It's a measure of **ionic bond strength**.

For example: $Na^+_{(g)} + Cl^-_{(g)} \rightarrow NaCl_{(s)}$ $\Delta H^{\ominus} = -787$ kJmol^{-1}
$Mg^{2+}_{(g)} + O^{2-}_{(g)} \rightarrow MgO_{(s)}$ $\Delta H^{\ominus} = -3791$ kJmol^{-1}

The **more negative** the lattice enthalpy, the **stronger** the bonding. So out of NaCl and MgO, **MgO** has stronger bonding.

Ionic Charge and Size Affects Lattice Enthalpy

The **higher the charge** on the ions, the **more energy** is released when an ionic lattice forms. More energy released means that the lattice enthalpy will be **more negative**. So the lattice enthalpies for compounds with **2+ or 2– ions** (e.g. Mg^{2+} or S^{2-}) are **more negative** than those with **1+ or 1– ions** (e.g. Na^+ or Cl^-).

For example, the lattice enthalpy of NaCl is only –787 kJ mol^{-1}, but the lattice enthalpy of $MgCl_2$ is –2526 kJ mol^{-1}. MgS has an even higher lattice enthalpy (–3299 kJ mol^{-1}) because both magnesium and sulfur ions have double charges.

Magnesium oxide has a **very exothermic** lattice enthalpy too, which means it is very resistant to heat. This makes it great as a **lining in furnaces**.

> The **smaller the ionic radii** of the ions involved, the **more exothermic** (more negative) the **lattice enthalpy**. Smaller ions attract **more strongly** because their **charge density** is higher.

Born-Haber Cycles can be Used to Calculate Lattice Enthalpies

Hess's law says that the **total enthalpy change** of a reaction is always the **same**, no matter which route is taken.

A **lattice enthalpy** is just the **enthalpy change** when a mole of a **solid ionic compound** is formed from **gaseous ions**. You can't calculate a lattice enthalpy **directly**, so you have to use a **Born-Haber cycle** to figure out what the enthalpy change would be if you took **another**, less direct, **route**.

Here's how to draw a Born-Haber cycle for calculating the lattice enthalpy of **NaCl**:

$Na^+_{(g)} + e^- + Cl_{(g)}$

3 The electron affinity goes up here...

First ionisation energy of sodium (+496 kJ mol^{-1}) ΔH4

$Na_{(g)} + Cl_{(g)}$ (gaseous atoms)

First electron affinity of chlorine (–349 kJ mol^{-1}) ΔH5

2 Then put the enthalpies of atomisation and ionisation above this.

Atomisation energy of sodium (+107 kJ mol^{-1}) ΔH3

$Na_{(s)} + Cl_{(g)}$

$Na^+_{(g)} + Cl^-_{(g)}$

Atomisation energy of chlorine (+122 kJ mol^{-1}) ΔH2

$Na_{(s)} + \frac{1}{2}Cl_{2(g)}$ (standard states)

Lattice enthalpy of sodium chloride ΔH6

1 Start with the enthalpy of formation here.

Enthalpy of formation of sodium chloride (–411 kJ mol^{-1}) ΔH1

$NaCl_{(s)}$ (ionic lattice)

4 ...and lattice enthalpy goes down here.

There are **two routes** you can follow to get from the elements in their **standard states** to the **ionic lattice**. The green arrow shows the **direct route** and the purple arrows show the **indirect route**. The enthalpy change for each is the **same**.

From Hess's law: $\Delta H6 = -\Delta H5 - \Delta H4 - \Delta H3 - \Delta H2 + \Delta H1$
$= -(-349) - (+496) - (+107) - (+122) + (-411) = \mathbf{-787}$ **kJ mol**$^{-1}$

You need a minus sign if you go the wrong way along an arrow.

Lattice Enthalpy and Born-Haber Cycles

Calculations involving Group 2 Elements are a Bit Different

Born-Haber cycles for compounds containing **Group 2 elements** have a few **changes** from the one on the previous page. Make sure you understand what's going on so you can handle whatever compound they throw at you.

Here's the Born-Haber cycle for calculating the lattice enthalpy of **magnesium chloride** ($MgCl_2$).

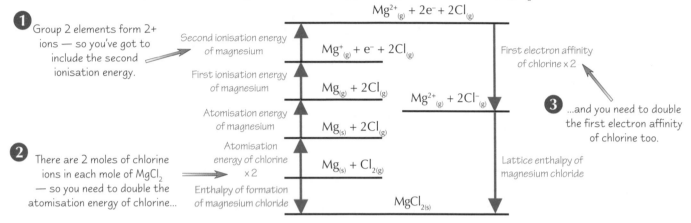

① Group 2 elements form 2+ ions — so you've got to include the second ionisation energy.

② There are 2 moles of chlorine ions in each mole of $MgCl_2$ — so you need to double the atomisation energy of chlorine...

③ ...and you need to double the first electron affinity of chlorine too.

Practice Questions

Q1 What is the definition of standard lattice enthalpy?

Q2 What does a very negative lattice enthalpy mean?

Q3 Why does magnesium chloride have a more negative lattice enthalpy than sodium chloride?

Q4 Why would lithium chloride have a more negative lattice enthalpy than sodium chloride?

Exam Questions

1   Using the data below:
   a)   Construct a Born-Haber cycle for potassium bromide (KBr).   [4 marks]
   b)   Use your Born-Haber cycle to calculate the lattice enthalpy of potassium bromide.   [3 marks]

   $\Delta H_f^\ominus$ [potassium bromide] $= -394$ kJ mol^{-1} $\Delta H_{at}^\ominus$ [bromine] $= +112$ kJ mol^{-1} $\Delta H_{at}^\ominus$ [potassium] $= +89$ kJ mol^{-1}
   $\Delta H_{ie1}^\ominus$ [potassium] $= +419$ kJ mol^{-1} $\Delta H_{e1}^\ominus$ [bromine] $= -325$ kJ mol^{-1}

2   Using the data below:
   a)   Construct a Born-Haber cycle for aluminium chloride ($AlCl_3$).   [5 marks]
   b)   Use your cycle to calculate the lattice enthalpy of aluminium chloride.   [3 marks]

   $\Delta H_f^\ominus$ [aluminium chloride] $= -706$ kJ mol^{-1} $\Delta H_{at}^\ominus$ [chlorine] $= +122$ kJ mol^{-1} $\Delta H_{at}^\ominus$ [aluminium] $= +326$ kJ mol^{-1}
   $\Delta H_{e1}^\ominus$ [chlorine] $= -349$ kJ mol^{-1} $\Delta H_{ie1}^\ominus$ [aluminium] $= +578$ kJ mol^{-1} $\Delta H_{ie2}^\ominus$ [aluminium] $= +1817$ kJ mol^{-1}
   $\Delta H_{ie3}^\ominus$ [aluminium] $= +2745$ kJ mol^{-1}

3   Using the data below:
   a)   Construct a Born-Haber cycle for aluminium oxide (Al_2O_3).   [5 marks]
   b)   Use your cycle to calculate the lattice enthalpy of aluminium oxide.   [3 marks]

   $\Delta H_f^\ominus$ [aluminium oxide] $= -1676$ kJ mol^{-1} $\Delta H_{at}^\ominus$ [oxygen] $= +249$ kJ mol^{-1} $\Delta H_{at}^\ominus$ [aluminium] $= +326$ kJ mol^{-1}
   $\Delta H_{ie1}^\ominus$ [aluminium] $= +578$ kJ mol^{-1} $\Delta H_{ie2}^\ominus$ [aluminium] $= +1817$ kJ mol^{-1} $\Delta H_{ie3}^\ominus$ [aluminium] $= +2745$ kJ mol^{-1}
   $\Delta H_{e1}^\ominus$ [oxygen] $= -141$ kJ mol^{-1} $\Delta H_{e2}^\ominus$ [oxygen] $= +844$ kJ mol^{-1}

Using Born-Haber cycles — it's just like riding a bike...

All this energy going in and out can get a bit confusing. Remember these simple rules: 1) It takes energy to break bonds, but energy is given out when bonds are made. 2) A negative ΔH means energy is given out (it's exothermic). 3) A positive ΔH means energy is taken in (it's endothermic). 4) Never return to a firework once lit.

Enthalpies of Solution

Once you know what's happening when you stir sugar into your tea, your cuppa'll be twice as enjoyable.

Dissolving Involves Enthalpy Changes

When a solid **ionic lattice** dissolves in water these **two** things happen:

1) The bonds between the ions **break** — this is **endothermic**. The enthalpy change is the **opposite** of the **lattice enthalpy**.

2) Bonds between the ions and the water are **made** — this is **exothermic**.
   The enthalpy change here is called the **enthalpy change of hydration**.

3) The **enthalpy change of solution** is the overall effect on the enthalpy of these two things.

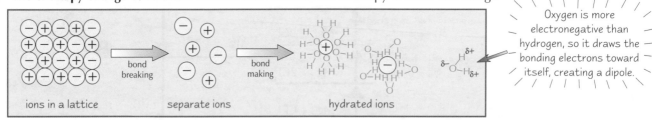

ions in a lattice   separate ions   hydrated ions

Oxygen is more electronegative than hydrogen, so it draws the bonding electrons toward itself, creating a dipole.

Substances generally **only** dissolve if the energy released is roughly the same, or **greater than** the energy taken in.

But enthalpy change isn't the only thing that decides if something will dissolve or not — **entropy change** is important too.

A reaction or state change is **more likely** when there is a **positive** entropy change. Dissolving normally causes an **increase** in entropy. But for **small**, **highly charged ions** there may be a **decrease** because when water molecules surround the ions, it makes things **more orderly**. The entropy changes are usually **pretty small** but they can sometimes **make the difference** between something being soluble or insoluble.

Entropy is a measure of disorder. It's covered in more detail on pages 76-77.

Enthalpy Change of Solution can be Calculated

You can work it out using a Born-Haber cycle — but one drawn a bit differently from those on page 72.

You just need to know the **lattice enthalpy** of the compound and the enthalpies of **hydration of the ions**.

Here's how to draw the enthalpy cycle for working out the **enthalpy change of solution** for **sodium chloride**.

1 Put the ionic lattice and the dissolved ions on the top — connect them by the enthalpy change of solution. This is the direct route.

2 Connect the ionic lattice to the gaseous ions by the reverse of the lattice enthalpy.
The breakdown of the lattice has the opposite enthalpy change to the formation of the lattice.

$$NaCl_{(s)} \xrightarrow{\text{Enthalpy change of solution} \atop \Delta H3} Na^+_{(aq)} + Cl^-_{(aq)}$$

– (lattice enthalpy) –(–787 kJ mol⁻¹) $\Delta H1$

$\Delta H2$ Enthalpy of hydration of Na⁺(g)(–406 kJ mol⁻¹)
Enthalpy of hydration of Cl⁻(g)(–364 kJ mol⁻¹)

$Na^+_{(g)} + Cl^-_{(g)}$

3 Connect the gaseous ions to the dissolved ions by the hydration enthalpies of **each** ion. This completes the indirect route.

From Hess's law: $\Delta H3 = \Delta H1 + \Delta H2 = +787 + (-406 + -364) = $ **+17 kJ mol⁻¹**

The enthalpy change of solution is **slightly endothermic**, but this is compensated for by a small increase in **entropy**, so sodium chloride still dissolves in water.

And here's another. This one's for working out the **enthalpy change of solution** for **silver chloride**.

$$AgCl_{(s)} \xrightarrow{\text{Enthalpy change of solution} \atop \Delta H3} Ag^+_{(aq)} + Cl^-_{(aq)}$$

– (lattice enthalpy) –(–905 kJ mol⁻¹) $\Delta H1$

$\Delta H2$ Enthalpy of hydration of Ag⁺(g)(–464 kJ mol⁻¹)
Enthalpy of hydration of Cl⁻(g)(–364 kJ mol⁻¹)

$Ag^+_{(g)} + Cl^-_{(g)}$

From Hess's law: $\Delta H3 = \Delta H1 + \Delta H2 = +905 + (-464 + -364) = $ **+77 kJ mol⁻¹**

This is much **more endothermic** than the enthalpy change of solution for sodium chloride. There is an **increase in entropy** again, but it's pretty small and not enough to make a difference — so silver chloride is **insoluble** in water.

Enthalpies of Solution

Ionic Charge and Ionic Radius Affect the Enthalpy of Hydration

The **two** things that can affect the lattice enthalpy (see page 72) can also affect the enthalpy of hydration.
They are the **size** and the **charge** of the ions.

Ions with a greater charge have a greater enthalpy of hydration.

Ions with a **higher charge** are better at **attracting** water molecules than those with lower charges. **More energy** is released when the bonds are **made** giving them a **more exothermic** enthalpy of hydration.

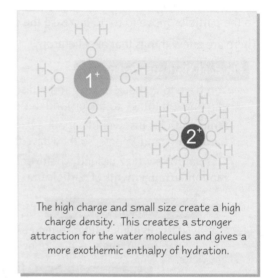

Smaller ions have a greater enthalpy of hydration.

Smaller ions have a **higher** charge density than bigger ions. They **attract** the water molecules **better** and have a **more exothermic** enthalpy of hydration.

The high charge and small size create a high charge density. This creates a stronger attraction for the water molecules and gives a more exothermic enthalpy of hydration.

E.g. a magnesium ion is smaller and more charged than a sodium ion, which gives it a much bigger enthalpy of hydration.
$Mg^{2+} = -1927$ kJ mol^{-1}, $Na^+ = -406$ kJ mol^{-1}

Practice Questions

Q1 What are the steps in producing a solution from a crystal?

Q2 Sketch a Born-Haber cycle to calculate the enthalpy change of solution of potassium bromide.

Q3 What factors affect the enthalpy of hydration of an ion?

Q4 Do soluble substances have exo- or endothermic enthalpies of solution in general?

Exam Questions

1   a) Draw an enthalpy cycle for the enthalpy change of solution of $AgF_{(s)}$. Label each enthalpy change.   [4 marks]
    b) Calculate the enthalpy change of solution for AgF from the following data: [2 marks]

$\Delta H^{\ominus}_{latt} [AgF_{(s)}] = -960$ kJ mol^{-1}, $\Delta H^{\ominus}_{hyd} [Ag^{+}_{(g)}] = -464$ kJ mol^{-1}, $\Delta H^{\ominus}_{hyd} [F^{-}_{(g)}] = -506$ kJ mol^{-1}.

2   a) Draw an enthalpy cycle for the enthalpy change of solution of $SrF_{2(s)}$. Label each enthalpy change.   [4 marks]
    b) Calculate the enthalpy change of solution for SrF_2 from the following data: [2 marks]

$\Delta H^{\ominus}_{latt} [SrF_{2(s)}] = -2492$ kJ mol^{-1}, $\Delta H^{\ominus}_{hyd} [Sr^{2+}_{(g)}] = -1480$ kJ mol^{-1}, $\Delta H^{\ominus}_{hyd} [F^{-}_{(g)}] = -506$ kJ mol^{-1}.

3   Show that the enthalpy change of solution for $MgCl_{2(s)}$ is -122 kJ mol^{-1}, given that: [3 marks]

$\Delta H^{\ominus}_{latt} [MgCl_{2(s)}] = -2526$ kJ mol^{-1}, $\Delta H^{\ominus}_{hyd} [Mg^{2+}_{(g)}] = -1920$ kJ mol^{-1}, $\Delta H^{\ominus}_{hyd} [Cl^{-}_{(g)}] = -364$ kJ mol^{-1}.

Enthalpy change of solution of the Wicked Witch of the West = 8745 kJ mol^{-1}...

Compared to the ones on page 72, these enthalpy cycles are an absolute breeze. You've got to make sure the definitions are firmly fixed in your mind though. Don't forget that a positive enthalpy change doesn't mean the stuff definitely won't dissolve — there might be an entropy change that'll make up for it. The delights of entropy are on the next two pages.

Free-Energy Change and Entropy Change

Free energy — I could do with a bit of that. My gas bill is astronomical.

Entropy *Tells you How Much* Disorder *there is*

Entropy is a measure of the **number of ways** that **particles** can be **arranged** and the **number of ways** that the **energy** can be shared out between the particles.

Substances really **like** disorder, they're actually more **energetically stable** when there's more disorder. So the particles move to try to **increase the entropy**.

There are a few things that affect entropy:

Physical State affects Entropy

You have to go back to the good old **solid-liquid-gas** particle explanation thingy to understand this.

Solid particles just wobble about a fixed point — there's **hardly any** randomness, so they have the **lowest entropy**.

Gas particles whizz around wherever they like. They've got the most **random arrangements** of particles, so they have the **highest entropy**.

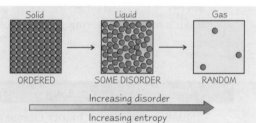

Solid — ORDERED   Liquid — SOME DISORDER   Gas — RANDOM

Increasing disorder
Increasing entropy

Dissolving affects Entropy

Dissolving a solid also increases its entropy — dissolved particles can **move freely** as they're no longer held in one place.

More Particles means More Entropy

It makes sense — the more particles you've got, the **more ways** they and their energy can be **arranged** — so in a reaction like $N_2O_{4(g)} \rightarrow 2NO_{2(g)}$, entropy increases because the **number of moles** increases.

Reactions Won't *Happen Unless the* Total Entropy Change *is* Positive

During a reaction, there's an entropy change between the **reactants and products** — the entropy change of the **system**. The entropy of the **surroundings** changes too (because **energy** is transferred to or from the system). The **TOTAL entropy change** is the sum of the entropy changes of the **system** and the **surroundings**.

The units of entropy are $J\ K^{-1}\ mol^{-1}$

$$\Delta S_{total} = \Delta S_{system} + \Delta S_{surroundings}$$

This equation isn't much use unless you know ΔS_{system} and $\Delta S_{surroundings}$. Luckily, there are formulas for them too:

This is just the difference between the entropies of the reactants and products. $\longrightarrow$ $$\Delta S_{system} = S_{products} - S_{reactants}$$ and $$\Delta S_{surroundings} = -\frac{\Delta H}{T}$$ $\longleftarrow$ *ΔH = enthalpy change (in $J\ mol^{-1}$) T = temperature (in K)*

Example: Calculate the total entropy change for the reaction of ammonia and hydrogen chloride under standard conditions.

$$NH_{3(g)} + HCl_{(g)} \rightarrow NH_4Cl_{(s)} \qquad \Delta H^{\ominus} = -315\ kJ\ mol^{-1}\ (at\ 298\ K)$$

$$S^{\ominus}[NH_{3(g)}] = 192.3\ J\ K^{-1}\ mol^{-1},\ S^{\ominus}[HCl_{(g)}] = 186.8\ J\ K^{-1}\ mol^{-1},\ S^{\ominus}[NH_4Cl_{(s)}] = 94.6\ J\ K^{-1}\ mol^{-1}$$

First find the entropy change of the **system**:

$$\Delta S^{\ominus}_{system} = S^{\ominus}_{products} - S^{\ominus}_{reactants} = 94.6 - (192.3 + 186.8) = -284.5\ J\ K^{-1}\ mol^{-1}$$

This shows a negative change in entropy. It's not surprising as 2 moles of gas have combined to form 1 mole of solid.

Now find the entropy change of the **surroundings**:

$$\Delta H^{\ominus} = -315\ kJ\ mol^{-1} = -315 \times 10^3\ J\ mol^{-1}$$ *Put $\Delta H^{\ominus}$ in the right units.*

$$\Delta S^{\ominus}_{surroundings} = -\frac{\Delta H^{\ominus}}{T} = \frac{-(-315 \times 10^3)}{298} = +1057\ J\ K^{-1}\ mol^{-1}$$

Finally you can find the **total** entropy

$$\Delta S^{\ominus}_{total} = \Delta S^{\ominus}_{system} + \Delta S^{\ominus}_{surroundings} = -284.5 + (+1057) = +772.5\ J\ K^{-1}\ mol^{-1}$$

*The total entropy has **increased**. The entropy increase in the surroundings was big enough to make up for the entropy decrease in the system.*

Free-Energy Change and Entropy Change

Entropy Increase May Explain Spontaneous Endothermic Reactions

A spontaneous (or feasible) change is one that'll **just happen** by itself — you don't need to give it energy.

But the weird thing is, some **endothermic** reactions are **spontaneous**. You'd normally have to supply **energy** to make an endothermic reaction happen, but if the **entropy** increases enough, the reaction will happen by itself.

1) Water evaporates at room temperature. This change needs **energy** to break the bonds between the molecules — but because it's **changing state** (from a liquid to a gas), the entropy increases.

2) The reaction of sodium hydrogencarbonate with hydrochloric acid is a **spontaneous endothermic reaction**. Again there's an **increase in entropy**.

$$NaHCO_{3(s)} + H^+_{(aq)} \rightarrow Na^+_{(aq)} + CO_{2(g)} + H_2O_{(l)}$$

1 mole solid   1 mole   1 mole   1 mole gas   1 mole liquid

aqueous ions   aqueous ions

The product has more particles — and gases and liquids have more entropy than solids too.

For Spontaneous Reactions ΔG must be Negative or Zero

The tendency of a process to take place is dependent on three things — the **entropy**, *ΔS*, the **enthalpy**, *ΔH*, and the **temperature**, *T*. When you put all these things **together** you get the **free energy change**, *ΔG*, and it tells you if a reaction is **feasible** or not.

Of course, there's a formula for it:

Even if ΔG shows that a reaction is theoretically feasible, it might have a really high activation energy and be so slow that you wouldn't notice it happening at all.

$$\Delta G = \Delta H - T\Delta S_{system}$$

$ΔH$ = enthalpy change (in J mol⁻¹)
T = temperature (in K)

Example: Calculate the free energy change for the following reaction at 298 K.

$$MgCO_{3(g)} \rightarrow MgO_{(s)} + CO_{2(g)} \qquad \Delta H^{\ominus} = +117\,000 \text{ J mol}^{-1}, \ \Delta S^{\ominus}_{system} = +175 \text{ J mol}^{-1}$$

$$\Delta G = \Delta H - T\Delta S_{system} = +117\,000 - (298 \times (+175)) = +64\,850 \text{ J mol}^{-1}$$

ΔG is positive — so the reaction isn't feasible at this temperature.

Practice Questions

Q1 What does the term 'entropy' mean?

Q2 In each of the following pairs choose the one with the greater entropy value.
a) 1 mole of $NaCl_{(aq)}$ and 1 mole of $NaCl_{(s)}$ b) 1 mole of $Br_{2(l)}$ and 1 mole of $Br_{2(g)}$
c) 1 mole of $Br_{2(g)}$ and 2 moles of $Br_{2(g)}$

Q3 Write down the formulas for:
a) total entropy change,   b) entropy change of the surroundings,   c) free energy change.

Exam Questions

1 a) Based on just the equation, predict whether the reaction below
   is likely to be spontaneous. Give a reason for your answer.
   $$Mg_{(s)} + \tfrac{1}{2}O_{2(g)} \rightarrow MgO_{(s)}$$
   [2 marks]

   b) Use the data on the right to calculate the entropy change for
   the system above.
   [3 marks]

   c) Does the result of the calculation indicate that the reaction
   will be spontaneous? Give a reason for your answer.
   [2 marks]

Substance	Entropy — standard conditions (J K⁻¹ mol⁻¹)
$Mg_{(s)}$	32.7
$\frac{1}{2}O_{2(g)}$	102.5
$MgO_{(s)}$	26.9

2 $S^{\ominus}[H_2O_{(l)}] = 70$ J K⁻¹ mol⁻¹, $S^{\ominus}[H_2O_{(s)}] = 48$ J K⁻¹ mol⁻¹, $\Delta H^{\ominus} = -6$ kJ mol⁻¹
   For the reaction $H_2O_{(l)} \rightarrow H_2O_{(s)}$:
   a) Calculate the total entropy change at   i) 250 K   ii) 300 K   [5 marks]
   b) Will this reaction be spontaneous at 250 K or 300 K? Explain your answer.   [2 marks]

Being neat and tidy is against the laws of nature...

There's a scary amount of scary looking formulas on these pages. They aren't too hard to use, but watch out for your units. Make sure the temperature's in kelvin — if you're given one in °C, you need to add 273 to change it to kelvin. And check that all your enthalpy and entropy values involve joules, not kilojoules (so J mol⁻¹, not kJ mol⁻¹, etc.).

Redox Equations

And now for something a bit different. Read on to learn more about redox...

If Electrons are Transferred, it's a **Redox Reaction**

1) A **loss** of electrons is called **oxidation**. A **gain** of electrons is called **reduction**.
2) Reduction and oxidation happen **simultaneously** — hence the term **"redox"** reaction.
3) An **oxidising agent accepts** electrons and gets reduced.
4) A **reducing agent donates** electrons and gets oxidised.

I couldn't find a red ox, so you'll have to make do with a multicoloured donkey instead.

$$\overset{-e^-}{\overbrace{Na + \tfrac{1}{2}Cl_2 \longrightarrow \underset{+e^-}{Na^+Cl^-}}}$$

Na is oxidised
Cl is reduced

Sometimes it's Easier to Talk About **Oxidation Numbers**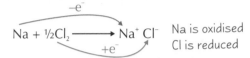

(It's also called oxidation <u>state</u>.)

There are lots of rules. Take a deep breath...

1) All atoms are treated as **ions** for this, even if they're covalently bonded.

2) Uncombined **elements** have an oxidation number of **0**.

3) Elements just bonded to **identical atoms**, like O_2 and H_2, also have an oxidation number of **0**.

4) The oxidation number of a simple **monatomic ion**, e.g. Na^+, is the same as its **charge**.

5) In **compounds** or **compound ions**, the **overall oxidation number** is just the ion charge.

SO_4^{2-} — overall oxidation number = –2,
oxidation number of O = –2 (total = –8), ◄—— Within an ion, the most electronegative element has a negative oxidation number (equal to its ionic charge). Other elements have more positive oxidation numbers.
so oxidation number of S = +6

6) The sum of the oxidation numbers for a **neutral compound** is 0.

Fe_2O_3 — overall oxidation number = 0, oxidation number of O = –2
(total = –6), so oxidation number of **Fe = +3**

There are a few exceptions to these but you don't need to know about them.

7) Combined **oxygen** is –2 (except in O_2 where it's 0). ◄——

8) Combined **hydrogen** is +1 (except in H_2 where it's 0).

If you see **Roman numerals** in a chemical name, it's an **oxidation number**
— it applies to the atom or group immediately before it.
E.g. copper has oxidation number **2** in **copper(II) sulfate**,
and manganese has oxidation number **7** in a **manganate(VII) ion** (MnO_4^-).

Oxidation States go **Up** or **Down** as Electrons are **Lost** or **Gained**

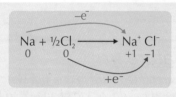

Oxidation No.

$$\overset{-e^-}{\overbrace{Na + \tfrac{1}{2}Cl_2 \longrightarrow \underset{+1 \quad -1}{Na^+Cl^-}}}$$
$$\underset{+e^-}{}$$

0   0   +1 –1

1) The oxidation state for an atom will **increase by 1** for each **electron lost**.

2) The oxidation state will **decrease by 1** for each **electron gained**.

Redox Equations

You can Separate Redox Reactions into **Half-Reactions**

1) A redox reaction is made up of an **oxidation half-reaction** and a **reduction half-reaction**.
2) You can write an **ionic half-equation** for each of these **half-reactions**.

> **Example:** **Zinc metal** displaces **silver ions** from silver nitrate solution to form **zinc nitrate** and a deposit of **silver metal**.
>
> | | |
> |---|---|
> | The zinc atoms each lose 2 electrons (oxidation) | $Zn_{(s)} \rightarrow Zn^{2+}_{(aq)} + 2e^-$ |
> | The silver ions each gain 1 electron (reduction) | $Ag^+_{(aq)} + e^- \rightarrow Ag_{(s)}$ |
>
> **Two silver ions** are needed to accept the **two electrons** released by each zinc atom.
> So you need to double the silver half-equation before the two half-equations can be combined: $\boxed{2Ag^+_{(aq)} + 2e^- \rightarrow 2Ag_{(s)}}$
>
> Now the number of electrons lost and gained
> balance, so the half-equations can be combined: $\boxed{Zn_{(s)} + 2Ag^+_{(aq)} \rightarrow Zn^{2+}_{(aq)} + 2Ag_{(s)}}$ — Electrons aren't included in the full equation.

H⁺ Ions May be Needed to **Reduce** Some **Oxidising Agents**

1) **Manganate(VII) ions**, MnO_4^-, contain Mn with an oxidation number of **+7**. When these ions are **reduced** they gain five electrons to become Mn^{2+} ions, with an oxidation number of **+2**.
2) In a **+2 state**, Mn can exist as simple $Mn^{2+}_{(aq)}$ ions. But in a **+7 state**, Mn has to combine with **oxygen** to form MnO_4^- ions, as $Mn^{7+}_{(aq)}$ ions wouldn't be stable.
3) MnO_4^- ions are good **oxidising agents**. The trouble is, when they get reduced to Mn^{2+} the four O^{2-} ions have to go somewhere. To solve this problem, **H⁺ ions** are added. The $4O^{2-}$ can now react with $8H^+$ to form $4H_2O$. This is why manganate(VII) ions are usually **acidified** before they're used as an oxidising agent.

> **Example:** Acidified manganate(VII) ions can be reduced by Fe^{2+} ions.
>
> The half-equations are: $MnO_4^-{}_{(aq)} + 8H^+_{(aq)} + 5e^- \rightarrow Mn^{2+}_{(aq)} + 4H_2O_{(l)}$
> $Fe^{2+}_{(aq)} \rightarrow Fe^{3+}_{(aq)} + e^-$
>
> To balance the electrons you have to multiply the second half-equation by 5: $5Fe^{2+}_{(aq)} \rightarrow 5Fe^{3+}_{(aq)} + 5e^-$
>
> Now you can combine both half-equations: $MnO_4^-{}_{(aq)} + 8H^+_{(aq)} + 5Fe^{2+}_{(aq)} \rightarrow Mn^{2+}_{(aq)} + 4H_2O_{(l)} + 5Fe^{3+}_{(aq)}$

Practice Questions

Q1 What is an oxidising agent?
Q2 Why do manganate(VII) ions have to be acidified to oxidise metals?

Exam Questions

1 What is the oxidation number of the following elements?
   a) Ti in $TiCl_4$ b) V in V_2O_5 c) Cr in CrO_4^{2-} d) Cr in $Cr_2O_7^{2-}$ [4 marks]

2 Acidified manganate(VII) ions will react with aqueous iodide ions to form iodine.
  The two half-equations for the changes that occur are:
    $MnO_4^-{}_{(aq)} + 8H^+_{(aq)} + 5e^- \rightarrow Mn^{2+}_{(aq)} + 4H_2O_{(l)}$ and $2I^-_{(aq)} \rightarrow I_{2(aq)} + 2e^-$

  a) Write a balanced equation to show the reaction taking place. [2 marks]
  b) Use oxidation numbers to explain the redox processes which have occurred. [4 marks]
  c) Suggest why a fairly reactive metal such as zinc will not react with aqueous iodide ions in a
     similar manner to manganate(VII) ions. [2 marks]

Redox — relax in a lovely warm bubble bath...

The words oxidation and reduction are tossed about a lot in chemistry — so they're important.
*Don't forget, oxidation is really about electrons being lost, **not** oxygen being gained.*
I suppose you ought to learn the most famous memory aid thingy in the world — here it is...

> **OIL RIG**
> - **Oxidation Is Loss**
> - **Reduction Is Gain**
> (of electrons)

Electrode Potentials

There are electrons toing and froing in redox reactions. And when electrons move, you get electricity.

Electrochemical Cells Make Electricity

Electrochemical cells can be made from **two different metals** dipped in salt solutions of their **own ions** and connected by a wire (the **external circuit**).

There are always **two** reactions within an electrochemical cell — one's an oxidation and one's a reduction — so it's a **redox process** (see page 78).

Here's what happens in the **zinc/copper** electrochemical cell on the right:

1) Zinc **loses electrons** more easily than copper. So in the half-cell on the left, zinc (from the zinc electrode) is **OXIDISED** to form $Zn^{2+}_{(aq)}$ ions. This releases electrons into the external circuit.

2) In the other half-cell, the **same number of electrons** are taken from the external circuit, **REDUCING** the Cu^{2+} ions to copper atoms.

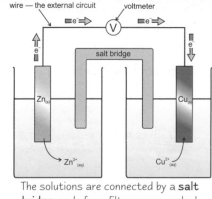

So **electrons** flow through the wire from the most reactive metal to the least.

A voltmeter in the external circuit shows the **voltage** between the two half-cells. This is the **cell potential** or **e.m.f.**, E_{cell}.

The solutions are connected by a **salt bridge** made from filter paper soaked in $KNO_{3(aq)}$. This allows ions to flow through and balance out the charges.

The boys tested the strength of the bridge, whilst the girls just stood and watched.

You can also have half-cells involving **solutions of two aqueous ions of the same element**, such as $Fe^{2+}_{(aq)}/Fe^{3+}_{(aq)}$.
The conversion from Fe^{2+} to Fe^{3+}, or vice versa, happens on the surface of the **electrode**.

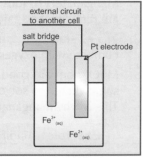

The Reactions at Each Electrode are Reversible

1) The **reactions** that occur at each electrode in the **zinc/copper cell** above are:

$$Zn^{2+}_{(aq)} + 2e^- \rightleftharpoons Zn_{(s)}$$
$$Cu^{2+}_{(aq)} + 2e^- \rightleftharpoons Cu_{(s)}$$

2) The **reversible arrows** show that both reactions can go in **either direction**. **Which direction** each reaction goes in depends on **how easily** each metal loses electrons (i.e. how easily it's **oxidised**).

3) How easily a metal is oxidised is measured using **electrode potentials**. A metal that's **easily oxidised** has a very **negative electrode potential**, while one that's harder to oxidise has a less negative or **a positive electrode potential**.

Half-cell	Electrode potential E° (V)
$Zn^{2+}_{(aq)}/Zn_{(s)}$	−0.76
$Cu^{2+}_{(aq)}/Cu_{(s)}$	+0.34

4) The table on the left shows the electrode potentials for the copper and zinc half-cells. The **zinc half-cell** has a **more negative** electrode potential, so **zinc is oxidised** (the reaction goes **backwards**), while **copper is reduced** (the reaction goes **forwards**).
Remember, the little ⊖ symbol next to the E means it's under standard conditions — 298 K and 100 kPa.

There's a Convention for Drawing Electrochemical Cells

It's a bit of a faff drawing pictures of electrochemical cells. There's a **shorthand** way of representing them though — this is the **Zn/Cu cell**:

There are a couple of important **conventions** when drawing cells:

1) The **half-cell** with the **more negative** potential goes on the **left**.

2) The **oxidised forms** go in the **centre** of the cell diagram.

$$Zn_{(s)} \mid Zn^{2+}_{(aq)} \mid\mid Cu^{2+}_{(aq)} \mid Cu_{(s)}$$

Changes go in this direction

reduced form	oxidised form	oxidised form	reduced form

If you follow the conventions, you can use the electrode potentials to calculate the overall cell potential.

$$E^{\circ}_{cell} = \left(E^{\circ}_{right\ hand\ side} - E^{\circ}_{left\ hand\ side}\right)$$

The symbol for electrode potential is E°.

The cell potential will always be a **positive voltage**, because the more negative E° value is being subtracted from the more positive E° value. For example, the cell potential for the Zn/Cu cell = +0.34 − (−0.76) = **+1.10 V**

Electrode Potentials

Electrode Potentials are Measured Against Standard Hydrogen Electrodes

You measure the electrode potential of a half-cell against a **standard hydrogen electrode**.

> The **standard electrode potential** E° of a half-cell is the **voltage measured** under **standard conditions** when the **half-cell** is connected to a **standard hydrogen electrode**.

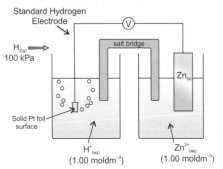

Standard conditions are:
1) Any solution must have a concentration of 1.00 mol dm^{-3}
2) The temperature must be 298 K (25 °C)
3) The pressure must be 100 kPa

1) The **standard hydrogen electrode** is always shown on the **left** — it doesn't matter whether or not the other half-cell has a more positive value. The standard hydrogen electrode half-cell has a value of **0.00 V**.

2) The whole cell potential = $E^\circ_{\text{right-hand side}} - E^\circ_{\text{left-hand side}}$.
   $E^\circ_{\text{left-hand side}} = 0.00$ V, so the **voltage reading** will be equal to $E^\circ_{\text{right-hand side}}$.
   This reading could be **positive** or **negative**, depending which way the **electrons flow**.

3) In an electrochemical cell, the half-cell with the **most negative** standard electrode potential is the one in which **oxidation** happens.

Practice Questions

Q1 $Fe^{3+} + e^- \rightleftharpoons Fe^{2+}$, $E^\circ = +0.77$ V $Mn^{3+} + e^- \rightleftharpoons Mn^{2+}$, $E^\circ = +1.48$ V
Calculate the standard cell potential for the above system.

Q2 What's the definition of standard electrode potential?

Q3 List the three standard conditions used when measuring standard electrode potentials.

Exam Questions

1 A cell is made up of a lead and an iron plate, dipped in solutions of lead(II) nitrate and iron(II) nitrate respectively and connected by a salt bridge. The electrode potentials for the two electrodes are:

$Fe^{2+}_{(aq)} + 2e^- \rightleftharpoons Fe_{(s)}$ $E^\circ = -0.44$ V $Pb^{2+}_{(aq)} + 2e^- \rightleftharpoons Pb_{(s)}$ $E^\circ = -0.13$ V

a) Which metal becomes oxidised in the cell? Explain your answer. [2 marks]
b) Which half-cell releases electrons into the circuit? Explain your answer. [2 marks]
c) Find the standard cell potential of this cell. [1 mark]

2 An electrochemical cell containing a zinc half-cell and a silver half-cell was set up using a potassium nitrate salt bridge. The cell potential at 25 °C was measured to be 1.40 V.

$Zn^{2+}_{(aq)} + 2e^- \rightleftharpoons Zn_{(s)}$ $E^\circ = -0.76$ V $Ag^+_{(aq)} + e^- \rightleftharpoons Ag_{(s)}$ $E^\circ = +0.80$ V

a) Use the standard electrode potentials given to calculate the standard cell potential for a zinc-silver cell. [1 mark]
b) Suggest two possible reasons why the actual cell potential was different from the value calculated in part (a). [2 marks]
c) Write an equation for the overall cell reaction. [1 mark]
d) Which half-cell released the electrons into the circuit? Why is this? [1 mark]

Half-equations are not straightforward reactions — they're reversible...

You've just got to think long and hard about this stuff. The metal on the left-hand electrode disappears off into the solution, leaving its electrons behind. This makes the left-hand electrode the negative one. So the right-hand electrode's got to be the positive one. It makes sense if you think about it. This electrode gives up electrons to turn the positive ions into atoms.

The Electrochemical Series

The electrochemical series is like a pop chart of the most reactive metals – except without the pop so it's really just a chart.

The **Electrochemical Series** Shows You What's **Reactive** and What's Not

1) The **more reactive** a **metal** is, the **more** it wants to **lose electrons** to form a **positive ion**.
   More reactive metals have **more negative standard electrode potentials**.

   > **Example:** Magnesium is **more reactive** than zinc — so it's more eager to form 2+ ions than zinc is.
   > The list of standard electrode potentials shows that Mg^{2+}/Mg has a **more negative** value than Zn^{2+}/Zn.
   >
   > In terms of oxidation and reduction, magnesium would **reduce** Zn^{2+} (or Zn^{2+} would **oxidise** magnesium).

2) The more reactive a **non-metal** the **more** it wants to **gain electrons** to form a **negative ion**.
   More reactive non-metals have **more positive standard electrode potentials**.

   > **Example:** Chlorine is **more reactive** than bromine — so it's more eager to form a negative ion than bromine is.
   > The list of standard electrode potentials shows that $Cl_2/2Cl^-$ is **more positive** than $Br_2/2Br^-$.
   >
   > In terms of oxidation and reduction, chlorine would **oxidise** Br^- (or Br^- would **reduce** chlorine).

3) Here's an **electrochemical series** showing some standard electrode potentials:

Chestnut wondered if his load was hindering his pulling potential.

Half-reaction	E°/V
$Mg^{2+}_{(aq)} + 2e^- \rightleftharpoons Mg_{(s)}$	−2.37
$Al^{3+}_{(aq)} + 3e^- \rightleftharpoons Al_{(s)}$	−1.66
$Zn^{2+}_{(aq)} + 2e^- \rightleftharpoons Zn_{(s)}$	−0.76
$Ni^{2+}_{(aq)} + 2e^- \rightleftharpoons Ni_{(s)}$	−0.25
$2H^+_{(aq)} + 2e^- \rightleftharpoons H_{2(g)}$	0.00
$Sn^{4+}_{(aq)} + 2e^- \rightleftharpoons Sn^{2+}_{(aq)}$	+0.15
$Cu^{2+}_{(aq)} + 2e^- \rightleftharpoons Cu_{(s)}$	+0.34
$Fe^{3+}_{(aq)} + e^- \rightleftharpoons Fe^{2+}_{(aq)}$	+0.77
$Ag^+_{(aq)} + e^- \rightleftharpoons Ag_{(s)}$	+0.80
$Br_{2(aq)} + 2e^- \rightleftharpoons 2Br^-_{(aq)}$	+1.08
$Cr_2O_7^{2-}_{(aq)} + 14H^+_{(aq)} + 6e^- \rightleftharpoons 2Cr^{3+}_{(aq)} + 7H_2O_{(l)}$	+1.33
$Cl_{2(aq)} + 2e^- \rightleftharpoons 2Cl^-_{(aq)}$	+1.36
$MnO_4^-_{(aq)} + 8H^+_{(aq)} + 5e^- \rightleftharpoons Mn^{2+}_{(aq)} + 4H_2O_{(l)}$	+1.51

More positive electrode potentials mean that:
1. The left-hand substances are more easily reduced.
2. The right-hand substances are more stable.

More negative electrode potentials mean that:
1. The right-hand substances are more easily oxidised.
2. The left-hand substances are more stable.

The **Anticlockwise Rule** Predicts Whether a Reaction Will Happen

To figure out if a metal will react with the aqueous ions of another metal, you can use the E° and the **anticlockwise rule**.

> **For example, will zinc react with aqueous copper ions?**
> First you write the two half-equations down, putting the one with the **more negative** standard electrode potential on **top**.
> Then you draw on some **anticlockwise arrows** — these give you the **direction** of each half-reaction.
>
> $Zn^{2+}_{(aq)} + 2e^- \rightleftharpoons Zn_{(s)} \quad E^{\circ} = -0.76\,V$
> $Cu^{2+}_{(aq)} + 2e^- \rightleftharpoons Cu_{(s)} \quad E^{\circ} = +0.34\,V$
>
> The **half-equations** are: $\quad Zn_{(s)} \rightleftharpoons Zn^{2+}_{(aq)} + 2e^-$
> $\qquad\qquad\qquad\qquad\qquad Cu^{2+}_{(aq)} + 2e^- \rightleftharpoons Cu_{(s)}$
>
> Which combine to give: $\quad Zn_{(s)} + Cu^{2+}_{(aq)} \rightleftharpoons Zn^{2+}_{(aq)} + Cu_{(s)}$
> So zinc **does** react with aqueous copper ions.
>
> To find the **cell potential** you always do $E^{\circ}_{bottom} - E^{\circ}_{top}$, so the cell potential for this reaction is $+0.34 - (-0.76) = +1.10\,V$.

You can also draw an **electrode potential chart**. It's the same sort of idea.

You draw an '**upside-down y-axis**' with the more negative number at the top.
Then you put both half-reactions on the chart and draw on your **anticlockwise** arrows which give you the **direction** of each half-reaction.

The **difference** between the values is the **cell potential** — in this case it's **+1.10 V**.

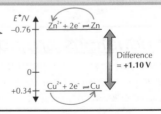

The Electrochemical Series

Sometimes the Prediction is Wrong

A **prediction** using $E°$ and the anticlockwise rule only states if a reaction is **possible** under **standard conditions**. The prediction might be **wrong if**...

...the conditions are not standard

1) Changing the **concentration** (or temperature) of the solution can cause the electrode potential to **change**.

2) For example the zinc/copper cell has these half equations in equilibrium...

$$Zn_{(s)} \rightleftharpoons Zn^{2+}_{(aq)} + 2e^-$$
$$Cu^{2+}_{(aq)} + 2e^- \rightleftharpoons Cu_{(s)}$$

3) ...if you **increase** the concentration of Zn^{2+}, the **equilibrium** will shift to the **left**, **reducing** the ease of **electron loss**. The whole cell potential will be lower.

4) ...if you **increase** the concentration of Cu^{2+}, the **equilibrium** will shift to the **right**, **increasing** the ease of **electron gain**. The whole cell potential will be higher.

Gary was hopeful, but Sue's high activation energy meant it was never going to happen

...the reaction kinetics are not favourable

1) The **rate of a reaction** may be so **slow** that the reaction might **not appear** to happen.

2) If a reaction has a **high activation energy**, this may stop it happening.

Practice Questions

Q1 Cu is less reactive than Pb.
Which half-reaction has a more negative standard electrode potential, $Pb^{2+} + 2e^- \rightleftharpoons Pb$ or $Cu^{2+} + 2e^- \rightleftharpoons Cu$?

Q2 Use electrode potentials to show that magnesium will reduce Zn^{2+}.

Q3 What is the anticlockwise rule used for? Outline how you use it.

Q4 Use the table on the opposite page to predict whether or not Zn^{2+} ions can oxidise Fe^{2+} ions to Fe^{3+} ions.

Exam Question

1 Use $E°$ values quoted on the opposite page to determine the outcome of mixing the following solutions.
If there is a reaction, determine the $E°$ value and write the equation. If there isn't a reaction, state this and explain why.
   a) Zinc metal and Ni^{2+} ions   [2 marks]
   b) Acidified MnO_4^- ions and Sn^{2+} ions   [2 marks]
   c) $Br_{2(aq)}$ and acidified $Cr_2O_7^{2-}$ ions   [2 marks]
   d) Silver ions and Fe^{2+} ions   [2 marks]

2 Potassium manganate(VII), $KMnO_4$, and potassium dichromate $K_2Cr_2O_7$, are both used as oxidising agents.
   a) From their electrode potentials, which would you predict is the stronger oxidising agent? Explain why.   [2 marks]
   b) Write equations to show each oxidising agent reacting with a solution of Fe^{2+} ions.   [2 marks]
   c) Calculate the cell potential for each reaction.   [2 marks]

3 A cell is set up with copper and nickel electrodes in 1 mol dm^{-3} solutions of their ions, Cu^{2+} and Ni^{2+}, connected by a salt bridge.
   a) Write equations for the reactions that occur in each half-cell.   [2 marks]
   b) Find the voltage of the cell.   [1 mark]
   c) What is the overall equation for this reaction?   [1 mark]
   d) How would the voltage of the cell change if:
      i) A more dilute copper solution was used?   [1 mark]
      ii) A more concentrated nickel solution was used?   [1 mark]

The forward reaction that happens is the one with the most positive $E^{\ominus}$ value...

To see if a reaction will happen, you basically find the two half-equations in the electrochemical series and check whether you can draw anticlockwise arrows on them to get from your reactants to your products. If you can — great. The reaction will have a positive electrode potential, so it should happen. If you can't — well, it ain't gonna work.

Storage and Fuel Cells

Yet more electrochemical reactions on these pages but you're nearly at the end of the section so keep going...

Energy Storage Cells are Like Electrochemical Cells

Energy storage cells (fancy name for a battery) have been around for ages and modern ones **work** just like an **electrochemical cell**. For example the nickel-iron cell was developed way back at the start of the 1900s and is often used as a back-up power supply because it can be repeatedly charged and is very robust. You can work out the **voltage** produced by these **cells** by using the **electrode potentials** of the substances used in the cell.

There are **lots** of different cells and you **won't** be asked to remember the E° for the reactions, but you might be **asked** to work out the **cell potential** or **cell voltage** for a given cell...so here's an example I prepared earlier.

Example

The nickel-iron cell has a nickel oxide hydroxide (NiOOH) cathode and an iron (Fe) anode with potassium hydroxide as the electrolyte. Using the half equations given:
a) write out the full equation for the reaction.
b) calculate the cell voltage produced by the nickel-iron cell.

$$Fe + 2OH^- \rightarrow Fe(OH)_2 + 2e^- \qquad E^\circ = -0.44 \text{ V}$$

$$NiOOH + H_2O + e^- \rightarrow Ni(OH)_2 + OH^- \qquad E^\circ = +0.76 \text{ V}$$

The **overall** reaction is...

$$2NiOOH + 2H_2O + Fe \rightarrow 2Ni(OH)_2 + Fe(OH)_2$$

For the first part you have to **combine** the two half equations together. The e^- and the OH^- are not shown because they cancel each other out.

To calculate the **cell voltage** you use the **same formula** for working out the **cell potential** (page 82).

So the **cell voltage** $= E^\circ_{bottom} - E^\circ_{top}$
$= +0.76 - (-0.44)$
$= 1.2 \text{ V}$

Fuel Cells Generate Electricity from Reacting a Fuel with an Oxidant

A **fuel cell** produces electricity by reacting a **fuel**, usually hydrogen, with an **oxidant**, which is most likely to be oxygen.

1) At the **anode** the platinum catalyst **splits** the H_2 into protons and electrons

2) The **polymer electrolyte membrane** (PEM) **only** allows the H^+ across and this **forces** the e^- to travel **around** the circuit to get to the cathode.

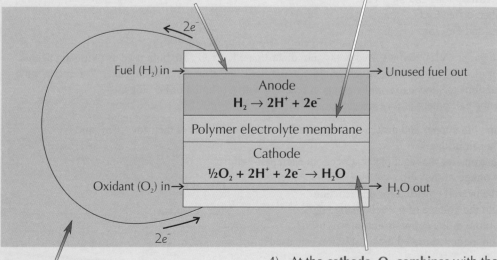

Fuel (H_2) in →
→ Unused fuel out

Anode
$$H_2 \rightarrow 2H^+ + 2e^-$$

Polymer electrolyte membrane

Cathode
$$\frac{1}{2}O_2 + 2H^+ + 2e^- \rightarrow H_2O$$

Oxidant (O_2) in→
→ H_2O out

$2e^-$

3) An **electric current** is created in the circuit, which is used to **power** something like a car or a bike or a dancing Santa.

4) At the **cathode**, O_2 **combines** with the H^+ from the anode and the e^- from the circuit to make H_2O. This is the only waste product.

Storage and Fuel Cells

Fuel Cell Vehicles use Fuel Cells For Power

Fuel cell vehicles are, unsurprisingly, electric vehicles powered by fuel cells as opposed to petrol or diesel. Using a **hydrogen** fuel cell does give FCVs some **important advantages** over regular cars.

1) They produce a lot **less pollution** because the only waste product is water.

2) The fuel cell is twice as **efficient** at converting fuel to power vs a petrol engine.

Fuel cells don't just use hydrogen — they can **also** be powered by **hydrogen-rich** fuels.

1) Hydrogen-rich fuels include **methanol**, **natural gas**, or **petrol**.

2) These are **converted** into **hydrogen gas** by a **reformer** before being used in the fuel cell.

3) Hydrogen rich fuels only release **small amounts** of **pollutants** and CO_2 when used in a fuel cell compared to burning them in a conventional engine.

Hydrogen Fuel Cells still have some Problems

Hydrogen might sound like the perfect fuel but there are some other things to think about...

... the fuel cells are not easy to make

1) The **platinum** catalysts and membrane are **expensive**.

2) The **production** of a fuel cell involves the use of **toxic chemicals**, which you need to dispose of afterwards.

3) Fuel cells only have a **limited life span** so need to be replaced, which means new ones have to be made, and old ones disposed of. **Disposing** of a fuel cell is an **expensive** process because of the chemicals they contain and the need to recycle some of the materials.

... storing and transporting hydrogen can be a pain

1) If you store it as a **gas** it is very **explosive**.

2) If you try to store it as a **liquid** you need really **expensive fridges** because it has such a low boiling point.

3) You can also store it **adsorbed** to the **surface** of a solid like charcoal or **absorbed** into a material like palladium but...

...these can be **very expensive** and often have a **limited life span**.

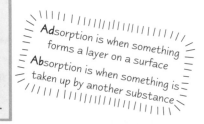

Adsorption is when something forms a layer on a surface. Absorption is when something is taken up by another substance.

Martin had seen the chocolate sundae and was ready to adsorb it to his face.

... manufacturing hydrogen takes energy

1) **Most** hydrogen is currently produced from **reacting natural gas** with steam, which **produces carbon dioxide** as a waste product.

2) Not only is one of the **reactants** a **fossil fuel**, but fossil fuels are also used to **heat** the process.

3) Hydrogen can be produced by the **electrolysis** of water but the **large** amounts of **electricity** needed are produced by conventional **power stations** using fossil fuels.

4) **Hydrogen** is described as a **energy carrier** and not an energy source because it requires energy to make it.

Storage and Fuel Cells

A *Hydrogen Economy* Uses Hydrogen Fuel For Its Energy

Lots of people think that hydrogen will be really important in the future. They think there will be a **hydrogen economy** instead of an **oil economy** where all the **energy needs** of cars, buildings and electronics will be **powered** by **hydrogen fuel cells**.

Sounds great but there are a few things to overcome first...

1) People **accepting** hydrogen as a fuel.

> Many people have concerns about the **safety** and **reliability** of hydrogen as a fuel. Most people are happy filling their cars with petrol but might think doing the same with hydrogen is more dangerous.

2) The **cost** of the new system.

> If hydrogen is going to be the future it needs to be as cheap or **cheaper** than **existing** energy systems to convince people to change. The **infrastructure** for hydrogen fuel supplies would also be **very expensive** to set up.

Sam pondered bottling horse wind to make hydrogen. It was cheap but often not clean.

3) Clean, renewable energy systems needed to **produce** the hydrogen are also **expensive**.

> Hydrogen is an **energy carrier**, which means it needs an energy source to make it. So if you want to make **clean hydrogen** you need to make it using a **clean energy source**, e.g. solar or wind energy. Unfortunately these methods are **expensive** and currently don't supply large amounts of energy.

Practice Questions

Q1 What are the half-equations for the reactions at each electrode in a hydrogen-oxygen fuel cell?

Q2 Give two ways that hydrogen fuel could be stored.

Q3 What is meant by a hydrogen-rich fuel?

Q4 Give two advantages of FCVs over conventional cars.

Exam Questions

1   a) Sketch a diagram showing the structure and operation of a hydrogen-oxygen fuel cell.
        Include the relevant half-equations.   [5 marks]
    b) Label the site of oxidation and the site of reduction on the diagram.   [2 marks]

2   a) Fuel cell vehicles use hydrogen as a fuel. Give one advantage and one disadvantage of fuel
        cells over conventional petrol engines.   [2 marks]
    b) It is possible that in the future we will move towards a 'hydrogen economy'. Explain what this means. [2 marks]
    c) Outline three issues that will need to be addressed before a hydrogen economy could be implemented. [3 marks]

3   The half equations for a lead-acid battery are as follows:

$$Pb + HSO_4^- \rightleftharpoons PbSO_4 + H^+ + 2e^- \qquad\qquad E^\circ = +0.35$$

$$PbO_2 + 3H^+ + HSO_4^- + 2e^- \rightleftharpoons PbSO_4 + 2H_2O \qquad E^\circ = +1.68$$

    a) Write out the overall equation for the reaction in its simplest form.   [2 marks]
    b) Calculate the voltage produced by the cell.   [1 mark]

In the olden days they used donkey-powered mills. They were called...wait for it...

...mule cells. Buddum tish. Oh dear, I'm really struggling today. Anyway, the hydrogen future is not upon us yet. It may have some advantages over the oil we use today but there are a lot of other things to overcome first. So maybe it will happen and maybe it won't. All we really know is it's the end of the section and that's got to be a good thing. Hurrah!!

Properties of Transition Elements

The transition elements are the metallic ones that sit slap bang in the middle of the periodic table. Thanks to their weird electronic structure, they make pretty-coloured solutions, and get involved in all sorts of fancy reactions.

Transition Elements are Found in the **d-Block**

The **d-block** is the block of elements in the middle of the periodic table.

Most of the elements in the d-block are **transition elements**.

You only need to know about the transition elements in the first row of the d-block — the ones from **titanium to copper**.

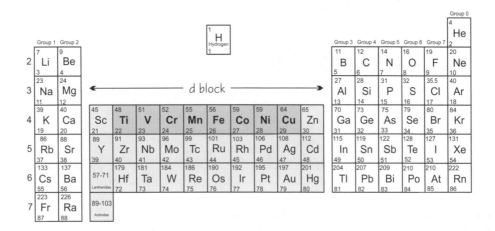

You Need to Know the **Electron Configurations** of the **Transition Elements**

1) Make sure you can write down the **electron configurations** of **all** the **Period 4 d-block elements** in sub-shell notation. Have a look at your AS notes if you've forgotten the details of how to do this. Here are a couple of examples:

$$V = 1s^2\ 2s^2\ 2p^6\ 3s^2\ 3p^6\ 3d^3\ 4s^2 \qquad Co = 1s^2\ 2s^2\ 2p^6\ 3s^2\ 3p^6\ 3d^7\ 4s^2$$

The 4s electrons fill up before the 3d electrons.
But chromium and copper are a trifle odd — see below.

2) Here's the definition of a transition element:

> A **transition element** is one that can form **at least one stable ion** with an **incomplete d sub-shell**.

3) A d sub-shell can hold **10** electrons. So transition metals must form **at least one ion** that has **between 1 and 9 electrons** in the d sub-shell. All the Period 4 d-block elements are transition metals apart from **scandium** and **zinc**. This diagram shows the 3d and 4s sub-shells of these elements:

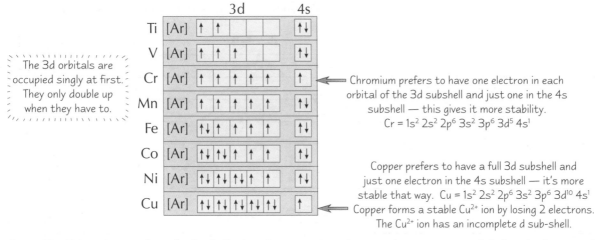

The 3d orbitals are occupied singly at first. They only double up when they have to.

Chromium prefers to have one electron in each orbital of the 3d subshell and just one in the 4s subshell — this gives it more stability.
$Cr = 1s^2\ 2s^2\ 2p^6\ 3s^2\ 3p^6\ 3d^5\ 4s^1$

Copper prefers to have a full 3d subshell and just one electron in the 4s subshell — it's more stable that way. $Cu = 1s^2\ 2s^2\ 2p^6\ 3s^2\ 3p^6\ 3d^{10}\ 4s^1$
Copper forms a stable Cu^{2+} ion by losing 2 electrons. The Cu^{2+} ion has an incomplete d sub-shell.

4) It's because of their **incomplete d sub-shells** that the transition elements have some **special chemical properties**. There's more about this on the next page.

Properties of Transition Elements

When Ions are Formed, the s Electrons are Removed First

When transition elements form **positive** ions, the **s electrons** are removed **first, then** the d electrons.

1) Iron can form Fe^{2+} ions and Fe^{3+} ions.

2) When it forms 2+ ions, it loses **both its 4s electrons**.
   $Fe = 1s^2\ 2s^2\ 2p^6\ 3s^2\ 3p^6\ 3d^6\ 4s^2 \rightarrow Fe^{2+} = 1s^2\ 2s^2\ 2p^6\ 3s^2\ 3p^6\ 3d^6$

3) Only once the 4s electrons are removed can a **3d electron** be removed.
   E.g. $Fe^{2+} = 1s^2\ 2s^2\ 2p^6\ 3s^2\ 3p^6\ 3d^6 \rightarrow Fe^{3+} = 1s^2\ 2s^2\ 2p^6\ 3s^2\ 3p^6\ 3d^5$

Sc and Zn Aren't Transition Metals

Scandium and zinc can't form **stable ions** with **incomplete d sub-shells**.
So neither of them fits the definition of a **transition metal.**

Scandium only forms one ion, Sc^{3+}, which has an **empty d sub-shell**.
Scandium has the electron configuration $1s^2\ 2s^2\ 2p^6\ 3s^2\ 3p^6\ 3d^1\ 4s^2$.
It loses three electrons to form Sc^{3+}, which has the electron configuration $1s^2\ 2s^2\ 2p^6\ 3s^2\ 3p^6$.

Zinc only forms one ion, Zn^{2+}, which has a **full d sub-shell**.
Zinc has the electron configuration $1s^2\ 2s^2\ 2p^6\ 3s^2\ 3p^6\ 3d^{10}\ 4s^2$.
When it forms Zn^{2+} it loses 2 electrons, both from the 4s sub-shell — so it keeps its full 3d sub-shell.

Transition Elements have Special Chemical Properties

1) Transition elements can form **complex ions** — see page 90.
   For example, iron forms a **complex ion with water** — $[Fe(H_2O)_6]^{2+}$.

2) They can exist in **variable oxidation states**.
   For example, iron can exist in the **+2** oxidation state as Fe^{2+} ions and in the **+3** oxidation state as Fe^{3+} ions.

3) They form **coloured ions**. E.g. Fe^{2+} ions are **pale green** and Fe^{3+} ions are **yellow**.

4) Transition metals and their compounds make **good catalysts** because they can **change oxidation states** by gaining or losing electrons within their **d orbitals**. This means they can **transfer electrons** to **speed up** reactions.

• **Iron** is the catalyst used in the **Haber process** to produce ammonia.
• **Vanadium(V) oxide**, V_2O_5, is the catalyst used in the **contact process** to make sulfuric acid.
• **Nickel** is the catalyst used to **harden margarine**.

Some common **coloured** ions and **oxidation states** are shown below. The colours refer to the **aqueous ions**.

oxidation state	+7	+6	+5	+4	+3	+2
			VO_2^+ (yellow)	VO^{2+} (blue)	V^{3+} (green)	V^{2+} (violet)
		$Cr_2O_7^{2-}$ (orange)			Cr^{3+} (green)	
	MnO_4^- (purple)					Mn^{2+} (pale pink)
					Fe^{3+} (yellow)	Fe^{2+} (pale green)
						Co^{2+} (pink)
						Ni^{2+} (green)
						Cu^{2+} (pale blue)
					Ti^{3+} (purple)	Ti^{2+} (violet)

These elements show **variable** oxidation states because the **energy levels** of the 4s and the 3d sub-shells are **very close** to one another. So different numbers of electrons can be gained or lost using fairly **similar** amounts of energy.

Properties of Transition Elements

Transition Metals Hydroxides are Brightly Coloured Precipitates

When you mix a solution of **transition metal ions** with **sodium hydroxide solution** you get a **coloured precipitate**.
You need to know the equations for the following reactions, and the colours of the hydroxide precipitates:

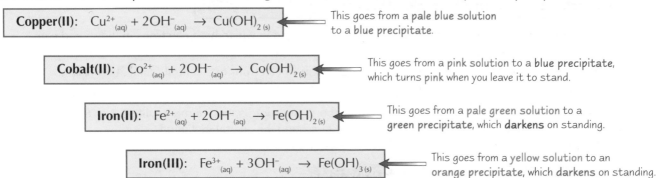

Copper(II): $Cu^{2+}_{(aq)} + 2OH^-_{(aq)} \rightarrow Cu(OH)_{2\,(s)}$ — This goes from a pale blue solution to a blue precipitate.

Cobalt(II): $Co^{2+}_{(aq)} + 2OH^-_{(aq)} \rightarrow Co(OH)_{2\,(s)}$ — This goes from a pink solution to a blue precipitate, which turns pink when you leave it to stand.

Iron(II): $Fe^{2+}_{(aq)} + 2OH^-_{(aq)} \rightarrow Fe(OH)_{2\,(s)}$ — This goes from a pale green solution to a green precipitate, which **darkens** on standing.

Iron(III): $Fe^{3+}_{(aq)} + 3OH^-_{(aq)} \rightarrow Fe(OH)_{3\,(s)}$ — This goes from a yellow solution to an orange precipitate, which **darkens** on standing.

If you know which **transition metal** ion produces which **colour** precipitate, you can use these reactions to **identify** a transition metal ion solution.

Practice Questions

Q1 What's the definition of a transition metal?

Q2 Give the electron configuration of: (a) a vanadium atom,   (b) a V^{2+} ion.

Q3 State four chemical properties which are characteristic of transition elements.

Q4 Write an equation for the reaction of iron(II) ions with hydroxide ions.
Describe the colour change that occurs during this reaction.

Exam Questions

1   When solid copper(I) sulfate is added to water, a blue solution forms with a red-brown precipitate of copper metal.
    a) Give the electron configuration of copper(I) ions.   [1 mark]
    b) Does the formation of copper(I) ions show copper acting as a transition metal? Explain your answer.   [2 marks]
    c) Identify the blue solution.   [1 mark]

2   Manganese and iron sit next to each other in the periodic table. Both are transition metals.
    Their most stable ions are Mn^{2+} and Fe^{3+} respectively.
    a) Write a balanced equation for the reaction of Fe^{3+} ions with hydroxide ions in solution.   [2 marks]
    b) What is the oxidation state of manganese in the following compounds:
        i) $KMnO_4$ [1 mark]
        ii) MnO_2 [1 mark]
        iii) Mn_2O_7 [1 mark]
    c) Sodium hydroxide solution is added to a test tube containing $FeCl_3$ solution.
        Describe the change that you would expect to observe in the test tube as the sodium hydroxide is added.   [2 marks]

3   Aluminium and iron are the two most common metals in the Earth's crust.
    Both can form an ion with a 3+ charge.
    a) i)   Give the electron configuration of the Fe^{3+} ion.   [1 mark]
        ii)   Give the electron configuration of the Al^{3+} ion.   [1 mark]
    b) With reference to oxidation states and colours of compounds,
        explain why iron is a typical transition metal and aluminium is not.   [4 marks]

4s electrons — like rats leaving a sinking ship...

Have a quick read of the electronic configuration stuff in your AS notes if it's been pushed to a little corner of your mind labelled, "Well, I won't be needing that again in a hurry". It should come flooding back pretty quickly. And don't forget to learn all the metal ion/hydroxide reactions at the top of this page — plus the colour changes that go with them...

Complex Ions

Transition metals are always forming complex ions. These aren't as complicated as they sound, though. Honest.

Complex Ions are Metal Ions Surrounded by Ligands

A **complex ion** is a **metal ion** surrounded by **coordinately bonded ligands**.

1) A **coordinate bond** (or dative covalent bond) is a covalent bond in which **both electrons** in the shared pair come from the **same atom**.

2) So a **ligand** is an atom, ion or molecule that **donates a pair of electrons** to a central metal atom or ion.

3) The **coordination number** is the **number** of **coordinate bonds** that are formed with the central metal ion.

4) In most of the complex ions that you need to know about, the coordination number will be **4** or **6**.
If the ligands are **small**, like H_2O, CN^- or NH_3, **6** can fit around the central metal ion.
But if the ligands are **larger**, like Cl^-, **only 4** can fit around the central metal ion.

6 COORDINATE BONDS MEAN AN <u>OCTAHEDRAL</u> SHAPE

Here are a few examples:

The ligands don't always have to be the same.

The different types of bond arrow show that the complex is 3-D. The wedge-shaped arrows represent bonds coming towards you and the dashed arrows represent bonds sticking out behind the molecule.

$[Cu(H_2O)_6]^{2+}{}_{(aq)}$ $[Co(NH_3)_6]^{2+}{}_{(aq)}$ $[Cu(NH_3)_4(H_2O)_2]^{2+}{}_{(aq)}$

4 COORDINATE BONDS USUALLY MEAN A <u>TETRAHEDRAL</u> SHAPE...

E.g. $[CuCl_4]^{2-}$, which is yellow and shown here, and $[CoCl_4]^{2-}$, which is blue.

...BUT NOT ALWAYS

In a **few** complexes, **4 coordinate bonds** form a **square planar** shape.
E.g. $[NiCl_2(NH_3)_2]$ — see the next page.

A Ligand Must Have at Least One Lone Pair of Electrons

A ligand must have **at least one lone pair of electrons**, or it won't have anything to form a **coordinate bond** with.

- Ligands that have **one lone pair** available for bonding are called **monodentate** — e.g. $H_2\ddot{O}$, $\ddot{N}H_3$, $\ddot{C}l^-$, $\ddot{C}N^-$.

- Ligands with **two lone pairs** are called **bidentate** — e.g. ethane-1,2-diamine: $\ddot{N}H_2CH_2CH_2\ddot{N}H_2$. *You might see ethane-1,2-diamine abbreviated to "en".*
Bidentate ligands can each form **two coordinate bonds** with a metal ion.

- Ligands with **more than two lone pairs** are called **multidentate**.

Complex Ions Can Show Optical Isomerism

Optical isomerism is a type of **stereoisomerism** (see the next page). With complex ions, it happens when an ion can exist in **two non-superimposable mirror images**.

This happens when **three bidentate ligands**, such as ethane-1,2-diamine, $H_2NCH_2CH_2NH_2$, use the lone pairs on **both** nitrogen atoms to coordinately bond with **nickel**.

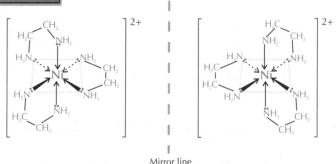

Mirror line

Complex Ions

Complex Ions Can Show Cis-Trans Isomerism

Cis-trans isomerism is a special case of **E/Z isomerism** (see page 32).
When there are only **two different groups** involved, you can use the *cis-trans* naming system.

Square planar complex ions that have **two pairs** of ligands show **cis-trans isomerism**.

[NiCl₂(NH₃)₂] is an example of this:

> E-Z is another type of **stereoisomerism**. In stereoisomerism, the atoms are joined together in the same order, but they have different orientations in space.

Cis isomers have the same groups on the <u>same</u> sides. ⟶

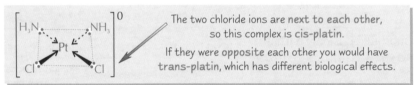

cis-[NiCl₂(NH₃)₂]   trans-[NiCl₂(NH₃)₂]

⟵ *Trans* isomers have the <u>same</u> groups <u>diagonally</u> across from each other.

Cis-platin Can Bind to DNA in Cancer Cells

Cis-platin is a complex of platinum(II) with two chloride ions and two ammonia molecules in a square planar shape. It is used as an anti-cancer drug.

> The two chloride ions are next to each other, so this complex is cis-platin.
>
> If they were opposite each other you would have trans-platin, which has different biological effects.

This is how it works:

1) The two **chlorine ligands** are very easy to displace. So the cis-platin loses them, and bonds to two **nitrogen atoms** on the **DNA molecule** inside the **cancerous cell** instead.

2) This **block** on its DNA prevents the cancerous cell from **reproducing** by division. The cell will **die**, since it is unable to repair the damage.

Practice Questions

Q1 Explain what the term 'coordination number' means in relation to a complex ion.

Q2 Draw the shape of the complex ion [Co(NH₃)₆]³⁺. Name the shape.

Q3 What is meant by the term 'bidentate ligand'? Give an example of one.

Q4 Draw the cis and trans isomers of the complex [NiBr₂(NH₃)₂].

Exam Questions

1   When potassium cyanide is added to iron(II) chloride solution, the complex ion [Fe(CN)₆]⁴⁻ is produced.
   a)   What is meant by the term 'complex ion'?   [1 mark]
   b)   Explain how the cyanide ions bond with the central iron ion.   [1 mark]
   c)   Draw a diagram to show the structure of the complex ion.   [1 mark]

2   Iron(III) can form the complex ion [Fe(C₂O₄)₃]³⁻ with three ethanedioate ions.
    The ethanedioate ion is a bidentate ligand. Its structure is shown on the right.
   a)   Explain the term 'bidentate ligand'.   [2 marks]
   b)   What is the coordination number of the [Fe(C₂O₄)₃]³⁻ complex?   [1 mark]
   c)   Use your answer from part (b) to suggest what shape the [Fe(C₂O₄)₃]³⁻ complex is.   [1 mark]

3   Cis-platin is a platinum-based complex ion that is used as an anti-cancer drug.
   a)   Draw the structure of cis-platin.   [3 marks]
   b)   Explain how cis-platin works as a cancer treatment.   [4 marks]

Put your hands up — we've got you surrounded...

You'll never get transition metal ions floating around by themselves in a solution — they'll always be surrounded by other molecules. It's kind of like what'd happen if you put a dish of sweets in a room of eight (or eighteen) year-olds. When you're drawing complex ions, you should always include some wedge-shaped bonds to show that it's 3-D.

UNIT 5: MODULE 3 — TRANSITION ELEMENTS

Substitution Reactions

There are more equations on this page than the number of elephants you can fit in a Mini.

Ligands can Exchange Places with One Another

One ligand can be **swapped** for another ligand — this is **ligand substitution**. It pretty much always causes a **colour change**.

1) If the ligands are of **similar size**, e.g. H_2O and NH_3, then the **coordination number** of the complex ion **doesn't change**, and neither does the **shape**.

$$[Co(H_2O)_6]^{2+}{}_{(aq)} + 6NH_{3(aq)} \rightleftharpoons [Co(NH_3)_6]^{2+}{}_{(aq)} + 6H_2O_{(l)}$$
octahedral   octahedral
pink   pale brown

2) If the ligands are **different sizes**, e.g. H_2O and Cl^-, there's a **change of coordination number** and a **change of shape**.

$$[Cu(H_2O)_6]^{2+}{}_{(aq)} + 4Cl^-{}_{(aq)} \rightleftharpoons [CuCl_4]^{2-}{}_{(aq)} + 6H_2O_{(l)}$$
octahedral   tetrahedral
pale blue   yellow

$$[Co(H_2O)_6]^{2+}{}_{(aq)} + 4Cl^-{}_{(aq)} \rightleftharpoons [CoCl_4]^{2-}{}_{(aq)} + 6H_2O_{(l)}$$
octahedral   tetrahedral
pink   blue

> The forward reaction is endothermic, so the equilibrium can be shifted to the right-hand side by heating. The equilibrium will also shift to the right if you add more concentrated hydrochloric acid. Adding water to this equilibrium shifts it back to the left.

3) Sometimes the substitution is only **partial**.

> This reaction only happens when you add an excess of ammonia — if you just add a bit, you get a blue precipitate of $[Cu(H_2O)_4(OH)_2]$ instead.

$$[Cu(H_2O)_6]^{2+}{}_{(aq)} + 4NH_{3(aq)} \rightleftharpoons [Cu(NH_3)_4(H_2O)_2]^{2+}{}_{(aq)} + 4H_2O_{(l)}$$
octahedral   elongated octahedral
pale blue   deep blue

Fe^{2+} in Haemoglobin Allows Oxygen to be Carried in the Blood

> Haem is a multidentate ligand.

1) **Haemoglobin** contains Fe^{2+} ions. The Fe^{2+} ions form **6 coordinate bonds**. Four of the **lone pairs** come from nitrogen atoms within a circular part of a molecule called '**haem**'. A fifth lone pair comes from a nitrogen atom on a protein (**globin**). The last position is the important one — this has a **water ligand** attached to the **iron**.

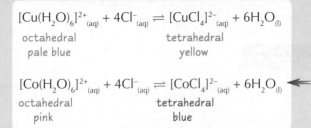

2) In the lungs the oxygen concentration is high, so the water ligand is **substituted** for an **oxygen molecule** (O_2), forming **oxyhaemoglobin**. This is carried around the body and when it gets to a place where oxygen is needed the oxygen molecule is exchanged for a water molecule again.

3) If **carbon monoxide** (**CO**) is inhaled, the **haemoglobin** swaps its **water** ligand for a **carbon monoxide** ligand, forming **carboxyhaemoglobin**. This is bad news because carbon monoxide is a **strong** ligand and **doesn't** readily exchange with oxygen or water ligands, meaning the haemoglobin **can't transport oxygen** any more.

Stability Constants are Special Equilibrium Constants

The **stability constant of a complex ion** is just what it sounds like — it tells you how stable a complex ion is in solution. Here's the official definition:

> If you want a reminder of how equilibrium constants work, look back at page 56.

> The **stability constant, K_{stab}**, of a **complex ion** is the **equilibrium constant** for the **formation** of the complex ion from its **constituent ions** in solution.

Example: Write an expression for the stability constant for the formation of the complex ion $[Fe(CN)_6]^{4-}$

Here is the equation for the formation of this ion in solution: $Fe^{2+}{}_{(aq)} + 6CN^-{}_{(aq)} \rightleftharpoons [Fe(CN)_6]^{4-}{}_{(aq)}$

So the stability constant for this reaction is: $K_{stab} = \dfrac{[(Fe(CN)_6)^{4-}]}{[Fe^{2+}][CN^-]^6}$

> The square brackets in the K_{stab} expression mean 'the concentrations of the ions'. Don't mix them up with the square brackets you'd use in the formula of a complex ion — they just keep everything together.

Substitution Reactions

K_{stab} Can Tell You If a Ligand Substitution Reaction Will Happen

1) All ligand substitution reactions are **reversible** — so you can write a ligand substitution reaction as an **equilibrium**.

2) The **equilibrium constant** will also be the **stability constant**, or K_{stab}, for this ligand substitution reaction.

3) If the complex that you start with **only** has **water** ligands, **don't** include $[H_2O]$ in the stability constant expression. Since all the ions are in solution, there's so much water around that the few extra molecules produced don't alter its concentration much — it's practically constant.

4) The size of the stability constant tells you how stable the new complex ion is, and how likely it is to form.

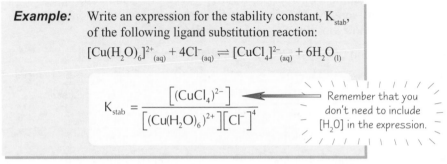

Example: Write an expression for the stability constant, K_{stab}, of the following ligand substitution reaction:

$$[Cu(H_2O)_6]^{2+}_{(aq)} + 4Cl^-_{(aq)} \rightleftharpoons [CuCl_4]^{2-}_{(aq)} + 6H_2O_{(l)}$$

$$K_{stab} = \frac{\left[(CuCl_4)^{2-}\right]}{\left[(Cu(H_2O)_6)^{2+}\right]\left[Cl^-\right]^4}$$

Remember that you don't need to include $[H_2O]$ in the expression.

The **stability constant** for the reaction in the example is 4.2×10^5 dm^{12} mol^{-4} at 291 K.

This is a **large** stability constant — which tells you that the $[CuCl_4]^{2-}$ complex ion is **very stable**.

So if you add **chloride ions** to a solution containing $[Cu(H_2O)_6]^{2+}$ ions, it's very likely that a **ligand substitution** reaction will happen, and you'll end up with $[CuCl_4]^{2-}$ ions.

Practice Questions

Q1 Give an example of a ligand substitution reaction that involves a change of coordination number.

Q2 What is the coordination number of the Fe^{2+} ion in the haemoglobin complex?

Q3 What does the size of the stability constant for a particular ligand substitution reaction tell you?

Exam Questions

1 a) Write an expression for the stability constant for the formation of the complex ion $[Co(NH_3)_6]^{2+}$.   [1 mark]

   b) Write an expression for the stability constant of the following ligand substitution reaction:

$$[Cu(H_2O)_6]^{2+}_{(aq)} + 6CN^-_{(aq)} \rightleftharpoons [Cu(CN)_6]^{4-}_{(aq)} + 6H_2O_{(l)}$$ [1 mark]

2 A sample of copper(II) sulfate powder is dissolved in pure water, giving a pale blue solution.

   a) Give the formula of the complex ion that is present in the pale blue solution.   [1 mark]

   b) When an excess of ammonia is added to the solution, its colour changes to deep blue.

      i) Write a balanced equation for the ligand substitution reaction that has taken place.   [2 marks]

      ii) Write an expression for the stability constant of this ligand substitution reaction.   [2 marks]

3 Haemoglobin is a complex ion that is found in the blood. It consists of an Fe^{2+} ion bonded to four nitrogen atoms from a haem ring, one nitrogen atom from a protein called globin, and one water molecule.

   a) When blood passes through the lungs, a ligand substitution reaction occurs.

      i) Which of the ligands in the haemoglobin complex is replaced, and by what?   [2 marks]

      ii) Why is this ligand substitution reaction important?   [1 mark]

   b) Explain how inhaling carbon monoxide can damage the human body.   [3 marks]

My friend suffers from Nativity Play Phobia — he's got a stable complex...

Four things to do with this page — One: learn what a ligand substitution reaction is, and why haemoglobin's an important example of one. Two: learn the definition of the stability constant of a complex ion. Three: make sure you can write an expression for K_{stab} for the formation of an ion, and a ligand substitution reaction. Four: fold it into a lovely origami crane.

94

Redox Reactions and Transition Elements

Transition elements love to swap electrons around, so they're always getting involved in redox reactions. That makes them handy for doing redox titrations — which are like acid-base titrations, but different (you don't need indicators for a start).

Transition Elements are Used as Oxidising and Reducing Agents

1) Transition elements can exist in many different **oxidation states** (see page 88).
2) They can **change** oxidation state by **gaining** or **losing electrons** in **redox reactions** (see page 78).
3) The ability to gain or lose electrons easily makes transition metal ions good **oxidising** or **reducing agents**.

Here are a couple of examples:

Acidified **potassium manganate(VII)** solution, $KMnO_{4\,(aq)}$, is used as an **oxidising agent**. It contains **manganate(VII) ions** (MnO_4^-), in which manganese has an oxidation state of **+7**. They can be reduced to Mn^{2+} ions during a **redox reaction**.

Example: The oxidation of Fe^{2+} to Fe^{3+} by manganate(VII) ions in solution.

Half equations:
$$MnO_4^- + 8H^+ + 5e^- \rightarrow Mn^{2+} + 4H_2O \quad \text{Manganese is \textbf{reduced}}$$
$$5Fe^{2+} \rightarrow 5Fe^{3+} + 5e^- \quad \text{Iron is \textbf{oxidised}}$$
$$\overline{MnO_4^- + 8H^+ + 5Fe^{2+} \rightarrow Mn^{2+} + 4H_2O + 5Fe^{3+}}$$

$MnO_4^-{}_{(aq)}$ is purple.
$[Mn(H_2O)_6]^{2+}{}_{(aq)}$ is colourless

During this reaction, you'll see a colour change from **purple** to **colourless**.

Acidified **potassium dichromate** solution, $K_2Cr_2O_{7\,(aq)}$, is another **oxidising agent**. It contains **dichromate(VI) ions** ($Cr_2O_7^{2-}$), in which chromium has an oxidation state of **+6**. They can be reduced to Cr^{3+} ions during a **redox reaction**.

Example: The oxidation of Zn to Zn^{2+} by dichromate(VI) ions in solution.

Half equations:
$$Cr_2O_7^{2-} + 14H^+ + 6e^- \rightarrow 2Cr^{3+} + 7H_2O \quad \text{Chromium is \textbf{reduced}}$$
$$3Zn \rightarrow 3Zn^{2+} + 6e^- \quad \text{Zinc is \textbf{oxidised}}$$
$$\overline{Cr_2O_7^{2-} + 14H^+ + 3Zn \rightarrow 2Cr^{3+} + 7H_2O + 3Zn^{2+}}$$

$Cr_2O_7^{2-}{}_{(aq)}$ is orange.
$[Cr(H_2O)_6]^{3+}{}_{(aq)}$ is violet, but usually looks green.

During this reaction, you'll see a colour change from **orange** to **green**.

Titrations Using Transition Element Ions are Redox Titrations

Redox titrations are used to find out how much **oxidising agent** is needed to **exactly** react with a quantity of **reducing agent**. You need to know the **concentration** of either the oxidising agent or the reducing agent. Then you can use the titration results to work out the concentration of the other.

You need to know about redox titrations in which **manganate(VII) ions** (MnO_4^-) are the oxidising agents.

1) First you measure out a quantity of **reducing agent**, e.g. aqueous Fe^{2+} ions, using a pipette, and put it in a conical flask.
2) You then add some **dilute sulfuric acid** to the flask — this is an excess, so you don't have to be too exact (about 20 cm³ should do it). The acid is added to make sure there are plenty of H⁺ ions to allow the oxidising agent to be reduced.
3) Now you add the aqueous MnO_4^- (the **oxidising agent**) to the reducing agent using a **burette**, **swirling** the conical flask as you do so.
4) You stop when the mixture in the flask **just** becomes tainted with the colour of the MnO_4^- (the **end point**) and record the volume of the oxidising agent added. This is the **rough titration**.
5) Now you do some **accurate titrations**. You need to do a few until you get **two or more** readings that are **within 0.20 cm³** of each other.

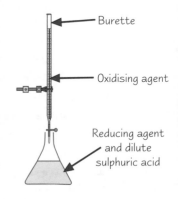

Burette

Oxidising agent

Reducing agent and dilute sulphuric acid

You can also do titrations the **other way round** — adding the reducing agent to the oxidising agent.

The Sharp Colour Change Tells You when the Reaction's Just Been Completed

1) **Manganate(VII) ions** (MnO_4^-) in **aqueous potassium manganate(VII)** ($KMnO_4$) are **purple**. When they're added to the reducing agent, they start reacting. This reaction will continue until **all** of the reducing agent is used up.
2) The **very next drop** into the flask will give the mixture the **purple colour of the oxidising agent**. The trick is to spot **exactly** when this happens.
(You could use a coloured reducing agent and a colourless oxidising agent instead — then you'd be watching for the moment that the colour in the flask disappears.)

UNIT 5: MODULE 3 — TRANSITION ELEMENTS

Redox Reactions and Transition Elements

You Can **Calculate** the **Concentration** of a Reagent from the **Titration Results**

Example: 27.5 cm³ of 0.020 moldm⁻³ aqueous potassium manganate(VII) reacted with 25.0 cm³ of acidified iron(II) sulfate solution. Calculate the concentration of Fe^{2+} ions in the solution.

$$MnO_{4\ (aq)}^{-} + 8H^{+}_{(aq)} + 5Fe^{2+}_{(aq)} \rightarrow Mn^{2+}_{(aq)} + 4H_2O_{(l)} + 5Fe^{3+}_{(aq)}$$

1) Work out the number of **moles of MnO_4^- ions** added to the flask.

Number of moles MnO_4^- added $= \dfrac{\text{concentration} \times \text{volume}}{1000} = \dfrac{0.020 \times 27.5}{1000} = 5.50 \times 10^{-4}$ moles

2) Look at the balanced equation to find how many moles of **Fe^{2+}** react with **every mole** of MnO_4^-. Then you can work out the **number of moles of Fe^{2+}** in the flask.

5 moles of Fe^{2+} react with 1 mole of MnO_4^-. So moles of $Fe^{2+} = 5.50 \times 10^{-4} \times 5 = 2.75 \times 10^{-3}$ moles.

3) Work out the **number of moles of Fe^{2+}** that would be in 1000 cm³ (1 dm) of solution — this is the **concentration**.

25.0 cm³ of solution contained 2.75×10^{-3} moles of Fe^{2+}.

1000 cm³ of solution would contain $\dfrac{(2.75 \times 10^{-3}) \times 1000}{25.0} = 0.11$ moles of Fe^{2+}.

So the concentration of Fe^{2+} is **0.11 moldm⁻³**.

Manganate 007, licensed to oxidise.

Practice Questions

Q1 Write a half equation to show manganate(VII) ions acting as an oxidising agent.

Q2 What is the change in the oxidation state of manganese during this reaction?

Q3 If you carry out a redox titration by slowly adding aqueous MnO_4^- ions to aqueous Fe^{2+} ions, how can you tell that you've reached the end point?

Q4 Why is dilute acid added to the reaction mixture in redox titrations involving MnO_4^- ions?

Exam Questions

1 Steel wool contains a high percentage of iron, and a small amount of carbon.
A 1.3 g piece of steel wool was dissolved in 50 cm³ of aqueous sulfuric acid.
The resulting solution was titrated with 0.4 mol dm⁻³ of potassium manganate(VII) solution.
11.5 cm³ of the potassium manganate(VII) solution was needed to oxidise all of the iron(II) ions to iron(III).

a) Write a balanced equation for the reaction between the manganate(VII) ions and the iron(II) ions. [3 marks]

b) Calculate the number of moles of iron(II) ions present in the original solution. [3 marks]

c) Calculate the percentage of iron present in the steel wool.
Give your answer to one decimal place. [3 marks]

2 A 10 cm³ sample of 0.5 mol dm⁻³ $SnCl_2$ solution was titrated with acidified potassium manganate(VII) solution.
Exactly 20 cm³ of 0.1 mol dm⁻³ potassium manganate(VII) solution was needed to fully oxidise the tin(II) chloride.

a) What type of reaction is this? [1 mark]

b) How many moles of tin(II) chloride were present in the 10 cm³ sample? [2 marks]

c) How many moles of potassium manganate(VII) were needed to fully oxidise the tin(II) chloride? [2 marks]

The half equation for acidified MnO_4^- acting as an oxidising agent is: $MnO_4^- + 8H^+ + 5e^- \rightarrow Mn^{2+} + 4H_2O$

d) Find the oxidation state of the oxidised tin ions present in the solution at the end of the titration. [4 marks]

And how many moles does it take to change a light bulb...

...two, one to change the bulb, and another to ask "Why do we need light bulbs? We're moles — most of the time that we're underground, we keep our eyes shut. We've mostly been using our senses of touch and smell to find our way around anyway. And we're not on mains, so the electricity must be costing a packet. We haven't thought this through properly..."

Iodine-Sodium Thiosulfate Titrations

This is another example of a redox titration — it's a handy little reaction that you can use to find the concentration of an oxidising agent. And since it's a titration, that also means a few more calculations to get to grips with...

Iodine-Sodium Thiosulfate Titrations are Dead Handy

Iodine-sodium thiosulfate titrations are a way of finding the concentration of an **oxidising agent**.
The **more concentrated** an oxidising agent is, the **more ions will be oxidised** by a certain volume of it.
So here's how you can find out the concentration of a solution of the oxidising agent **potassium iodate(V)**:

STAGE 1: Use a sample of oxidising agent to oxidise as much iodide as possible.

1) Measure out a certain volume of **potassium iodate(V)** solution (**KIO$_3$**) (the oxidising agent) — say **25 cm^3**.

2) Add this to an excess of acidified **potassium iodide** solution (**KI**).
   The iodate(V) ions in the potassium iodate(V) solution
   oxidise some of the **iodide ions to iodine**. ⟹ $$IO_3^-{}_{(aq)} + 5I^-{}_{(aq)} + 6H^+{}_{(aq)} \rightarrow 3I_2{}_{(aq)} + 3H_2O$$

STAGE 2: Find out how many moles of iodine have been produced.

You do this by **titrating** the resulting solution with **sodium thiosulfate** (**Na$_2$S$_2$O$_3$**).
(You need to know the concentration of the sodium thiosulfate solution.)

The iodine in the solution reacts
with **thiosulfate ions** like this: ⟹ $$I_2 + 2S_2O_3^{2-} \rightarrow 2I^- + S_4O_6^{2-}$$

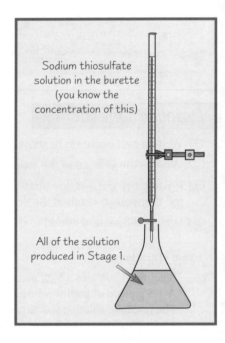

Sodium thiosulfate solution in the burette (you know the concentration of this)

All of the solution produced in Stage 1.

Titration of Iodine with Sodium Thiosulfate

1) Take the flask containing the solution that was produced in Stage 1.

2) From a burette, add sodium thiosulfate solution to the flask drop by drop.

3) It's hard to see the end point, so when the iodine colour fades to a pale yellow, add 2 cm^3 of starch solution (to detect the presence of iodine). The solution in the conical flask will go dark blue, showing there's still some iodine there.

4) Add sodium thiosulfate <u>one drop at a time</u> until the blue colour disappears.

5) When this happens, it means all the iodine has <u>just</u> been reacted.

6) Now you can <u>calculate</u> the number of moles of iodine in the solution.

Here's how you'd do the titration calculation to find the **number of moles of iodine** produced in Stage 1.

 The iodine in the solution produced in Stage 1 reacted fully with 11.1 cm^3 of 0.12 mol dm^{-3} thiosulfate solution.

$$I_2 + 2S_2O_3^{2-} \rightarrow 2I^- + S_4O_6^{2-}$$
$$\text{11.1 cm}^3$$
$$\text{0.12 mol dm}^{-3}$$

Number of moles of thiosulfate = $\dfrac{\text{concentration} \times \text{volume (cm}^3)}{1000} = \dfrac{0.12 \times 11.1}{1000} = \mathbf{1.332 \times 10^{-3} \text{ moles}}$

1 mole of iodine reacts with **2 moles** of thiosulfate.

So number of **moles of iodine** in the solution = $1.332 \times 10^{-3} \div 2 = \mathbf{6.66 \times 10^{-4} \text{ moles}}$

Iodine-Sodium Thiosulfate Titrations

STAGE 3: Calculate the concentration of the oxidising agent.

1) Now you look back at your original equation: $\boxed{IO_3^-{}_{(aq)} + 5I^-{}_{(aq)} + 6H^+{}_{(aq)} \rightarrow 3I_{2(aq)} + 3H_2O}$

2) 25 cm³ of potassium iodate(V) solution produced **6.66 × 10⁻⁴ moles of iodine**.
The equation shows that **one mole** of iodate(V) ions will produce **three moles** of iodine.

3) That means there must have been **6.66 × 10⁻⁴ ÷ 3 = 2.22 × 10⁻⁴ moles of iodate(V) ions** in the original solution.
So now it's straightforward to find the **concentration** of the potassium iodate(V) solution, which is what you're after:

$$\text{number of moles} = \frac{\text{concentration} \times \text{volume (cm}^3)}{1000} \quad \Rightarrow \quad 2.22 \times 10^{-4} = \frac{\text{concentration} \times 25}{1000}$$

$$\Rightarrow \textbf{concentration of potassium iodate(V) solution} = \textbf{0.0089 mol dm}^{-3}$$

Practice Questions

Q1 How can an iodine-sodium thiosulfate titration help you to work out the concentration of an oxidising agent?

Q2 How many moles of thiosulfate ions react with one mole of iodine molecules?

Q3 What is added during an iodine-sodium thiosulfate titration to make the end point easier to see?

Q4 Describe the colour change at the end point of the iodine-sodium thiosulfate titration.

Exam Questions

1 10 cm³ of potassium iodate(V) solution was reacted with excess acidified potassium iodide solution.
All of the resulting solution was titrated with 0.15 mol dm⁻³ sodium thiosulfate solution.
It fully reacted with 24.0 cm³ of the sodium thiosulfate solution.

   a) Write an equation showing how iodine is formed in the reaction between iodate(V) ions and
   iodide ions in acidic solution. [2 marks]

   b) How many moles of thiosulfate ions were there in 24.0 cm³ of the sodium thiosulfate solution? [1 mark]

   c) In the titration, iodine reacted with sodium thiosulfate according to this equation:
   $$I_{2(aq)} + 2Na_2S_2O_{3(aq)} \rightarrow 2NaI_{(aq)} + Na_2S_4O_{6(aq)}$$
   Calculate the number of moles of iodine that reacted with the sodium thiosulfate solution. [1 mark]

   d) How many moles of iodate(V) ions produce 1 mole of iodine from potassium iodide? [1 mark]

   e) What was the concentration of the potassium iodate(V) solution? [2 marks]

2 An 18 cm³ sample of potassium manganate(VII) solution was reacted with an excess of acidified potassium
iodide solution. The resulting solution was titrated with 0.3 mol dm⁻³ sodium thiosulfate solution.
12.5 cm³ of sodium thiosulfate solution were needed to fully react with the iodine.

   When they were mixed, the manganate(VII) ions reacted with the iodide ions according to this equation:
   $$2MnO_4^-{}_{(aq)} + 10I^-{}_{(aq)} + 16H^+ \rightarrow 5I_{2(aq)} + 8H_2O_{(aq)} + 2Mn^{2+}{}_{(aq)}$$

   During the titration, the iodine reacted with sodium thiosulfate according to this equation:
   $$I_{2(aq)} + 2Na_2S_2O_{3(aq)} \rightarrow 2NaI_{(aq)} + Na_2S_4O_{6(aq)}$$

   Calculate the concentration of the potassium manganate(VII) solution. [5 marks]

Two vowels went out for dinner — they had an iodate...

_This might seem like quite a faff — you do a redox reaction to release iodine, titrate the iodine solution, do a sum to find
the iodine concentration, write an equation, then do another sum to work out the concentration of something else.
The thing is though, it does work, and you do have to know how. If you're rusty on the calculations, look back to page 69._

Practical and Investigative Skills

You're going to have to do some practical work too — and once you've done it, you have to make sense of your results...

Make it a **Fair Test** — Control your **Variables**

You probably know this all off by heart but it's easy to get mixed up sometimes. So here's a quick recap:

> **Variable** — A variable is a **quantity** that has the **potential to change**, e.g. mass.
> There are two types of variable commonly referred to in experiments:
> • **Independent variable** — the thing that you **change** in an experiment.
> • **Dependent variable** — the thing that you **measure** in an experiment.

When drawing graphs, the dependent variable should go on the y-axis, the independent on the x-axis.

So, if you're investigating the effect of **temperature** on rate of reaction using the apparatus on the right, the variables will be:

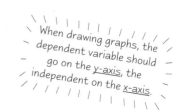

Independent variable	Temperature
Dependent variable	Amount of gas produced — you can measure this by collecting it in a gas syringe
Other variables — you MUST keep these the same	Concentration and volume of solutions, mass of solids, pressure, the presence of a catalyst and the surface area of any solid reactants

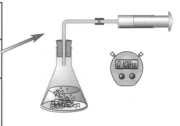

Know Your Different Sorts of **Data**

Experiments always involve some sort of measurement to provide **data**.
There are different types of data — and you need to know what they are.

> **Discrete** — you get discrete data by **counting**. E.g. the number of bubbles produced in a reaction would be discrete. You can't have 1.25 bubbles. That'd be daft. Shoe size is another good example of a discrete variable.

> **Continuous** — a continuous variable can have **any value** on a scale. For example, the volume of gas produced or the mass of products from a reaction. You can never measure the exact value of a continuous variable.

> **Categoric** — a categoric variable has values that can be sorted into **categories**. For example, the colours of solutions might be blue, red and green. Or types of material might be wood, steel, glass.

> **Ordered (ordinal)** — Ordered data is similar to categoric, but the categories can be **put in order**. For example, if you classify reactions as 'slow', 'fairly fast' and 'very fast' you'd have ordered data.

Organise Your Results in a **Table** — And Watch Out For **Anomalous** Ones

Before you start your experiment, make a **table** to write your results in.
You'll need to repeat each test at least three times to check your results are reliable.

This is the sort of table you might end up with when you investigate the effect of **temperature** on **reaction rate**.
(You'd then have to do the same for **different temperatures**.)

Temperature	Time (s)	Volume of gas evolved (cm³) Run 1	Volume of gas evolved (cm³) Run 2	Volume of gas evolved (cm³) Run 3	Average volume of gas evolved (cm³)
	10	8	7	8	7.7
20 °C	20	17	19	20	18.7
	30	28	20	30	29

Find the average of each set of repeated values.

You need to add them all up and divide by how many there are.

E.g.: $(8 + 7 + 8) \div 3 = 7.7 \ cm^3$

Watch out for **anomalous results**. These are ones that don't fit in with the other values and are likely to be wrong. They're likely to be due to random errors — here the syringe plunger may have got stuck.
Ignore anomalous results when you calculate the average.

Practical and Investigative Skills

Graphs: *Line, Bar or Scatter* — Use the **Best Type**

You'll usually be expected to make a **graph** of your results. Not only are graphs **pretty**, they make your data **easier to understand** — so long as you choose the right type.

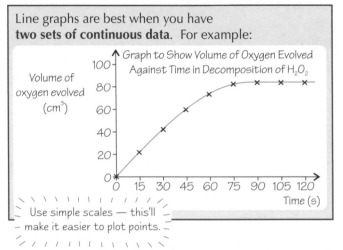

Line graphs are best when you have **two sets of continuous data**. For example:

Graph to Show Volume of Oxygen Evolved Against Time in Decomposition of H_2O_2

Volume of oxygen evolved (cm^3)

Time (s)

Use simple scales — this'll make it easier to plot points.

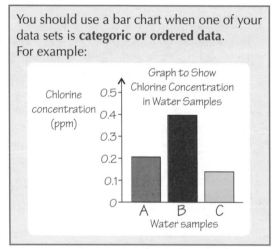

You should use a bar chart when one of your data sets is **categoric or ordered data**. For example:

Graph to Show Chlorine Concentration in Water Samples

Chlorine concentration (ppm)

Water samples

Scatter plots are great for showing how two sets of data are related (or **correlated**).

Don't try to join all the points — draw a **line of best fit** to show the **trend**.

Scatter Graph to Show Relationship Between Relative Molecular Masses and Melting Points of Straight-Chain Alcohols

Melting point (K)

Relative Molecular Mass

Scatter Graphs Show the Relationship Between Variables

Correlation describes the **relationship** between two variables — the independent one and the dependent one.

Data can show:

1) **Positive correlation** — as one variable **increases** the other **increases**. The graph on the left shows positive correlation.

2) **Negative correlation** — as one variable **increases** the other **decreases**.

3) **No correlation** — there is **no relationship** between the two variables.

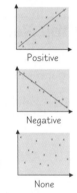

Positive

Negative

None

There are also pie charts. These are normally used to display categoric data.

Whatever type of graph you make, you'll ONLY get full marks if you:
- Choose a sensible scale — don't do a tiny graph in the corner of the paper.
- Label both axes — including units.
- Plot your points accurately — using a sharp pencil.

Correlation **Doesn't Necessarily** Mean **Cause** — Don't Jump to Conclusions

1) Ideally, only **two** quantities would **ever** change in any experiment — everything else would remain **constant**.

2) But in experiments or studies outside the lab, you **can't** usually control all the variables. So even if two variables are correlated, the change in one may **not** be causing the change in the other. Both changes might be caused be a **third variable**.

Watch out for bias too — for instance, a bottled water company might point these studies out to people without mentioning any of the doubts.

Example

For example: Some studies have found a correlation between **drinking chlorinated tap water** and the risk of developing certain cancers. So some people argue that this means water shouldn't have chlorine added.

BUT it's hard to control all the variables (e.g. lifestyle factors) between people who do drink tap water and people who don't.

Or, the cancer risk could be affected by something else in tap water — or by whatever the non-tap water drinkers drink instead...

Practical and Investigative Skills

Don't Get Carried Away When Drawing Conclusions

The **data** should always **support** the conclusion. This may sound obvious but it's easy to **jump** to conclusions. Conclusions have to be **specific** — not make sweeping generalisations.

Example

The rate of an enzyme-controlled reaction was measured at **10 °C, 20 °C, 30 °C, 40 °C, 50 °C and 60 °C**. All other variables were kept constant, and the results are shown in this graph.

A science magazine **concluded** from this data that enzyme X works best at **40 °C**. The data **doesn't** support this.

The enzyme **could** work best at 42 °C or 47 °C but you can't tell from the data because **increases** of **10 °C** at a time were used. The rate of reaction at in-between temperatures **wasn't** measured.

All you know is that it's faster at **40 °C** than at any of the other temperatures tested.

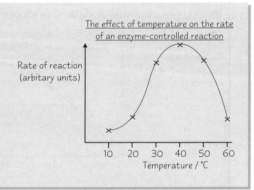

The effect of temperature on the rate of an enzyme-controlled reaction

Rate of reaction (arbitrary units)

Temperature / °C

Example

The experiment above **ONLY** gives information about this particular enzyme-controlled reaction. You can't conclude that **all** enzyme-controlled reactions happen faster at a particular temperature — only this one. And you can't say for sure that doing the experiment at, say, a different constant pressure, wouldn't give a different optimum temperature.

You Need to Look Critically at Your Results

There are a few bits of lingo that you need to understand. They'll be useful when you're evaluating how convincing your results are.

1) **Valid results** — Valid results answer the original question. For example, if you haven't **controlled all the variables** your results won't be valid, because you won't be testing just the thing you wanted to.

2) **Accurate** — Accurate results are those that are **really close** to the **true** answer.

3) **Precise results** — These are results taken using **sensitive instruments** that measure in **small increments**, e.g. pH measured with a meter (pH 7.692) will be **more precise** than pH measured with paper (pH 7).

It's possible for results to be precise **but not** accurate, e.g. a balance that weighs to 1/1000 th of a gram will give precise results but if it's not **calibrated** properly the results won't be accurate.

You may have to calculate the percentage error of a measurement.
E.g. if a balance is calibrated to within 0.1 g, and you measure a mass as 4 g, then the percentage error is: $(0.1 \div 4) \times 100 = 2.5\%$.
Using a larger quantity reduces the percentage error. E.g. a mass of 40 g has a percentage error of: $(0.1 \div 40) \times 100 = 0.25\%$.

4) **Reliable results** — **Reliable** means the results can be **consistently reproduced** in independent experiments. And if the results are reproducible they're more likely to be **true**. If the data isn't reliable for whatever reason you **can't draw** a valid **conclusion**.

For experiments, the **more repeats** you do, the **more reliable** the data. If you get the **same result** twice, it could be the correct answer. But if you get the same result **20 times**, it's much more reliable. And it would be even more reliable if everyone in the class got about the same results using different apparatus.

Work Safely and Ethically — Don't Blow Up the Lab or Harm Small Animals

In any experiment you'll be expected to show that you've thought about the **risks and hazards**. It's generally a good thing to wear a lab coat and goggles, but you may need to take additional safety measures, depending on the experiment. For example, anything involving nasty gases will need to be done in a fume cupboard.

You need to make sure you're working **ethically** too. This is most important if there are other people or animals involved. You have to put their welfare first.

Unit 4: Module 1 — Rings, Acids and Amines

Page 5 — Benzene

1 a) C_7H_8 or $C_6H_5CH_3$ **[1 mark]**
   b) Aromatic OR arene **[1 mark]**
   c) A: 1,3-dichlorobenzene **[1 mark]**
      B: nitrobenzene **[1 mark]**
      C: 2,4-dimethylphenol **[1 mark]**
2 a) The model suggests that there should be two different bond lengths in the molecule, corresponding to C=C and C–C **[1 mark]**
   b) X-ray diffraction **[1 mark]**
   c) X-ray diffraction shows that all the carbon–carbon bond lengths in benzene are actually the same, which doesn't fit the Kekulé model. **[1 mark]**

Page 7 — Reactions of Benzene

1 a) 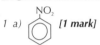 **[1 mark]**

   b) 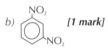 **[1 mark]**

   c) Electrophilic substitution **[1 mark]**

   d)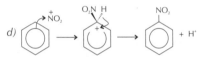

   [3 marks available — 1 mark for each stage above given either as a diagram or a description.]
   You need to get used to working out structures of compounds from their names. In 1,3-dinitrobenzene, dinitro tells you that the nitro group NO_2 appears twice and the 1 and 3 tell you where the two nitro groups appear.
2 a) Cyclohexene would decolorise bromine water, benzene would not. **[1 mark]**
   b) Bromine reacts with the cyclohexene – the bromine atoms are added to the cyclohexene molecules, forming a dibromocycloalkane and leaving a clear solution **[1 mark]**. Benzene does not react. **[1 mark]**
   c) i) It acts as a halogen carrier **[1 mark]**

   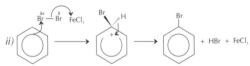

   [3 marks available — 1 mark for each stage above given either as a diagram or a description.]

Page 9 — Phenols

1 a) **[1 mark]**

   b) $2K + 2C_7H_7OH \rightarrow 2C_7H_7OK + H_2$ **[1 mark]**
   c) 4.8 dm^3 of H_2 = 4.8 ÷ 24 = 0.2 moles **[1 mark]**
      From eqn:
      2 moles of C_7H_7OH give 1 mole of H_2
      So 0.4 moles of C_7H_7OH give 0.2 moles of H_2 **[1 mark]**
      M_r of C_7H_7OH is (7 × 12) + (7 × 1) + 16 + 1 = 108
      Mass of 0.4 moles of C_7H_7OH is 108 × 0.4 = 43.2g **[1 mark]**
2 a) With benzene, there will be no reaction **[1 mark]** but with phenol a reaction will occur which decolorises the bromine water / gives a precipitate / smells of antiseptic **[1 mark for any of these observations]**
   b) 2,4,6-tribromophenol **[1 mark]**
   c) Electrons from one of oxygen's p-orbitals overlap with the benzene ring's delocalised system, increasing its electron density **[1 mark]**. This makes the ring more likely to be attacked by electrophiles. **[1 mark]**
   d) Electrophilic substitution **[1 mark]**

Page 12 — Aldehydes and Ketones

1 a) Y is a ketone **[1 mark]**.
      It cannot be an acid as it has a neutral pH **[1 mark]** and it cannot be an aldehyde as there is no reaction with Tollens' reagent OR because an aldehyde heated under reflux would be oxidised to an acid **[1 mark]**.
   b) It must be a secondary alcohol as they are the only ones oxidised to ketones. **[1 mark]**
   c) E.g. add Brady's reagent **[1 mark]** and then find the melting point of the precipitate that is formed. This will identify the ketone **[1 mark]**.
2 a) $H_3C — C — C_2H_5$ with ║ and O below

   [2 marks for correct answer or 1 mark for correct functional group.]
   b) Butan-2-ol **[1 mark]** $H_3C — C — C_2H_5$ with OH below **[1 mark]**
3 a) Reflux propan-1-ol with acidified potassium dichromate(VI) **[1 mark]**.
   b) To make propanal you would gently heat the same mixture as in a), but with excess alcohol and distil the aldehyde off as it is produced. **[1 mark]**
   c) Testing the pH would identify the acid **[1 mark]**.
      Tollens' reagent **[1 mark]** will then distinguish between the alcohol and the aldehyde as only the aldehyde will give a silver mirror when heated with Tollens' reagent **[1 mark]**.

Page 15 — Carboxylic Acids and Esters

1 a) 2-methylpropyl ethanoate **[1 mark]**
   b) Food flavouring/perfume **[1 mark]**
   c) Ethanoic acid **[1 mark]**   (structure of ethanoic acid) **[1 mark]**

      2-methylpropan-1-ol **[1 mark]**   (structure of 2-methylpropan-1-ol) **[1 mark]**

      This is acid hydrolysis **[1 mark]**
   d) With sodium hydroxide, sodium ethanoate is produced, but in the reaction in part (c), ethanoic acid is produced **[1 mark]**.
2 a) Propanol **[1 mark]**
   b) Ethanoic acid **[1 mark]**
      Ethanoic anhydride **[1 mark]**
   c) (structures of molecules)

      [2 marks — 1 for each correctly drawn molecule]
      Esters are pretty complicated molecules, but remember that they're basically an alcohol (-OH group) and carboxylic acid (-COOH) with H_2O removed.

Page 18 — Fatty Acids and Fats

1 a) $C_{17}H_{35}COOH$ or $C_{18}H_{36}O_2$ **[1 mark]**
   b) i) Triglycerides **[1 mark]**
      ii) The triester is saturated as there are no double bonds OR because stearic acid and glycerol are both saturated / contain no double bonds. **[1 mark]**
2 a) 'Cis' means that the hydrogen atoms attached to the carbon atoms either side of the double bond are on the same side **[1 mark]**
   b) Trans fatty acids increase the levels of 'bad' cholesterol/decrease the level of 'good' cholesterol in the body. **[1 mark]** 'Bad' cholesterol increases the risk of heart disease and strokes/'good' cholesterol decreases the risk of heart disease and strokes. **[1 mark]**

Answers

Page 21 — Amines

1 a) propylamine, dipropylamine and tripropylamine
   [2 marks available — 1 each for any two.]
   b) Fractional distillation **[1 mark]**
   c) React nitrobenzene with tin **[1 mark]** and hydrochloric acid **[1 mark]** under reflux **[1 mark]**, then react the product with sodium hydroxide **[1 mark]**

2 a) Azo dyes **[1 mark]**
   b) The -N=N- group **[1 mark]**
   c)

[1 mark]

[1 mark]

As a first step make sure you remember the basic overall reaction, e.g. phenylamine + phenol = azo dye, then learn the actual equations and reaction conditions.

Unit 4: Module 2 — Polymers and Synthesis

Page 23 — Polymers

1 a) Addition polymerisation **[1 mark]**
   b)

   [1 mark]
   c)

   [1 mark]
   d) Polymers formed from alkenes are very stable **[1 mark]** — they cannot be broken down easily, e.g. by hydrolysis **[1 mark]**.
2 Water in the body slowly hydrolyses **[1 mark]** the ester links **[1 mark]** in the polyester. Poly(propene) does not hydrolyse/is chemically unreactive/inert **[1 mark]**.

Page 25 — Polyesters and Polyamides

1 a) i)

   [1 mark each]

   ii) Amide/peptide link **[1 mark]**

   b) i)

   or

[1 mark]

   ii) For each link formed, one water molecule is eliminated **[1 mark]**.

2 a)

repeating unit

[2 marks — 1 mark for correctly drawing 3 repeating units and 1 mark for correctly labelling 1 repeating unit.]
   b) Polyesters **[1 mark]**

Page 27 — Amino Acids and Proteins

1 a) An amino acid in which the amino and carboxyl groups are attached to the same carbon atom **[1 mark]**.
   b)

   [1 mark — structure of NH_2 and COOH not required]
   c) The CH_3 group **[1 mark]**.
   d) Alanine has a central carbon atom with four different groups attached to it OR it has enantiomers/optical isomers. **[1 mark]**
   e)

   [1 mark]
2 a) A molecule made by joining 2 amino acids **[1 mark]**.
   b)

   OR

   [1 mark — structure of NH_2 and COOH not required]
   c) A condensation reaction involves a water molecule being removed as two other molecules are joined **[1 mark]**.
   d) Hydrolysis **[1 mark]**.
   e) Glycine is not chiral as the central carbon atom is not joined to four different groups **[1 mark]**.

Page 29 — Organic Synthesis

1 Step 1: The methanol is refluxed **[1 mark]** with $K_2Cr_2O_7$ **[1 mark]** and acid **[1 mark]** to form methanoic acid **[1 mark]**.
   Step 2: The methanoic acid is reacted under reflux **[1 mark]** with ethanol **[1 mark]** using an acid catalyst **[1 mark]** to make ethyl methanoate.
2 Step 1: React propane with bromine **[1 mark]** in the presence of UV light **[1 mark]**. Bromine is toxic and corrosive **[1 mark]** so great care should be taken. Bromopropane is formed **[1 mark]**.
   Step 2: Bromopropane is then refluxed **[1 mark]** with sodium hydroxide solution **[1 mark]**, again a corrosive substance so take care **[1 mark]**, to form propanol.

Answers

Page 31 — Functional Groups

1 a) A — hydroxyl *[1 mark]*
   B — hydroxyl and alkenyl *[1 mark]*
   C — hydroxyl and phenyl *[1 mark]*
  b) C *[1 mark]*
  c) A *[1 mark]*
  d) C *[1 mark]*
2 a) carbonyl / ketone OR amide (–CONH$_2$) *[1 mark]*
   and (primary) amine / amino *[1 mark]*
  b) i) C=O *[1 mark]*
   ii) It is a double-ended molecule *[1 mark]*
      with 2 amine / amino groups *[1 mark]*.
3 a) phenyl *[1 mark]*, hydroxyl *[1 mark]* and ester *[1 mark]*
  b) ester *[1 mark]*
  c) Expanded structure (with C and H atoms showing):

   So molecular formula of methyl salicylate is C$_8$H$_8$O$_3$. *[1 mark]*
  d)

   [1 mark]

   Look back at esters on p13 if you had trouble with this one.

Page 33 — Stereoisomerism and Chirality

1 a)

   * is the chiral carbon atom, or chiral centre.
   [3 marks available — 1 mark for each correct diagram.]
  b)

   [2 marks available — 1 mark for each correct diagram.]
  c) They rotate plane-polarised light *[1 mark]*.
2 a)   *[1 mark]*

   The chiral carbon is the one with 4 different groups attached.
  b) i) Smaller doses needed *[1 mark]*, fewer side-effects
      (because there's no D-DOPA enantiomer) *[1 mark]*.
   ii) A mixture containing equal quantities of each enantiomer of an
      optically active compound *[1 mark]*.
   iii) The other enantiomer may have unexpected and dangerous side
      effects or completely different effects *[1 mark]*.

Unit 4: Module 3 — Analysis

Page 35 — Chromatography

1 a) R_f value = $\dfrac{\text{Distance travelled by spot}}{\text{Distance travelled by solvent}}$ *[1 mark]*

   R_f value of spot A = 7 ÷ 8 = 0.875 *[1 mark]*
   The R_f value has no units, because it's a ratio.
  b) Substance A has moved further up the plate because it's less strongly
     adsorbed *[1 mark]* onto the stationary phase *[1 mark]* than
     substance B *[1 mark]*.
2 a) The peak at 5 minutes *[1 mark]*.
  b) The mixture may contain another chemical with a similar retention
     time, which would give a peak at 5 minutes *[1 mark]*.
3 a) The mixture is injected into a stream of carrier gas, which takes it
     through a tube over the stationary phase *[1 mark]*. The components
     of the mixture dissolve in the stationary phase *[1 mark]*, evaporate
     into the mobile phase *[1 mark]*, and redissolve, gradually travelling
     along the tube to the detector *[1 mark]*.
  b) The substances separate because they have different solubilities in the
     stationary phase *[1 mark]*, so they take different amounts of time to
     move through the tube *[1 mark]*.
  c) The areas under the peaks will be proportional to the relative amount
     of each substance in the mixture OR the area under the benzene
     peak will be three times greater than the area under the ethanol peak
     [1 mark].

Page 38 — Mass Spectrometry and Chromatography

1 a) 88 *[1 mark]*
  b) A has a mass of 43, so it's probably CH$_3$CH$_2$CH$_2$ *[1 mark]*.
     B has a mass of 45, so it's probably COOH *[1 mark]*.
     C has a mass of 73, so it's probably CH$_2$CH$_2$COOH *[1 mark]*.
  c) Since the molecule is a carboxylic acid that contains the three
     fragments that you found in part (b), it must have this structure:

     [1 mark]

     This is butanoic acid *[1 mark]*.
2 a) Several alkanes/compounds have similar GC retention times *[1 mark]*,
     but different masses, so they would give different peaks on a mass
     spectrum *[1 mark]*.
  b) Formula of molecular ion: CH$_3$CH$_3^+$ *[1 mark]*
     Mass = (12 × 2) + (1 × 6) = 24 + 6 = 30 *[1 mark]*
  c) i) CH$_3$CH$_2^+$ *[1 mark]*
   ii) CH$_3^+$ *[1 mark]*

Page 41 — NMR Spectroscopy

1 a) The peak at δ = 0 is produced by the reference compound,
     tetramethylsilane/TMS *[1 mark]*.
  b) All three carbon atoms in the molecule CH$_3$CH$_2$CH$_2$NH$_2$ are in
     different environments *[1 mark]*. There are only two peaks on the
     carbon-13 NMR spectrum shown *[1 mark]*.
     The ^{13}C NMR spectrum of CH$_3$CH$_2$CH$_2$NH$_2$ has three peaks of equal height
     — because it has three carbon environments, and one carbon atom in each.
  c) Structure: *[1 mark]*.

     This molecule has two carbon environments, with two carbons in
     one, and one carbon in the other *[1 mark]*. So it would produce the
     spectrum shown.
     The 2 carbon environments are CH$_3$–CH(NH$_2$)–CH$_3$ and CH(NH$_2$)–(CH$_3$)$_2$

Answers

Page 43 — More NMR Spectroscopy

1 a) A CH_2 group adjacent to a halogen *[1 mark]*.
You've got to read the question carefully — it tells you it's an alkyl halide. So the group at 3.6 p.p.m. can't have oxygen in it. It can't be halogen-CH_3 either, as this has 3 hydrogens in it.

b) A CH_3 group *[1 mark]*.

c) CH_2 added to CH_3 gives a mass of 29, so the halogen must be chlorine with a mass of 35 *[1 mark]*.
So a likely structure is CH_3CH_2Cl *[1 mark]*.

d) The quartet at 3.6 p.p.m. is caused by 3 protons on the adjacent carbon *[1 mark]*. The n + 1 rule tells you that 3 protons give 3 + 1 = 4 peaks *[1 mark]*.
Similarly the triplet at 1.3 p.p.m. is due to 2 adjacent protons *[1 mark]* giving 2 + 1 = 3 peaks *[1 mark]*.

Page 45 — Infrared Spectroscopy

1 a) A's due to an O–H group in a carboxylic acid *[1 mark]*.
B's due to a C=O as in an aldehyde, ketone, acid or ester *[1 mark]*.
C's due to a C–O as in an alcohol, ester or acid *[1 mark]*.

b) The spectrum suggests it's a carboxylic acid, so it's got a COOH group *[1 mark]*. This group has a mass of 45, so the rest of the molecule has a mass of 74 – 45 = 29, which is likely to be C_2H_5 *[1 mark]*.
So the molecule could be C_2H_5COOH — propanoic acid *[1 mark]*.

2 a) X is due to an O–H group in an alcohol or phenol *[1 mark]*.
Y is due to C–H bonds *[1 mark]*.
Z is due to a C–O group in an alcohol, ester or acid *[1 mark]*.

b) The spectrum suggests it's an alcohol, so it's got an OH group *[1 mark]*. This group has a mass of 17, so the rest of the molecule has a mass of 46 – 17 = 29, which is likely to be C_2H_5 *[1 mark]*.
So the molecule could be C_2H_5OH — ethanol *[1 mark]*.

Page 47 — More on Spectra

1 a) Mass of molecule = 73 *[1 mark]*.
You can tell this from the mass spectrum — the mass of the molecular ion is 73.

b) Structure of the molecule: 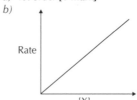 *[1 mark]*

Explanation: Award *1 mark* each for the following pieces of reasoning, up to a total of *[5 marks]*:
The infrared spectrum of the molecule shows a strong absorbance at about 3200 cm^{-1}, which suggests that the molecule contains an amine or amide group.
It also has a trough at about 1700 cm^{-1}, which suggests that the molecule contains a C=O group.
The ^{13}C NMR spectrum tells you that the molecule has three carbon environments, with the same number of carbons in each.
One of the ^{13}C NMR peaks has a chemical shift of about 170, which corresponds to a carbonyl group in an amide.
The ^1H NMR spectrum has a quartet at $\delta \approx 2$, and a triplet at $\delta \approx 1$ — to give this splitting pattern the molecule must contain a CH_2CH_3 group.
The ^1H NMR spectrum has a singlet at $\delta \approx 6$, corresponding to H atoms in an amine or amide group.
The mass spectrum shows a peak at m/z = 15 which corresponds to a CH_3 group.
The mass spectrum shows a peak at m/z = 29 which corresponds to a CH_2CH_3 group.
The mass spectrum shows a peak at m/z = 44 which corresponds to a $CONH_2$ group.

2 a) Mass of molecule = 60 *[1 mark]*.
You can tell this from the mass spectrum — the mass of the molecular ion is 60.

b) Structure of the molecule: H–C–C–C–OH *[1 mark]*

Explanation: Award *1 mark* each for the following pieces of reasoning, up to a total of *[5 marks]*:
The ^{13}C NMR spectrum tells you that the molecule has three carbon environments, with the same number of carbons in each.
One of the ^{13}C NMR peaks has a chemical shift of 60 — which corresponds to a C–O group.
The infrared spectrum of the molecule has a trough at about 3300 cm^{-1}, which suggests that the molecule contains an alcoholic OH group.
It also has a trough at about 1200 cm^{-1}, which suggests that the molecule also contains a C–O group.
The mass spectrum shows a peak at m/z = 15 which corresponds to a CH_3 group.
The mass spectrum shows a peak at m/z = 17 which corresponds to an OH group.
The mass spectrum shows a peak at m/z = 29 which corresponds to a C_2H_5 group.
The mass spectrum shows a peak at m/z = 31 which corresponds to a CH_2OH group.
The mass spectrum shows a peak at m/z = 43 which corresponds to a C_3H_7 group.
The ^1H NMR spectrum has 4 peaks, showing that the molecule has 4 proton environments.
The ^1H NMR spectrum has a singlet at $\delta \approx 2$, corresponding to H atoms in an OH group.
The ^1H NMR spectrum has a sextuplet with an integration trace of 2 at $\delta \approx 1.5$, a quartet with an integration trace of 2 at $\delta \approx 3.5$, and a triplet with an integration trace of 3 at $\delta \approx 1$ — to give this splitting pattern the molecule must contain a $CH_3CH_2CH_2$ group.

Unit 5: Module 1 — Rates, Equilibrium and pH

Page 49 — Rate Graphs and Orders

1 a) 1st order *[1 mark]*

b)

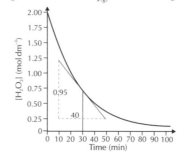

[1 mark for correctly labelled axes, 1 mark for correct line]

c) The volume *[1 mark]* of hydrogen gas produced in a unit time *[1 mark]*.

2 a) E.g. Gas volume of $O_{2(g)}$ *[1 mark]* using, e.g. a gas syringe *[1 mark]*.

b)

Rate after 30 minutes = 0.95 ÷ 40
≈ 0.024 *[1 mark]* mol dm^{-3} min^{-1} *[1 mark]*
Accept rate within range 0.024 ± 0.005.
[1 mark for [$H_2O_{2(aq)}$] on y-axis and time on x-axis. 1 mark for points accurately plotted. 1 mark for best-fit smooth curve. 1 mark for tangent to curve at 30 minutes.]

Answers

Page 51 — Initial Rates and Half-Life

1   Experiments 1 and 2:
    [D] doubles and the initial rate quadruples (with [E] remaining
    constant) *[1 mark]*. So it's 2nd order with respect to [D] *[1 mark]*.
    Experiments 1 and 3:
    [E] doubles and the initial rate doubles (with [D] remaining constant)
    [1 mark]. So it's 1st order with respect to [E] *[1 mark]*.
    Always explain your reasoning carefully — state which
    concentrations are constant and which are changing.

2 a)

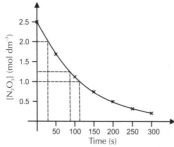

   *[[N₂O₅] on y-axis and time on x-axis 1 mark, points plotted
   accurately 1 mark, best-fit smooth curve 1 mark.]*

 b) i) Horizontal dotted line from 1.25 on y-axis to curve and
       vertical dotted line from curve to x-axis *[1 mark]* .
       Time value = 85s *[1 mark, allow 85 ± 2]*
    ii) Vertical dotted line from curve at 2.0 mol dm⁻³ and same at 1.0
       mol dm⁻³ *[1 mark]*. Time value difference = 113 (± 2) − 28 (± 2)
       = 85 *[1 mark, allow 85 ± 4]*
 c) The order of reaction = 1 *[1 mark]* because the half-life of ≈ 85 is
    independent of concentration *[1 mark]*.

Page 53 — Rate Equations

1 a) Rate = $k[NO_{(g)}]^2[H_{2(g)}]$
    [1 mark for correct orders, 1 mark for the rest]
 b) i) $0.00267 = k \times (0.004)^2 \times 0.002$ *[1 mark]*
      $k = 8.34 \times 10^4\ dm^6\,mol^{-2}\,s^{-1}$
      [1 mark for answer, 1 mark for units].
      Units: $k = mol\ dm^{-3}\ s^{-1} \div [(mol\ dm^{-3})^2 \times (mol\ dm^{-3})]$
      $= mol^{-2}\,dm^6\,s^{-1}$.
    ii) It would decrease *[1 mark]*.
      If the temperature decreases, the rate decreases too.
      A lower rate means a lower rate constant.
2 a) Rate = $k[CH_3COOC_2H_5][H^+]$ *[1 mark]*
 b) $2.2 \times 10^{-3} = k \times 0.25 \times 2.0$ *[1 mark]*
    $k = 2.2 \times 10^{-3} \div 0.5 = 4.4 \times 10^{-3}$ *[1 mark]*
    The units are:
    $k = (mol\ dm^{-3}\ s^{-1}) \div (mol\ dm^{-3})(mol\ dm^{-3})$
    $= mol^{-1}\ dm^3\ s^{-1}$ *[1 mark]*
 c) If the volume doubles, the concentration of each reactant halves to
    become 1 mol dm⁻³ and 0.125 mol dm⁻³ respectively *[1 mark]*.
    So the rate = $4.4 \times 10^{-3} \times 1 \times 0.125 = 5.5 \times 10^{-4}\ mol\ dm^{-3}\ s^{-1}$ *[1 mark]*.
3   The rate equation is: Rate = k[X][Y] *[1 mark]*
    Rate is proportional to [X], so increasing [X] by 3.33% increases the
    rate by 3.33% also *[1 mark]*.
    However, increasing the temperature by 10K doubles the rate.
    So temperature has a greater effect *[1 mark]*.

Page 55 — Rates and Reaction Mechanisms

1 a) rate = $k[H_2][ICl]$ *[1 mark]*
 b) i) One molecule of H_2 and one molecule of ICl *[1 mark]*.
       If the molecule is in the rate equation, it must be in the
       rate-determining step *[1 mark]*.
    ii) Incorrect *[1 mark]*. H_2 and ICl are both in the rate
       equation, so they must both be in the rate-determining
       step OR the order of the reaction with respect to ICl is 1,
       so there must be only one molecule of ICl in the
       rate-determining step *[1 mark]*.
2 a) The rate equation is first order with respect to HBr and O_2 *[1 mark]*
    So only 1 molecule of HBr (and O_2) is involved in the
    rate-determining step *[1 mark]*
    There must be more steps as 4 molecules of HBr are in the equation
    [1 mark].

 b) $HBr + O_2 \rightarrow HBrO_2$ (rate-determining step) *[1 mark]*
    $HBr + HBrO_2 \rightarrow 2HBrO$ *[1 mark]*
    $HBr + HBrO \rightarrow H_2O + Br_2$ *[1 mark]*
    $HBr + HBrO \rightarrow H_2O + Br_2$ *[1 mark]*
    Part b) is pretty tricky — you need to do a fair bit of detective work and
    some trial and error. Make sure you use all of the clues in the question...

Page 57 — The Equilibrium Constant

1 a) $K_c = \dfrac{[NH_3]^2}{[N_2][H_2]^3}$

   *[1 mark for correct reactants on top and bottom,
   1 mark for correct powers.]*

 b) $K_c = \dfrac{0.150^2}{1.06 \times 1.41^3}$ *[1 mark]*

    $= 7.6 \times 10^{-3}$ *[1 mark]* $mol^{-2}dm^6$ *[1 mark]*
2 a) i) moles = mass ÷ M_r = 42.5 ÷ 46 = 0.92 *[1 mark]*
    ii) moles of O_2 = mass ÷ M_r = 14.1 ÷ 32 = 0.44 *[1 mark]*
       moles of NO = 2 × moles of O_2 = 0.88 *[1 mark]*
       moles of NO_2 = 0.92 − 0.88 = 0.04 *[1 mark]*
 b) $[O_2]$ = 0.44 ÷ 22.8 = 0.019 mol dm⁻³
    [NO] = 0.88 ÷ 22.8 = 0.039 mol dm⁻³
    $[NO_2]$ = 0.04 ÷ 22.8 = 1.75 × 10⁻³ mol dm⁻³
    [1 mark]

    $K_c = \dfrac{[NO]^2[O_2]}{[NO_2]^2}$ *[1 mark]*

    $\Rightarrow K_c = \dfrac{(0.039)^2 \times (0.019)}{(1.75 \times 10^{-3})^2}$ *[1 mark]* = 9.4 *[1 mark]* mol dm⁻³ *[1 mark]*
    (Units = (mol dm⁻³)² × (mol dm⁻³) ÷ (mol dm⁻³)² = mol dm⁻³)

Page 59 — More on the Equilibrium Constant

1 a) T_2 is lower than T_1 *[1 mark]*.
    A decrease in temperature shifts the position of equilibrium in the
    exothermic direction, producing more product *[1 mark]*.
    More product means K_c increases *[1 mark]*.
    A negative ΔH means the forward reaction is exothermic
    — it gives out heat.
 b) The yield of SO_3 increases *[1 mark]*. (A decrease in volume means
    an increase in pressure. This shifts the equilibrium position to the
    right.) K_c is unchanged *[1 mark]*.

2 a) $K_c = \dfrac{[CO][H_2]^3}{[CH_4][H_2O]}$

   *[1 mark for correct reactants on top and bottom,
   1 mark for correct powers.]*
 b) i) K_c will increase *[1 mark]* as the forward (endothermic)
       reaction is favoured.
    ii) No effect *[1 mark]*.
 c) Increasing the pressure will move the reaction to the left,
    so amounts of CH_4 and H_2O will increase *[1 mark]*
    and amounts of CO and H_2 will decrease *[1 mark]*.

Page 61 — Acids and Bases

1 a) H^+ or H_3O^+ and SO_4^{2-} *[1 mark]*
 b) $2H^+_{(aq)} + Mg_{(s)} \rightarrow Mg^{2+}_{(aq)} + H_{2(g)}$ *[1 mark]*
 c) SO_4^{2-} *[1 mark]*
 d) The acid dissociates / ionises in water as follows:
    $H_2SO_4 + 2H_2O \rightleftharpoons 2H_3O^+ + SO_4^{2-}$ *[1 mark]*
    The equilibrium position lies almost completely to the right *[1 mark]*.
2 a) $HCN + H_2O \rightleftharpoons H_3O^+ + CN^-$ *[1 mark]*
 b) The equilibrium position lies to the left *[1 mark]*.
 c) The pairs are HCN and CN^- *[1 mark]*
    AND H_2O and H_3O^+ *[1 mark]*.
 d) H^+ *[1 mark]*
3 a) $NH_3 + H_2O \rightleftharpoons NH_4^+ + OH^-$ *[1 mark]*
 b) An acid *[1 mark]* as it donates a proton *[1 mark]*
 c) OH^- *[1 mark]*

Answers

Page 63 — pH

1 a) K_c is the equilibrium constant for water
$K_c = [H^+][OH^-] \div [H_2O]$ **[1 mark]**
But $[H_2O]$ is assumed to be constant.
So $K_c \times [H_2O]$ is constant $= K_w$
This gives $K_w = [H^+][OH^-]$ **[1 mark]**.
b) It's a strong monobasic acid, so $[H^+] = [HBr] = 0.32$ **[1 mark]**
$pH = -\log_{10} 0.32 = 0.49$ **[1 mark]**
c) More H^+ are produced in solution as it is more dissociated **[1 mark]**
So the pH is lower **[1 mark]**.
2 a) $2.5\,g = 2.5 \div 40 = 0.0625$ moles **[1 mark]**
1 mole of NaOH gives 1 mole of OH^-
So $[OH^-] = [NaOH] = 0.0625$ mol dm^{-3} **[1 mark]**
b) $K_w = [H^+][OH^-]$ **[1 mark]**
$[H^+] = 1 \times 10^{-14} \div 0.0625 = 1.6 \times 10^{-13}$ **[1 mark]**
$pH = -\log_{10}(1.6 \times 10^{-13}) = 12.8$ (1 d.p.) **[1 mark]**
c) The value of K_c and hence K_w is temperature dependent **[1 mark]**.
3 $K_w = [H^+][OH^-]$ **[1 mark]**
$[OH^-] = 0.0370$ **[1 mark]**
$[H^+] = K_w \div [OH^-] = (1 \times 10^{-14}) \div 0.0370 = 2.70 \times 10^{-13}$ **[1 mark]**
$pH = -\log_{10}[H^+] = -\log_{10}(2.70 \times 10^{-13}) = 12.57$ **[1 mark]**

Page 65 — More pH Calculations

1 a) $K_a = \dfrac{[H^+][A^-]}{[HA]}$ **[1 mark]**

b) $K_a = \dfrac{[H^+]^2}{[HA]}$ $\Rightarrow$ [HA] is 0.280 because very few HA will dissociate

[1 mark].

$[H^+] = \sqrt{(5.60 \times 10^{-4}) \times 0.280} = 0.0125$ mol dm^{-3} **[1 mark]**
$pH = -\log_{10}[H^+] = -\log_{10}(0.0125) = 1.90$ **[1 mark]**
2 a) $[H^+] = 10^{-2.65} = 2.24 \times 10^{-3}$ mol dm^{-3} **[1 mark]**
$K_a = \dfrac{[H^+]^2}{[HX]}$ **[1 mark]** $= \dfrac{[2.24 \times 10^{-3}]^2}{[0.150]}$
$= 3.34 \times 10^{-5}$ **[1 mark]** mol dm^{-3} **[1 mark]**
b) $pK_a = -\log_{10}K_a = -\log_{10}(3.34 \times 10^{-5})$ **[1 mark]** $= 4.48$ **[1 mark]**
3 $K_a = 10^{-pK_a} = 10^{-4.2} = 6.3 \times 10^{-5}$ **[1 mark]**
$K_a = \dfrac{[H^+]^2}{[HA]}$ **[1 mark]**
So $[H^+] = \sqrt{K_a[HA]}$
$= \sqrt{(6.3 \times 10^{-5}) \times (1.6 \times 10^{-4})} = \sqrt{1.0 \times 10^{-8}}$
$= 1.0 \times 10^{-4}$ mol dm^{-3} **[1 mark]**
$pH = -\log_{10}[H^+] = -\log_{10} 1.0 \times 10^{-4} = 4$ **[1 mark]**

Page 67 — Buffer Action

1 a) $K_a = \dfrac{[C_6H_5COO^-][H^+]}{[C_6H_5COOH]}$ **[1 mark]**

$\Rightarrow [H^+] = 6.4 \times 10^{-5} \times \dfrac{0.40}{0.20} = 1.28 \times 10^{-4}$ mol dm^{-3} **[1 mark]**

$pH = -\log_{10}[1.28 \times 10^{-4}] = 3.9$ **[1 mark]**
b) $C_6H_5COOH \rightleftharpoons H^+ + C_6H_5COO^-$ **[1 mark]**
Adding H_2SO_4 increases the concentration of H^+ **[1 mark]**.
The equilibrium shifts left to reduce the concentration of H^+, so the
pH will only change very slightly **[1 mark]**.
2 a) $CH_3(CH_2)_2COOH \rightleftharpoons H^+ + CH_3(CH_2)_2COO^-$ **[1 mark]**
b) $[CH_3(CH_2)_2COOH] = [CH_3(CH_2)_2COO^-]$,
so $[CH_3(CH_2)_2COOH] \div [CH_3(CH_2)_2COO^-] = 1$ **[1 mark]**
and $K_a = [H^+]$. $pH = -\log_{10}[1.5 \times 10^{-5}]$ **[1 mark]** $= 4.8$
[1 mark]
If the concentrations of the weak acid and the salt are equal, they cancel
from the K_a expression and the buffer pH = pK_a.

Page 69 — pH Curves, Titrations and Indicators

1 The pH at equivalence for nitric acid is 7, whereas the pH at
equivalence for ethanoic acid is greater than 7.
The pH at the start for nitric acid is lower than for ethanoic acid.
The near-vertical bit is bigger/slightly steeper for nitric acid than for
ethanoic acid.
[1 mark for each difference, up to a maximum of 2]
2 a) moles of ethanoic acid = $(25.0 \times 0.350) \div 1000$
$= 0.00875$ **[1 mark]**
Volume of KOH = (number of moles $\times$ 1000) $\div$ molar concentration
$= (0.00875 \times 1000) \div 0.285$ **[1 mark]**
$= 30.7\ cm^3$ **[1 mark]**
b) Thymol blue **[1 mark]**. It's a weak acid/strong base titration so the
equivalence point is above pH 8 **[1 mark]**.

Unit 5: Module 2 — Energy

Page 71 — Neutralisation and Enthalpy

1 a) $H_2SO_4 + 2NaOH \rightarrow Na_2SO_4 + 2H_2O$ **[1 mark]**
b) 200 ml of 2.75 mol dm^{-3} acid will contain $2.75 \times 0.2 = 0.55$ moles
[1 mark]
The volume of the solution is 400 ml, so the mass of the solution is
0.4 kg, so m = 0.4.
$\Delta H = -mc\Delta T = -0.4 \times 4.18 \times 38 = -63.54\ kJ$ for 0.55 moles of acid
[1 mark]
1 mole of water is given by 0.5 moles of acid.
So 0.5 moles of acid will produce $0.5 \div 0.55 \times -63.54 = -57.76\ kJ$
[1 mark]
2 a) $HCl + KOH \rightarrow H_2O + KCl$ **[1 mark]**
$H_2SO_4 + 2KOH \rightarrow K_2SO_4 + 2H_2O$ **[1 mark]**
$H_3PO_4 + 3KOH \rightarrow K_3PO_4 + 3H_2O$ **[1 mark]**
b) The enthalpy change of neutralisation is the energy change when 1
mole of water is formed by the reaction of an acid and a base.
[1 mark]
1 mole of H_3PO_4 will give 3 moles of water, so the energy released
per mole of acid will be $3 \times 57\ kJ$, whereas H_2SO_4 would give 2×57
and HCl just 57 kJ. So the neutralisation of H_3PO_4 is the most
exothermic and would result in the largest temperature rise. **[1 mark]**
3 $HCl + KOH \rightarrow H_2O + KCl$ **[1 mark]**
From the equation 1 mole of acid gives 1 mole of water.
$\Delta H = -mc\Delta T = -0.2 \times 4.18 \times 3.4 = -28.42\ kJ$ **[1 mark]**
In 100 ml of X mol dm^{-3} acid there are 0.1X moles. **[1 mark]**
So if 0.1X mol gives 28.42 kJ and 1 mole of acid gives 57 kJ
then X $= 28.42 \div (57 \times 0.1) = 5$ mol dm^{-3} **[1 mark]**

Page 73 — Lattice Enthalpy and Born-Haber Cycles

1 a)

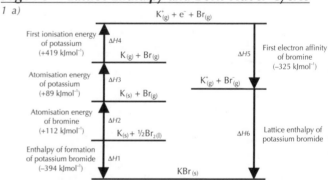

**[1 mark for left of cycle. 1 mark for right of cycle. 1 mark for
formulas/state symbols. 1 mark for correct directions of arrows.]**
b) Lattice enthalpy, $\Delta H6 = -\Delta H5 - \Delta H4 - \Delta H3 - \Delta H2 + \Delta H1$
$= -(-325) - (+419) - (+89) - (+112) + (-394)$ **[1 mark]**
$= -689$ **[1 mark]** kJ mol^{-1} **[1 mark]**
Award marks if calculation method matches cycle in part (a).

2 a)

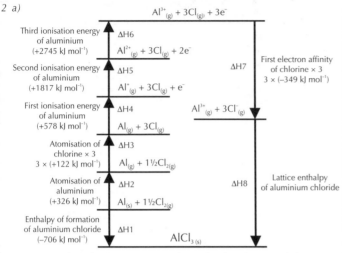

[1 mark for left of cycle. 1 mark for right of cycle. 1 mark for formulas/state symbols. 1 mark for correctly multiplying all the enthalpies. 1 mark for correct directions of arrows.]

b) Lattice enthalpy,
$\Delta H8 = -\Delta H7 - \Delta H6 - \Delta H5 - \Delta H4 - \Delta H3 - \Delta H2 + \Delta H1$
$= -3(-349) - (+2745) - (+1817) - (+578) - 3(+122) - (+326)$
$+ (-706)$ *[1 mark]*
$= -5491$ *[1 mark]* $kJ\ mol^{-1}$ *[1 mark]*

3 a)

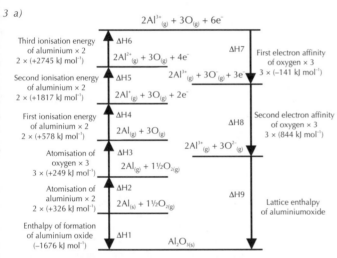

[1 mark for left of cycle. 1 mark for right of cycle. 1 mark for formulas/state symbols. 1 mark for correctly multiplying all the enthalpies. 1 mark for correct directions of arrows.]

b) Lattice enthalpy, $\Delta H9 = -\Delta H8 - \Delta H7 - \Delta H6 - \Delta H5 - \Delta H4 - \Delta H3$
$- \Delta H2 + \Delta H1$
$= -3(+844) - 3(-141) - 2(+2745) - 2(+1817) - 2(+578) -$
$3(+249) - 2(+326) + (-1676)$ *[1 mark]*
$= -15\ 464$ *[1 mark]* $kJ\ mol^{-1}$ *[1 mark]*

Page 75 — Enthalpies of Solution

1 a)

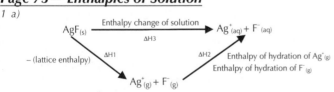

[1 mark for a complete correct cycle, 1 mark for each of the three arrows correctly labelled.]

b) $\Delta H3 = \Delta H1 + \Delta H2$
$= -(-960) + (-506) + (-464)$ *[1 mark]* $= -10\ kJ\ mol^{-1}$ *[1 mark]*

2 a)

SrF$_{2\,(s)}$ — Enthalpy change of solution ($\Delta H3$) → Sr$^{2+}_{(aq)}$ + 2F$^-_{(aq)}$
– (lattice enthalpy) $\Delta H1$ ... $\Delta H2$ Enthalpy of hydration of Sr$^{2+}_{(g)}$
Enthalpy of hydration of 2F$^-_{(g)}$
Sr$^{2+}_{(g)}$ + 2F$^-_{(g)}$

[1 mark for a complete correct cycle, 1 mark for each of the 3 arrows correctly labelled.]
Don't forget — you have to double the enthalpy of hydration for F$^-$ because there are two in SrF$_2$.

b) $-(-2492) + (-1480) + (2 \times -506)$ *[1 mark]* $= 0\ kJ\ mol^{-1}$
[1 mark]

3 By Hess's law:
Enthalpy change of solution ($MgCl_{2(s)}$)
$= -lattice\ enthalpy\ (MgCl_{2(s)})$
$+ enthalpy\ of\ hydration\ (Mg^{2+}_{(g)})$
$+ [2 \times enthalpy\ of\ hydration\ (Cl^-_{(g)})]$ *[1 mark]*
$= -(-2526) + (-1920) + [2 \times (-364)]$ *[1 mark]*
$= 2526 - 1920 - 728 = -122\ kJ\ mol^{-1}$ *[1 mark]*

Page 77 — Free-Energy Change and Entropy Change

1 a) The reaction is not likely to be spontaneous *[1 mark]*
because there is a decrease in entropy *[1 mark]*.
Remember — more particles means more entropy.
There's 1½ moles of reactants and only 1 mole of products.

b) $\Delta S_{system} = 26.9 - (32.7 + 102.5)$ *[1 mark]*
$= -108.3$ *[1 mark]* $J\ K^{-1}\ mol^{-1}$ *[1 mark]*

c) Reaction is not likely to be spontaneous *[1 mark]* because
ΔS_{system} is negative/there is a decrease in entropy *[1 mark]*.

2 a) (i) $\Delta S_{system} = 48 - 70 = -22\ JK^{-1}mol^{-1}$ *[1 mark]*
$\Delta S_{surroundings} = -(-6000)/250 = +24\ JK^{-1}mol^{-1}$ *[1 mark]*
$\Delta S_{total} = \Delta S_{system} + \Delta S_{surroundings} = -22 + 24 = +2\ JK^{-1}mol^{-1}$
[1 mark]

(ii) $\Delta S_{surroundings} = -(-6000)/300 = +20\ JK^{-1}mol^{-1}$ *[1 mark]*
$\Delta S_{total} = \Delta S_{system} + \Delta S_{surroundings} = -22 + 20 = -2\ JK^{-1}mol^{-1}$
[1 mark]

b) It will be spontaneous at 250 K, but not at 300 K *[1 mark]*, because
ΔS_{total} is positive at 250 K but negative at 300 K
[1 mark].

Page 79 — Redox Reactions

1 a) $Ti + (4 \times -1) = 0,\ Ti = +4$ *[1 mark]*
b) $(2 \times V) + (5 \times -2) = 0,\ V = +5$ *[1 mark]*
c) $Cr + (4 \times -2) = -2,\ Cr = +6$ *[1 mark]*
d) $(2 \times Cr) + (2 \times -7) = -2,\ Cr = +6$ *[1 mark]*

2 a) $2MnO_4^-{}_{(aq)} + 16H^+{}_{(aq)} + 10I^-{}_{(aq)} \rightarrow 2Mn^{2+}{}_{(aq)} + 8H_2O_{(l)} + 5I_{2(aq)}$
[1 mark for correct reactants and products,
1 mark for correct balancing]
You have to balance the number of electrons before you can combine the
half-equations. And always double-check that your equation definitely
balances. It's easy to slip up and throw away marks.

b) Mn has been reduced *[1 mark]* from +7 to +2 *[1 mark]*
I$^-$ has been oxidised *[1 mark]* from –1 to 0 *[1 mark]*

c) Reactive metals have a tendency to lose electrons, so are good
reducing agents *[1 mark]*. I$^-$ is already in its reduced form *[1 mark]*.

Page 81 — Electrode Potentials

1 a) Iron *[1 mark]* as it has a more negative electrode potential/ it loses
electrons more easily than lead *[1 mark]*
b) The iron half-cell *[1 mark]* as it loses electrons *[1 mark]*
c) Standard cell potential $= -0.13 - (-0.44) = +0.31\ V$ *[1 mark]*

2 a) $+0.80\ V - (-0.76\ V) = 1.56\ V$ *[1 mark]*
b) The concentration of Zn^{2+} ions or Ag$^+$ ions was not 1.00 mol dm^{-3}
[1 mark]. The pressure wasn't 100 kPa *[1 mark]*.
c) $Zn_{(s)} + 2Ag^+{}_{(aq)} \rightarrow Zn^{2+}{}_{(aq)} + 2Ag_{(s)}$ *[1 mark]*
d) The zinc half-cell. It has a more negative standard electrode potential
[1 mark].

Answers

Page 83 — The Electrochemical Series

1 a) $Zn_{(s)} + Ni^{2+}_{(aq)} \rightleftharpoons Zn^{2+}_{(aq)} + Ni_{(s)}$ **[1 mark]**

   $E^\circ = (-0.25) - (-0.76) = +0.51 V$ **[1 mark]**

   b) $2MnO_4^-_{(aq)} + 16H^+_{(aq)} + 5Sn^{2+}_{(aq)} \rightleftharpoons$
      $2Mn^{2+}_{(aq)} + 8H_2O_{(l)} + 5Sn^{4+}_{(aq)}$ **[1 mark]**

   $E^\circ = (+1.51) - (+0.15) = +1.36 V$ **[1 mark]**

   c) No reaction **[1 mark]**. Both reactants are in their oxidised form **[1 mark]**.

   d) $Ag^+_{(aq)} + Fe^{2+}_{(aq)} \rightleftharpoons Ag_{(s)} + Fe^{3+}_{(aq)}$ **[1 mark]**

   $E^\circ = (+0.80) - (+0.77) = +0.03 V$ **[1 mark]**

2 a) $KMnO_4$ **[1 mark]** because it has a more positive/less negative electrode potential **[1 mark]**

   b) $MnO_4^- + 8H^+ + 5Fe^{2+} \rightarrow MnO_2 + 4H_2O + 5Fe^{3+}$ **[1 mark]**
      $Cr_2O_7^{2-} + 14H^+ + 6Fe^{2+} \rightarrow 2Cr^{3+} + 7H_2O + 6Fe^{3+}$ **[1 mark]**

   c) Cell potential for the first reaction is $+1.51 - 0.77 = 0.74 V$ **[1 mark]**
      Cell potential for the second reaction is $+1.33 - 0.77 = 0.56 V$ **[1 mark]**

3 a) $Cu^{2+}_{(aq)} + 2e^- \rightleftharpoons Cu_{(s)}$ **[1 mark]**
      $Ni^{2+}_{(aq)} + 2e^- \rightleftharpoons Ni_{(s)}$ **[1 mark]**

   b) $0.34 - (-0.25) = 0.59 V$ **[1 mark]**

   c) If the copper solution was more dilute, the E of the copper half-cell would be lower, so the overall cell potential would be smaller. **[1 mark]**
   If the nickel solution was more concentrated, the E of the nickel half-cell would be higher (more positive/ less negative), so the overall cell potential would be lower. **[1 mark]**

Page 86 — Storage and Fuel Cells

1 a)

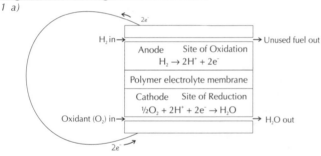

   [1 mark for naming anode and cathode. 1 mark for anode half equation. 1 mark for cathode half equation. 1 mark for showing H_2/ fuel and O_2/ oxidant in and unused fuel and H_2O out. 1 mark for showing correct direction of flow of electrons in circuit.]

   b) Correctly label anode as site of oxidation **[1 mark]** and cathode as site of reduction. **[1 mark]**

2 a) Possible advantages – more efficient/release less pollution **[1 mark]**
   Possible disadvantages – problems storing and transporting hydrogen/ manufacturing hydrogen currently requires energy from fossil fuels/ fuel cells are expensive **[1 mark]**

   b) Hydrogen would be used as the basic fuel for everything (e.g. vehicles, buildings and electronic equipment) **[1 mark]**
   Replacing fossil fuels (oil, gas) **[1 mark]**

   c) Clean production of hydrogen from renewable power **[1 mark]**
   Improved fuel cell design to reduce costs in manufacture and disposal **[1 mark]**
   Building/ creating of hydrogen infrastructure – supply, delivery and storage in a safe way **[1 mark]**

3 a) $Pb + 2H_2SO_4 + PbO_2 \rightleftharpoons 2PbSO_4 + 2H_2O$ **[2 marks, otherwise 1 mark for correct equation but not simplified by cancelling H^+]**

   b) Voltage = $1.68 - 0.35 = 1.33 V$ **[1 mark]**

Unit 5: Module 3 — Transition Elements

Page 89 — Properties of Transition Elements

1 a) $1s^2\ 2s^2\ 2p^6\ 3s^2\ 3p^6\ 3d^{10}$ or $[Ar]\ 3d^{10}$ **[1 mark]**

   b) No, it doesn't **[1 mark]**. A transition metal is an element that can form at least one stable ion with an incomplete d-subshell, but Cu^+ ions have a full 3d subshell **[1 mark]**.

   c) copper(II) sulfate ($CuSO_{4(aq)}$) **[1 mark]**

2 a) $Fe^{3+}_{(aq)} + 3OH^-_{(aq)} \rightarrow Fe(OH)_{3(s)}$
   [1 mark for balanced equation, 1 mark for state symbols].

   b) i) +7 **[1 mark]**
      ii) +4 **[1 mark]**
      iii) +7 **[1 mark]**
   Oxide ions, O^{2-}, have an oxidation state of –2. Potassium ions, K^+, have an oxidation state of +1. All three compounds are neutral, so the charge on the manganese ions must balance out the charges on the other ions in each compound.

   c) The $FeCl_3$ solution is yellow **[1 mark]**. When you add the sodium hydroxide solution, an orange precipitate forms **[1 mark]**.
   The orange precipitate is iron(III) hydroxide, $Fe(OH)_3$.

2 a) i) $1s^2\ 2s^2\ 2p^6\ 3s^2\ 3p^6\ 3d^5$ **[1 mark]**
      ii) $1s^2\ 2s^2\ 2p^6$ **[1 mark]**

   b) Iron can exist in two different oxidation states, Fe^{2+} and Fe^{3+} **[1 mark]**. Aluminium can only exist in one oxidation state, Al^{3+} **[1 mark]**.
   Iron can form coloured compounds/solutions **[1 mark]**.
   Aluminium forms only colourless/clear/white compounds/solutions **[1 mark]**.

Page 91 — Complex Ions

1 a) A complex ion is a metal ion surrounded by coordinately bonded ligands **[1 mark]**.

   b) A lone pair of electrons from the N atom is donated to/forms a coordinate bond with the central iron ion **[1 mark]**.

   c) 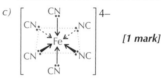 **[1 mark]**

2 a) A bidentate ligand has two lone pairs of electrons **[1 mark]**, so it can form two coordinate bonds with the central metal ion **[1 mark]**.

   b) 6 **[1 mark]**
   Each ethanedioate ligand forms two bonds with the Fe^{3+} ion — so that's 6 altogether.

   c) Octahedral **[1 mark]**
   Complex ions with a coordination number of 6 are usually octahedral.

3 a)

   [1 mark for four correct ligands, 1 mark for square planar shape, 1 mark for chloride ions being adjacent]

   b) The two chloride ligands are displaced **[1 mark]** and their places taken by two nitrogen atoms from the cancer cell's DNA **[1 mark]**. This stops the cell from reproducing **[1 mark]**. The cell is unable to repair the damage, and dies **[1 mark]**.

Page 93 — Substitution Reactions

1 a) The equation for the formation of the ion is:
   $Co^{2+}_{(aq)} + 6NH_{3(aq)} \rightleftharpoons [Co(NH_3)_6]^{2+}_{(aq)}$

   So $K_{stab} = \dfrac{[(Co(NH_3)_6)^{2+}]}{[Co^{2+}][NH_3]^6}$ **[1 mark]**

   b) $K_{stab} = \dfrac{[(Cu(CN)_6)^{4-}]}{[(Cu(H_2O)_6)^{2+}][CN^-]^6}$ **[1 mark]**

2 a) $[Cu(H_2O)_6]^{2+}$ **[1 mark]**.

   b) i) $[Cu(H_2O)_6]^{2+}_{(aq)} + 4NH_{3(aq)} \rightleftharpoons [Cu(NH_3)_4(H_2O)_2]^{2+}_{(aq)} + 4H_2O_{(l)}$
   [1 mark for correct formula of the new complex ion formed, 1 mark for the rest of the equation being correctly balanced]

   ii) $K_{stab} = \dfrac{[(Cu(NH_3)_4(H_2O)_2)^{2+}]}{[(Cu(H_2O)_6)^{2+}][NH_3]^4}$
   [1 mark for top of fraction correct, 1 mark for bottom of fraction correct]

Answers

3 a) i) The water [1 mark] ligand is replaced with an oxygen [1 mark]
ligand.
ii) It is the basis of the oxygen transportation mechanism in
the bloodstream [1 mark].
b) Carbon monoxide will bind strongly to the haemoglobin complex
[1 mark]. It is a strong ligand, and will not exchange with an oxygen
(or water) ligand [1 mark]. The haemoglobin can't transport oxygen
any more, so the cells of the body will get less oxygen [1 mark].

Page 95 — Redox Reactions and Transition Elements

1 a) $MnO_4^- + 8H^+ + 5Fe^{2+} \rightarrow Mn^{2+} + 4H_2O + 5Fe^{3+}$
[1 mark for MnO_4^- and Mn^{2+} correct, 1 mark for $5Fe^{2+}$ and $5Fe^{3+}$
correct, 1 mark for $8H^+$ and $4H_2O$ correct].
b) Number of moles = (concentration × volume) ÷ 1000
Moles of MnO_4^- = (0.4 × 11.5) ÷ 1000 = 4.6×10^{-3} [1 mark]
Moles of Fe^{2+} = moles of MnO_4^- × 5 [1 mark] = 2.3×10^{-2} [1 mark]
c) Mass of substance = moles × relative atomic mass
Mass of iron in solution = (2.3×10^{-2}) × 55.8 = 1.2834 g [1 mark]
% iron in steel wool = (1.2834 ÷ 1.3) × 100 [1 mark] = 98.7 % [1 mark]
2 a) A redox reaction [1 mark].
b) Number of moles = (concentration × volume) ÷ 1000
Number of moles = (0.5 × 10) ÷ 1000 [1 mark] = 0.005 [1 mark]
c) Number of moles = (concentration × volume) ÷ 1000
Number of moles = (0.1 × 20) ÷ 1000 [1 mark] = 0.002 [1 mark]
d) 1 mole of MnO_4^- ions needs 5 moles of electrons to be reduced.
So to reduce 0.002 moles of MnO_4^-, you need
(0.002 × 5) = 0.01 moles of electrons [1 mark].
The 0.005 moles of tin ions must have lost 0.01 moles of
electrons as they were oxidised OR all of these electrons must have
come from the tin ions [1 mark].
Each tin ion changed its oxidation state by 0.01 ÷ 0.005 = 2 [1 mark].
The oxidation state of the oxidised tin ions is (+2) + 2 = +4 [1 mark].

Page 97 — Iodine-Sodium Thiosulfate Titrations

1 a) $IO_3^- + 5I^- + 6H^+ \rightarrow 3I_2 + 3H_2O$
[1 mark for correct reactants and products, 1 mark for balancing]
b) Number of moles = (concentration × volume) ÷ 1000
Number of moles of thiosulfate = (0.15 × 24) ÷ 1000
= 3.6×10^{-3} [1 mark]
c) 2 moles of thiosulfate react with 1 mole of iodine,
so there were (3.6×10^{-3}) ÷ 2 = 1.8×10^{-3} moles of iodine [1 mark]
d) 1/3 mole of iodate(V) ions produces 1 mole of iodine molecules
[1 mark]
e) There must be 1.8×10^{-3} × 3 = 6×10^{-4} moles of iodate(V) in the
solution [1 mark].
So concentration of potassium iodate(V) =
6×10^{-4} moles × 1000 ÷ 10 = 0.06 mol dm⁻³ [1 mark].
2 Number of moles = (concentration × volume) ÷ 1000
Number of moles of thiosulfate = (0.3 × 12.5) ÷ 1000
= 3.75×10^{-3} [1 mark]
2 moles of thiosulfate react with 1 mole of iodine.
So there must have been (3.75×10^{-3}) ÷ 2 = 1.875×10^{-3} moles
of iodine produced [1 mark].
2 moles of manganate(VII) ions produce 5 moles of iodine molecules
So there must have been (1.875×10^{-3}) × (2 ÷ 5) [1 mark]
= 7.5×10^{-4} moles of manganate(VII) in the solution [1 mark].
Concentration of potassium manganate(VII)
= $(7.5 \times 10^{-4}$ moles$)$ ÷ (18 ÷ 1000) = 0.042 mol dm⁻³ [1 mark]

Index

anyone before he was done. A chainsaw is also a harder tool to control, especially if your aim is precision.' He examined the body and the bed for a while longer before moving away from it and approaching the coffee table and the morbid sculpture.

Both of Mr. Nicholson's arms were awkwardly twisted and bent at the wrist joints, forming two distinct, but meaningless shapes. His feet had been cut off and bundled together in a peculiar way with the arms and hands. All of it was held in place by thin but solid pieces of metal wire. Wire had also been used to attach a few of his severed toes to the edges of the two pieces. His legs had been laid flat side-by-side, and formed the base to the sculpture. Everything was covered in blood.

Hunter circled it slowly, trying to take every detail in.

'Whatever this is,' Doctor Hove said, 'it's not something anyone can put together in a couple of minutes. This takes time.'

'And if the killer took the time to put it together,' Garcia added, moving closer, 'it's gotta mean something.'

Hunter took a few steps back and stared at the macabre piece from a distance. It meant nothing to him.

'Do you think your lab could create a life-size replica of this?' he asked Doctor Hove.

Under her surgical mask, she twisted her mouth from side to side. 'I don't see why not. It's already been photographed, but I'll call the photographer back in and ask him to get a snapshot from all angles. I'm sure the lab can get it done.'

'Let's do it,' Hunter said. 'We're not gonna figure this out here and now.' He turned towards the far wall and froze. It was so covered in blood that he almost didn't notice it. 'What in the world is that?'

Garcia's stare moved to Hunter and then back to the wall.

He breathed out a heavy sigh.

'That . . . is everybody's worst nightmare.'

stare moved back to the revolting body-part sculpture. 'I'd say that was done first, before he was dismembered.'

'He was alone in the house?'

'Yes,' Garcia answered. 'Melinda, the student nurse you saw downstairs, spends the weekends here, but she sleeps in the guesthouse above the garage you saw up front. According to her, Mr. Nicholson's daughters came by every day and spent a couple of hours with him, sometimes more. They left last night at around 9:00 p.m. After putting him to sleep and finishing up in the house, Melinda left Mr. Nicholson at around 11:00 p.m. She went back to the guesthouse and stayed up until three-thirty in the morning, studying for an exam.'

It wasn't hard for Hunter to understand why the nurse never heard anything. The garage was all the way up front and about twenty yards away from the main building. The room they were in was right at the back of the house, the last one down the corridor. Its windows faced the backyard. They could've had a party in here and she wouldn't have heard it.

'No panic button?' Hunter asked.

Garcia pointed to one of the evidence bags in the corner of the room. Inside it was a piece of electric wire with a click button at the end of it. 'The wire was snipped.'

Hunter's attention focused on the blood splatters all over the bed, furniture and wall next to it. 'Was the weapon found?'

'No, not yet,' Garcia replied.

'The spit-like blood pattern and the jagged edge of the wounds inflicted indicate that the killer used some sort of electrical sawing device,' Doctor Hove said.

'Like a chainsaw?' Garcia asked.

'Possibly.'

Hunter shook his head. 'A chainsaw would be too noisy. Too risky. The last thing the killer would've wanted would be to alert

'You've gotta be kidding me,' Hunter whispered to himself. 'I'm not even going to ask. 'Cos I know you've never seen anything like this before, Robert,' Doctor Carolyn Hove said from the far corner of the room. 'None of us have.'

Doctor Hove was the Chief Medical Examiner for the Los Angeles County Department of Coroner. She was tall and slim with deep penetrating green eyes. Her long, chestnut hair was tucked away under the hood of her white coverall, her full lips and petite nose hidden under her surgical mask.

Hunter's attention moved to her for a couple of seconds and then to the large blood pools on the floor. He hesitated for a moment. There was no way he could walk into that room without treading on them.

'It's OK,' Doctor Hove said, motioning him and Garcia inside. 'The entire floor has been photographed.'

Still, Hunter did his best to circumvent the blood. He approached the bed and what was left of Mr. Nicholson's body. His face was caked in blood. His eyes and mouth were wide open, as if his last terrified scream had been frozen before it came out. The bed sheets, the pillows and the mattress were ripped and torn in several places.

'He was killed on that bed,' Doctor Hove said, coming up to Hunter.

He kept his attention on the body.

'Judging by the splatters and the amount of blood we have here,' she continued, 'the killer inflicted as much pain as the victim could handle before allowing him to die.'

'The killer cut him up first?'

The doctor nodded. 'And the killer started with the small, non-life-threatening pieces.'

Hunter frowned.

'All his toes were cut off, together with his tongue.' Her

Four

Hunter stood by the open door to the large bedroom. His eyes registered the scene in front of him, but his logical mind was having trouble comprehending it.

Centered against the north wall was an adjustable double bed. To its right he could see a small oxygen tank and mask on a wooden bedside table. A wheelchair occupied the space by the end of the bed. There was also an antique-looking chest of drawers, a mahogany writing desk, and a large shelf unit on the wall opposite the bed. Its centerpiece was a flat-screen TV set.

Hunter breathed out but didn't move, didn't blink, didn't say a word.

'Where do we start?' Garcia whispered by his side.

Blood was everywhere – on the bed, floor, rug, walls, ceiling, curtains, and on most of the furniture. Mr. Nicholson's body was on the bed. Or at least what was left of it. He'd been dismembered. Both legs and both arms had been ripped from his body. One of his arms had been hacked at the joints into smaller pieces. Both of his feet had also been separated from his legs.

But what baffled everyone who entered that room was the sculpture.

On a small coffee table by the window, the victim's severed and hacked body parts had been bundled up and arranged together into a bloody, twisted, incomprehensible shape.

As he took the steps up, Hunter was careful not to interfere with the forensic agents as they worked. The first-floor landing resembled a waiting room – two chairs, two leather armchairs, a small bookshelf, a magazine holder, and a sideboard covered with stylish picture frames. A dimly lit corridor led them deeper into the house, and to the four bedrooms and two bathrooms. Garcia took Hunter all the way to the last door on the right and paused outside.

'I know you've seen a lot of sick stuff before, Robert. God knows I have.' He rested his latex-gloved hand on the door-knob. 'But this . . . not even in nightmares.' He pushed the door open.

a large study. Inside, sitting on a vintage leather Chesterfield sofa, was a young woman dressed all in white. Her hair was tied back. Her eyes were raspberry red and puffed up from crying. Resting on her knees was a cup of coffee that she was holding with both hands. Her stare seemed lost and distant. Hunter noticed that she was rocking her upper body back and forth ever so slightly. She was clearly in shock. A uniformed officer was in the room with her.

'Anybody tried talking to her yet?'

'I did,' Garcia nodded. 'Managed to get some basic information out of her, but she's psychologically shutting down, and I'm not surprised. Maybe you could try later. You're better at these things than I am.'

'She was here on a Sunday?' Hunter asked.

'She's only here on weekends,' Garcia clarified. 'Her name is Melinda Wallis. She goes to UCLA. She's just finishing a degree in Nursing and Caretaking. This is part of her work experience. She got the job a week after Mr. Nicholson was diagnosed with his illness.'

'How about the rest of the week?'

'Mr. Nicholson had another nurse.' Garcia unzipped his coverall and reached inside his breast pocket for his notebook. 'Amy Dawson,' he read the name. 'Unlike Melinda, Amy isn't a student. She's a professional nurse. She took care of Mr. Nicholson during the week. Also, his two daughters came to visit him every day.'

Hunter's eyebrow arched.

'They haven't been contacted yet.'

'So the victim lived here alone?'

'That's right. His wife of twenty-six years died in a car accident two years ago.' Garcia returned the notebook to his pocket. 'The body is upstairs.' He motioned to the staircase.